# BEST
# FOOD
## WRITING

# 2003

# BEST
# FOOD
# WRITING

## 2003

EDITED BY

## Holly Hughes

Marlowe & Company
New York

Best Food Writing 2003

Compilation and introductions copyright © 2003 by Holly Hughes
and Avalon Publishing Group Incorporated

Published by
Marlowe & Company
A Division of Avalon Publishing Group Incorporated
161 William Street
16th floor
New York, NY 10038

Photography: © Judd Pilossof/Foodpix

Library of Congress Cataloging-in-Publication Data is available.

ISBN: 1-56924-440-5

Book Design: Michael Walters and Susan Canavan

Printed in the United States of America

Distributed by Publishers Group West

# Home Cooking

# Contents

## Someone's in the Kitchen

## Personal Tastes

# Introduction

## by Holly Hughes

Last February, I clicked into a lively discussion board on the foodie website eGullet.com, starring as guest host John Thorne (who, I'll say up front, is one of my favorite writers on the topic of food and cooking). All sorts of cooks and eaters and writers weighed in on the question: What is food writing? The consensus, if any, seemed to be that old cartoon punch line about modern art: we can't define it, but we all know what we like.

Food writers are split from the get-go because, not surprisingly, they all tend to write about what they're interested in. What a range of topics that embraces: luxury dining, discovering cheap ethnic eats, cooking precisely like a master chef, free-wheeling self-expression at the stove, shopping for just the right ingredients. Each writer also, whether he/she admits it or not, has a different platform. A member of the food writing establishment—and let's not try to pretend there isn't one—has a very different agenda from the hungry freelancer angling for free meals or the novelist who's "slumming" as a food writer. There's a political edge to all this, too (where isn't there a political edge, these days?), with the celebrators of fat-cat gastronomy grazing on an entirely different planet from the think-globally-eat-locally slow foodies. The great thing about putting together an anthology like this one is that the whole rich variety can be included between these covers.

In the course of the eGullet chat, there was a brief slam against "best of" anthologies (of which, to my knowledge, this is the only annual one), dismissing them as a collection of "essays and memoirs about food," not food writing. But give me a break: M.F.K. Fisher and A. J. Liebling wrote "just" essays about food, and if they aren't among the best food writers ever, I don't know who is. The comment did, however, make me consider why I choose what I choose for this annual collection. I've been editing *Best Food Writing* annuals for four years now: It's time to come clean.

I start out with imagining where you are when you're reading this—and I bet that you're not standing at the kitchen counter, apron on, whisk in hand, ready to cook. This is no cookbook, although there are recipes (delicious ones, too) included with some pieces. It's also not a dining guide that you riffle through hastily, phone in hand, ready to dial for reservations, although there are reviews of specific restaurants or food sources included. Instead, I envision you, the reader, dipping into this book at leisure. You're in the mood to read, and right now you've chosen to read about food—probably because you love it.

As I plow through piles of magazines and newspapers and books, as I scan streams of on-line text, I inevitably focus on the "writing" part of food writing. The prose has to be good enough to make me keep reading past the first couple of paragraphs. This, of course, is always subjective, but I do have certain rules of thumb. While food writing is by nature an adjective-heavy discipline, after months of reading submissions I feel downright allergic to flowery (or floury?) gushing about the taste of this or that—to me, it's the first sign of an inexperienced food writer. By now, I can spot a food-writing cliche a block away, so I appreciate writers who come to the table with fresh taste buds, so to speak. I also have to own up to a preference for colloquial, anecdotal writing—which often means a first-person voice, if only to lend personality (definitely not the same thing as ego). I like a sense of place and time as well as character.

And the piece has to say something worth reading about, something that resonates. That's why so many local newspaper reviews don't make my final cut: however well written, they rarely go beyond an "eat here/don't eat here" recommendation. (It can be done, though—read how Jonathan Gold and Min Liao handle the challenge.) Just as I want a meal that satisfies my hunger, I look for food writing that stays with me. Dave Gardetta's and Eric Levin's pieces cast light on the current state of the restaurant business; Adam Gopnik, Benjamin Wallace, John T. Edge, and Gabrielle Hamilton shine light into the psyche of a chef. Food movements in the news? Read Corby Kummer's book excerpt about the Slow Food folks, or Michael Pollan's article on a farmer who goes way beyond organic agriculture. Health issues? Try Jason Epstein's essay about adopting the Atkins diet, or Elmer Grossman's account of searching for healthy lard.

Tragedy is easy; comedy is hard—that's why I warm to food writers who can make me laugh. My slush pile is full of sentimental twaddle about Mom's cookies or apoplectic rants about fat-laden fast food, but anyone who can do it with a killer wit earns my vote. The master of this, of course, is Calvin Trillin, but many others in this collection have followed his lead.

But the more I thought about it, the more I realized that my number one criterion for excellent food writing is simply this: It has to make me hungry. One of the occupational hazards of reading so much food writing in the course of a year is the constant appetite it triggers (though if I'm lucky, a good article makes me hungry for *just that one thing;* no substitutions will do). Colman Andrews' essay made me lust for a good burger, John Kessler's had me grilling like a maniac in midwinter, Pete Wells' initiated a bacon habit that lasted for weeks. (By April I began to notice this year's weird plethora of writing about meat, especially cured meats. Next year, folks, do me a favor and write well about green salads, okay?) Sometimes just a chance phrase in the middle of a piece flicks my appetite switch, as when Matthew Amster-Burton describes the clutter of sugars and teas in his cupboards, or David Leite describes the devastating white-chocolate cake he plans to bake in his new Viking stove. Sometimes that's all it takes to convince me that the writer is alive to the importance of food.

Every year people ask me what themes stood out in the year's food writing. In 2003 the post-9/11 comfort-food mantras still simmered on the stove (though recipes for root vegetables and casseroles supplanted last year's mashed potatoes and mac-'n'-cheese), but I sensed a broader nostalgia coming to a boil—ex-chef food writers like Jason Sheehan recalling their kitchen careers, Zuni Café's Judy Rodgers fondly remembering the master chefs who taught her her trade. I found grail-like quests for old-style local treats (Robb Walsh, Andrea Strong, Ann Patchett, Fran Gage) as well as Proustian memories of Mom's/Dad's cooking, whether drenched in fondness (Miriam Sauls, Sara Roahen, Rick Nichols) or spiky with ambivalence (John Haney, Lucian Truscott IV, Dara Moskowitz).

Curiously, despite the Francophobia sparked by the Iraq war, French food turned up everywhere this year (most notably in Jacques Pepin's glorious memoir *The Apprentice*). It was as if the diplomatic spat caused epicures to sit up and declare, "Politics be damned! We still want our runny cheeses, our Bordeaux wines, our garlicky snails, our crisp frites, and our tartes tatin." Parisian baker Lionel Poilane was fondly remembered, and souls were searched over the suicide of master chef Bernard Loiseau (killed by the prospect of losing a Michelin star?).

More and more food memoirs seemed to crowd the shelves this season, but skim carefully before you buy—several are unworthy of the genre, merely tacking recipes onto flimsy travelogues that wouldn't have been published otherwise. As far as cookbooks go, the glossy celebrity chef collections of show-off recipes seemed superseded by a spate of equally glossy kitchen primers—basic recipes, step-by-step techniques, glossaries of ingredients, suggestions for adapting recipes, often overlaid with culinary philosophy (Nigel Slater's *Appetite* amused me with its dogmatic insistence that no cook should be bound by any culinary dogma). We've come a long way from the haute prescriptions of Julia Child.

Well, food fashions come and go; so do trends in food writing. But when the table is cleared, what's left is people who love food, writing about it because they love it. It's that passion I look for, that communicated appetite. When I read it, I taste it. And that's about as scientific as any definition of food writing is likely to get.

# Tools of the Trade

# Kit

by Nigel Slater

from *Appetite*

A U.K. best-seller, *Appetite* is more than a cookbook, more than a kitchen primer—it's a philosophy lesson for the home cook. Slater's bracing, no-nonsense style is like a fresh breeze clearing out stale kitchen air.

There is a lot of precious twaddle talked about kit: the right pan for this, the correct knife for that. The fact is that if it feels comfortable in your hand and it does the job you need it for, then it is the right pan or the correct knife. After all, you are the one who is going to cook with it. And don't believe that the most expensive is necessarily the best. Yes, of course, you tend to get what you pay for, but if that two-dollar potato peeler feels right, why buy the one that costs fifteen dollars just because some big-shot designer has got his name on it?

If you are going to cook you will need a few pans and a couple of knives, plus odd bits and pieces such as a sieve, a ladle, and the like, but don't be persuaded that you need a whole load of fancy stuff. You don't. Really. It will just gather dust. You could, if push came to shove, boil, steam, fry, braise, and probably even roast in a single wok, providing you unscrew the wooden handle to put it in the oven. But even I, a confirmed kitchen minimalist, think that is a bit desperate. It is a little like gardening, I guess. You could get away with having nothing more than a spade, but having a fork, a trowel, and a rake would make life a lot easier.

What you will need is a couple of deep saucepans, a frying pan, a roasting pan, and some sort of ridged grill pan or griddle, and it will be safer and easier if you invest in a couple of well-made knives, but you can cheerfully ignore much of what you see on sale in kitchen shops. A lot of it is there for heavyweight cooks who are into it all in a big, big way, or who simply must have an authentic couscous steamer/paella pan/fish kettle, or who probably have a fetish for kitchen equipment. Oh, and I don't know anyone who has ever used their Moroccan tagine more than twice.

There is enormous pleasure to be had in cooking the same dish year in year out in a favorite pan. I cannot emphasize this enough. A pan that has a history and in which the recipe feels right. I have an old, round-bottomed cooking pot I picked up for pennies in India several years ago. As rough as guts, it has now mellowed and developed a certain patina—for which you can read a thick layer of blackened fat. I use it for frying small quantities of food, even though it wobbles about unnervingly—this is not a recommendation—and yet I would miss it so much if it disappeared. Black, tatty, and as cheap as chips, it has become part of my kitchen, and therefore my cooking. I might add, though, that it is not worth getting overly attached to your equipment; things break and chip, snap and shatter, and that kind friend who helped peel the potatoes will chuck your favorite knife out with the peelings.

## Your Pans

You'll need some pans, but not half as many as you think. As a general rule, you will get better value from one or two well-chosen, probably rather expensive pans than an entire set you can order for fifty dollars from a mail-order catalogue. Never has the saying "quality not quantity" made more sense. Don't even consider those thin, light, nonstick pans with plastic handles and arty enameling on the outside. They are mostly rubbish. Avoid, too, those mirror-finish so-called professional pans—they spit menacingly when they get hot. I suggest you go for a pan that is heavy for its size and preferably made of stainless steel. Think big. You can't cook fettuccine in a small saucepan.

The pans you end up with should have a heavy, solid base so they don't buckle. It doesn't matter if they are enameled cast iron or stainless steel, but do make sure they have heatproof handles so they can go in the oven as well as on the stovetop. Make certain, too, that they will go in the dishwasher. Frankly, I'd sooner part with my television than my dishwasher. And no matter what you have heard elsewhere, don't even think of buying aluminum pans; they send your cooking gray.

At the end of the day, it is down to which pan feels comfortable in your hand and what you can afford. Just rummage through all the pans in the kitchen shop, hold them, feel them, and imagine what it will be like to cook with them day in day out. I recommend you buy one and live with it for a while before you go back and buy more. I started out with three pans that cost me almost a month's wages. It was the most extravagant purchase I had ever made, yet I still have them, eighteen years on, and use them every day. For the record, they are Italian, stainless steel, with a layer of copper in the base. Love 'em.

### ELECTRIC MIXERS AND STUFF

When people walk into my kitchen they are often surprised, shocked even, by how basic it is. No gadgets, no copper pans hanging from the ceiling, and no state-of-the-art cookware. A place to cook and eat that is devoid of all bells and whistles. That is how I like it, and its utilitarianism suits my style of cooking.

I do, though, recognize something that will make my life easier when I see it. Machines that will beat, whisk, chop, purée, and blend for you cut out some of the most mind-numbingly boring bits of cooking and let you get on with the fun side of it. I value my mixer, a great, whirring Kitchen Aid, for beating cake batters and meringue, for making crumble, pastry, and mayonnaise. I could, I suppose, live without it, but I doubt whether you would ever get a cake out of me again.

Whereas an electric mixer can be, if you choose the right one, a thing of beauty, a food processor will always be the ugliest creature in the kitchen. But I am willing to forgive the looks of my shiny plastic whizzer and blitzer in return for its doing almost every kitchen job I hate. Anyone can cook without a machine that will purée soup, make crumble, rub in pastry, chop herbs (though it is not very good at parsley), blitz nuts and dried fruit (though it hates dried apricots), and whiz up spice pastes. But would you want to?

### LITTLE KIT

Small things matter. It is just as important to have the right potato peeler as it is to have the right oven. It is pointless going to all the effort and expense of finding the perfect oven if your can opener pinches your fingers every time you use it. Comfort, rather than price or design, is the heart of the matter. I find I get quite attached to some small kitchen equipment, particularly peelers and little knives. There is a sentimentality attached to the right paring knife or pastry brush, simply because it works so well and becomes part of your life. Sometimes the cheapest ones work beautifully. Ruthlessly edit what you are offered in shops; it is amazing what you can do without. Clutter is the refuge of an insecure cook.

Sort yourself out a user-friendly example of each of the following, bearing in mind that your first choice may not be quite right. Expect to kiss a few frogs before you find your prince.

- **A metal, swivel-bladed vegetable peeler.**
- **A screwpull wine opener.** The most efficent there is, gets the cork out whole every time.
- **A cheap bottle opener for beer bottles.** In my

(considerable) experience, the worst are the ones attached to fancy corkscrews.

• **A couple of wooden spoons.** Try to get at least one with a corner to it for getting into the corners of saucepans.

• **A hand-held can opener.**

• **A pepper mill.** Avoid the explicitly large ones, however tempting they may be, the tiddlers (obviously), and any designer numbers. Go for a medium-sized one with a lifetime guarantee.

• **A salt mill.** Similar to a pepper mill but with a plastic mechanism so that it does not corrode. I know you can crumble sea salt flakes between your fingers, but sometimes you will find yourself with coarse salt crystals and sometimes you just need really fine salt.

• **A pestle and mortar.** Strange that all the food processors, spice mills, and space-age gadgets have not defeated the good old pestle and mortar. Besides the fact that you can grind spices and mash herbs in them with ease, they are also one of the most pleasing pieces of all to use. As you pound at the spices and herbs with the pestle, the fragrance that comes up is pure aromatherapy. Once you have ground cardamom seeds and pounded basil leaves in a mortar you will understand why I have been banging on about them for so long.

• **Rubber spatulas.** Invaluable. You can never have too many of these. They will get every last smear of cake batter, every last crumb of crumble, and every drop of spice paste from your bowls and pans. The cheap ones tend to be as effective as the dearer ones. Whichever sort you get, they will eventually go soft in the dishwasher and the top will come away from the handle.

• **Tongs.** Although they have been around for years, a

pair of long, strong tongs has become the *de rigueur* kitchen accessory, and with good reason. The joy of them is that you can lift meat, fish, and veggies from the pan without poking them with a fork, which would let some of the juices out, and you can get a firm grip on something without squeezing the life out of it. After years of cooking without them, I now find I have three pairs.

• **Mixing bowls.** Stainless steel or heatproof glass. Big ones about 12 inches for bread and pastry making and for marinating; smaller ones for storing bits and pieces in the fridge. The cheap, light ones are really useful. I have found ones with a hook on the side so I can hang them up—useful if, like me, you don't have much cupboard space.

• **Measuring spoons.** Go for metal rather than plastic, as you are less likely to melt them.

• **A small handheld grater.** I use a tiny one I have had for years, but the Microplane ones with their fat handles are brilliant.

Despite what every kitchen shop might have you believe, you do not need honey dippers, game scissors, pizza wheels, wicker baguette baskets, jelly bags, or porridge spurtles. You may want them, and there is no reason why you shouldn't buy them. It is just that you don't need them. Oh, and you do not, and will not, ever need a pastry bag.

Whatever kitchen equipment you end up buying, you will probably find that, like me, you assemble a mixture of exquisite design statements and comfy old tat. Rather like my wardrobe. At the end of the day it is not so much a point of adhering to tradition and the right-pan-for-the-right-job correctness, it is simply what feels comfortable and friendly and what works for you.

## The Art of Washing Up

Dinner is gone and there is the contented murmur of a full dishwasher from somewhere behind you in the kitchen. Everyone is fed. You have put the leftovers in the fridge to pick at much later, silently, secretly, when everyone else has gone to bed. (No matter how beautiful a set table looks, there is much solace to be had eating in the dark, the room lit only by the light from the open fridge.) This is when I curl up in a squashy chair, my feet tucked under me, to finish off the wine and to read or watch something unchallenging, trashy. I would honestly rather part with my television, my stereo, possibly even the odd relative, than lose my dishwasher.

I have met those who tell me they enjoy dishwashing by hand. I can see the appeal of dipping your hands in hot, soapy water. I don't, after all, put everything in the dishwasher. I do see how it could be faintly relaxing, especially if you have the water at the perfect temperature and were to take your time over it, rather than rush at it just to get it done. As much as I adore the warm stainless steel of a hot dishwasher, I do like the paraphernalia of dishwashing: the old-fashioned wooden brushes that a friend's mother sends me from her shop; the French string pot-scrubbers that I buy from the most beautiful kitchen shop in London; the old, soft, honey-colored linen dishtowels that have done years of service, not to mention the froth of bubbles of the same brand of dishwashing detergent my mother always used.

There is much satisfaction in getting things clean, in basking in the moment when everyone is quiet and the dishes are shining in their cupboard (am I alone in loving my dishwasher but hating, absolutely loathing, emptying it when it's finished?). The great thing about having done the dishwashing is the feeling of calm and quiet accomplishment that goes with it. You have made yourself and others something nice to eat. You can close down, check out, sign off . . . until breakfast.

# Cutting School

## by Joyce Chang

from the *New York Times Magazine* Style & Entertaining

> If skilled knife technique is the one thing that separates professional cooks from amateurs, why are so many chefs' hands etched with scars? *Times* reporter Chang waded into the macho world of slicing and dicing to get a handle on things.

A boy I was dating once offered to cook me dinner. He arrived with a grocery bag in one hand and his own set of knives in the other.

"What do you think that means?" I asked a friend later. "Are my knives not good enough for him?"

What I did not know then was that this particular boy would prove moody and pretentious—and, more important, that people who love to cook love their knives.

"I have always had a crush on them," says Daniel Boulud, his face lighting up, the most masterful of chefs reduced to adolescent ardor.

Boulud's crush has evolved into such a passion that he will unveil his own line of knives, made by Sabatier, in June. Eric Ripert is no less passionate; he prefers Nenox for delicate work and Wüsthof for heavier tasks. Todd English, who owns the chain of Olives restaurants, gave Mac knives to his five executive chefs for Christmas.

While I was growing up, the only knives I encountered were a huge cleaver that my grandmother used to cut everything, from pork shoulders to cucumbers that she julienned into translucent blades of grass, and her paring knife, which she used to peel apples, removing the skin in an uninterrupted ribbon. My mother preferred long hours at work to slaving at the stove. So the array of knives I encountered on my quest for knife skills was a whole new world for me.

Knife skills are the building blocks for any cook. Technique is as important as the quality of the knives themselves. At the Institute of Culinary Education (formerly known as Peter Kump's New York Cooking School), Norman Weinstein, a knife-skills instructor there since 1995, favors Wüsthof knives. He considers these basics: a chef's knife (an 8-inch is standard; a 10-inch, according to Weinstein, even better), a serrated knife (for bread, cakes, tomatoes and citrus), a 4½-inch utility knife and a paring knife. A good cook can do just about anything with one 8-inch chef's knife. But knives, like shoes for the fashion-conscious, can become an addiction. It seems no coincidence that a cook's collection of knives is known as her wardrobe.

Though Weinstein's groups are small—typically twelve to fourteen students a class—it is like any other school environment. Cliques form, and it becomes clear which ones have the skills and which don't. The haves talk about what kind of knives they own and ask questions about how often to use a steel (a sharpener that looks like a ski pole for dolls). The have-nots stand stupidly silent, making a mess of carrot bits at their stations. I kicked my wayward carrots underneath the chopping island.

"Shake hands with your knife," Weinstein told us. The proper grip is like a squash grip, relaxed and not club-fisted. Choke up on your knife so that the back knuckle of your index finger rests where the blade meets the handle. Keep your arm relaxed. Your stance should be open. Move your food, not your body. We learned to cut celery with a gliding motion. The motion of your fingers along the celery defines the thickness and uniformity of the cut.

We learned the carrot cut. Unlike the celery cut, the carrot cut enables the knife to lift off the board. The motion should still be fluid, Weinstein emphasized.

By the time we got to potatoes, I was pooped. Weinstein called us to his station to observe his technique.

"I don't want to hear this," he said, making chopping noises on his cutting board. "Do you know where you hear a lot of that?" he asked me.

I hesitated.

He swept his arm in my direction. "In Chinatown!" he exclaimed.

I snorted, appalled at being singled out in class not for praise or correction but for my ethnicity, as if I were somehow predisposed to bad chopping. Recognizing my dismay, he quickly added that he taught Chinese cooking and knew lots of Chinese chefs who had rare and amazing knife skills.

I returned to my station, the blood rushing to my face. I chopped my potato—loudly—like the Chinese person that I am. And with some effort, found calm in the motion, losing myself in a rhythm.

Asian knife skills are different. Chinese chefs prefer to use cleavers, like the one my grandmother used. Japanese knives are famous for their sharpness, their single-sided edge and the hardness of their steel. I decided to explore my native knife skills and got a lesson at the high-end Chinese restaurant Shun Lee West. Michael Tong, the owner, prizes his China-trained chefs, who are as much craftsmen as they are cooks. "The other night," he said, "one of my chefs made a centerpiece, a garden of vegetables and chestnuts with two pandas playing ball."

Under the tutelage of the chef Sun Dao Man, whose hands were as gnarled as an old oak, I learned to cut ginger and tofu into paper thin slices with a cleaver that looked more like a weapon.

"Slowly, slowly," he cautioned as I wielded my mini hatchet. We communicated in a mixture of English, Mandarin and sign. "I am afraid for you," he said. "But you can't be afraid of the knife. Otherwise you'll never learn." I cut a ginger root into blocks. Laying one piece flat on the board, I rested my fingers on top, and cut into the ginger horizontally, less than a millimeter thick. I could see the blade beneath the surface. Two short saws, and one deeper stroke, and I was through.

He showed me how he chopped carrots until they looked like flying-fish roe. His cleaver sounded like a woodpecker against the board. When I tried, it was not nearly so fast or so fine.

"Use the power," he said, gleefully. "Oh, you're gonna feel it tonight." I could already feel the bite of a blister on my index finger where it rubbed against the thick steel spine of the cleaver. But then my personal knife Yoda became more serious. "Use your power wisely," he said. "If you must chop for hours, you will be so tired. Power is not for wasting. And watch that little finger of yours. It has no home, and if you're not careful, you'll lose it."

The last stop on my knife-skill odyssey was the restaurant Daniel, where I arranged a lesson with the owner and chef, Daniel Boulud.

"A knife is a companion," he said. "I like to play with new ones, but I have a lot of old ones, too." He took one from his "tool kit," a wooden case that once held a bottle of 1995 vintage Cristal Champagne but now holds a dozen knives that have captivated his interest. He held up an old chef's knife with a worn wooden handle wrapped in green tape. "Here are my initials carved in," he said. "You see, sometimes other chefs would steal your knives. That is the worst thing a chef can do."

With an impish smile, he led me down the stairs from his office into the kitchen. "Let's go play," he said, his toolbox tucked under his arm.

"Before you start, wet a towel to put underneath your board so that it won't slip," he began.

We cut a chicken and filleted a fish. He held my hand as I slid the flexible boning knife against the skeleton of the fish. Keep the blade flat, he advised. "The tip should not come up. Your hand should be off the board so that you can keep your blade as flat against the bone as possible."

We julienned leeks. We trimmed turnips. We skinned squash, following the curve of the vegetable and using a small cut to stay close to the skin. We diced potatoes. We removed the rind and contoured a blood orange with a bird's-beak knife. We pared artichokes, cleaning the stem, removing the outer leaves until we got to the heart.

Looking at the ragged, wounded heart I had produced, he said, "You left your heart here." He pointed to the leaves lying on the cutting board. I took another. He waited anxiously as I slowly and deliberately pared.

"They come in a box of 120," he said. "How long do you think it would take you?"

"A week," I ventured.

"It takes my guy 20 minutes to do them downstairs. When it's 5 P.M. and you're in the weeds, that's when you learn."

"What does 'in the weeds' mean?"

"It means you're in trouble."

When at last I finished, he held them both up for another chef to see. They dissolved into a pitter-patter of French and bursts of laughter. I could feel my cheeks burning, not just from the heat of the stoves.

The kitchen was full of men—good-looking, French-speaking men. They winked and flirted to my giddy delight. Had I not read Anthony Bourdain's book, *Kitchen Confidential*, which details the womanizing ways of chefs, I might have doled out my business card in the name of research more liberally. During the course of the afternoon, I could not tell whether I was developing a crush on knives or on my teacher. I was sad to leave. My kitchen is much less electric.

To test my new skills, I threw a birthday party for my friend

Kelley. I planned to make a warm artichoke-and-chicory salad. I also planned to borrow Boulud's recipe for *paupiette* of sea bass (sea bass wrapped in thin slices of potato seared in a pan) over leeks with a Barolo sauce. I bought two whole sea bass and skinned and filleted them myself. The potatoes required a mandoline. Since any good Chinese chef could make origami cranes with a cleaver if he wanted, I figured I could at least cut paper-thin potatoes. With guests arriving at eight, I realized at seven that I was not a good Chinese chef and that the trick I needed to perform would be brainstorming a Plan B for my sea bass—fast. Four massacred artichokes later, I gave up trying to "choke" them. With an hour to go and without a first or main course, I was in the weeds.

I raced out to the market and grabbed some tomatoes, peppers, cucumbers, whatever looked fresh. I made a chopped salad like the kind I love to eat in Los Angeles and can't seem to get done right in New York. The potatoes originally destined for the *paupiette* became mashed. I minced leeks like a madwoman, the steel ringing a perfect pitch against my board. A friend arrived early— luckily she was the one friend who had gone to culinary school— and helped me get ready.

"You're the chopper—cut this onion," she commanded.

"Yes, chef."

I was in a state of chop.

We made a bed of leeks and onions in a roasting pan, laid my lovely salt-and-peppered fillets on it, sprinkled on some thyme, drizzled it with olive oil and sealed it in tinfoil. Twenty minutes later, I served my filleted sea bass with mashed potatoes and more buttery sautéed leeks. I drizzled my Barolo sauce from Boulud's recipe, and my friends were none the wiser.

As my guests left, I sent them each home with the remainder of the chocolate cake I baked. I returned to the crumb-covered plate, having saved the best for last. Picking up my new Wüsthof knife, cake still clinging to the blade, I ran a finger along its side and tasted the sweetness.

# The Torch Is Passed, Handle First

by Amanda Hesser
from the *New York Times*

In her frequent *Times* pieces Hesser contemplates not only the hautest of haute cuisines but also the homely kitchen rituals that bind friends and family together. Here she celebrates a tool that fits her hand like she was born to it.

A cook, no matter how well equipped, is apt to favor some tools over others. One may be a sauté pan, loved for the way its handle lies in the palm like a smooth, heavy stone. Or perhaps a spatula, bent from age and rounded to the contours of the bowl it scrapes. Or a rolling pin whose grain is bright from years of absorbing butter in pastry doughs.

These objects tend to wear with use and show their age. They often are beautiful to look at or gain character over time, as they change color or shape. Unlike many modern tools, which can be admired for their design and efficiency, these tools rarely have a brand. (If they do, the stamp or label has long since been rubbed off.) You may like your OXO peeler, but it's doubtful that you will ever feel such affection for it.

For at least four generations in my family, the beloved tools have been antique bone-handle forks. Although they vary in shape and size—so much that it is nearly impossible to find two that are identical—all of ours share a few qualities. They are about seven inches long, with handles secured by rivets. The carbon steel tines are long, as slim as toothpicks and quite flat. Each has the weight of an expensive fountain pen.

Thomas Keller, the chef at the French Laundry in Yountville, California, does not let his cooks use tongs, as the curved ends can damage delicate foods like eggplant, and, in his view, tongs lack finesse. And many other chefs prohibit their cooks from using long-tine roasting forks when turning food. None would look kindly on the bone-handle fork. I have been through stages of using tongs, which are handy for turning heavy meats, and roasting forks. I have tried wooden tongs and offset spatulas. But again and again, I return to the three bone-handle forks I own. One was given to me by my mother on my thirtieth birthday. My grandmother gave me another when I was married. That's how valuable they are to cooks in my family.

Both had scoured antique shops for them and saved them to give to me on those special occasions. Bone-handle forks are usually at least one hundred years old, and can date to the Civil War era. Most were made in England and New England.

"I've been trying to reproduce them for years," said Peri Wolfman, the vice president for product design at Williams-Sonoma. "Not in bone, of course, but in a good polymer or good plastic. But I haven't convinced Williams-Sonoma to do it."

The forks are utilitarian, never meant for fine tables. They are made of sturdy, long-lasting materials.

"The first fork that we know about in Europe was recorded by Peter Damian around 1060," said Carolin C. Young, a food historian. For a long time, they were rare, seen only in homes of the wealthy, and even then were not necessarily used for eating, but for picking up things like preserved fruits. Louis XIV, Ms. Young added, considered eating with a fork to be unmanly, and refused to. It wasn't until the middle of the eighteenth century that most people really began using forks.

Wood was sometimes used, rather than bone, to make the handles of forks for people with lower incomes. Bone-handle forks were later sold in sets with knives—a nineteenth-century Sears catalog offered a set of six forks and knives for $1.50, Ms. Wolfman said.

Now, a quick search at eBay on the Web (under "bone handle fork") will turn up a handful, many already worn, some with tines aslant from years of use by a right-handed person. Rarely do opening bids exceed five dollars.

One of my forks was made with just two tines, which suggests, according to Andre Burgos, a collector of bone-handle forks and an antiques dealer in Warwick, New York, that it may have been made in the eighteenth century, when stabbing food to hoist it from a passing platter was a necessity. Ms. Wolfman said it could also have been a bread or a potato fork, meant for piercing and lifting. Another has three tines, also a sign of its age. Mr. Burgos said three-tine forks tended to be made in the nineteenth century, and four-tine versions suggest the twentieth century or later. All three are unmistakably old.

The metals are the color of slate; the tines are all different lengths. On one fork, a concavity has been worn into the back of the handle by a right-hander's index finger. Someone loved this fork long before I did. It's hard to imagine just how many years it was used to conform to that finger. What did he or she eat with it?

Although bone-handle forks were designed to be used for eating, my mother, grandmother and great-grandmother always used them in cooking, where their thin, sharp tines can be a great advantage. You can slip one under a steak to see if it's browning, without damaging the meat. You can use it to pierce a simmering carrot for tenderness, or to check whether a piece of braised lamb has softened. The thin, sharp tines won't get stuck in the carrot or lamb, and they leave barely a mark.

I have used mine to urge a cake to let go of the sides of a pan, to scrape up pan drippings when making gravy and to turn onions in a roasting pan. When I am cooking, a fork becomes an extension of my own hand, a set of fine claws to deftly manipulate things I cannot touch. And whatever the task, the bone handle stays cool.

The handles of such forks are often made of cow bone, sometimes horn, Mr. Burgos said. The metal is usually carbon steel, and if the fork comes from the late nineteenth century or after, it might be plated with nickel.

Cleaning one requires the same attention as when washing a well-seasoned iron pan. Bone-handle forks should never be put in the dishwasher. Instead, rinse them quickly in hot sudsy water, and dry immediately. Ms. Wolfson said that to shine up the metal, scrub it with Bar Keepers Friend, applied with a fine steel-wool pad.

My grandmother's fork is just barely surviving. Having lifted and turned soft-shell crabs and having pierced a lifetime of steamed cauliflower, it has been rendered frail by its journeys from hot stove to soapy water. The slivers of bone have pulled away from the slender steel base. She now uses a pink rubber band to hold it together. Mine are comparatively polished—intact, untarnished and ready to age along with me.

# A Man and His Stove

## by David Leite
from *Bon Appétit*

Leave the low-tech tools to cooks like
Amanda Hesser—when men take over the
kitchen, they often want to crank the power
up to eleven. At least David Leite, proprietor
of the website leitesculinaria.com, has kept
a sense of humor about his kitchen
predilections.

It got to the point where I couldn't walk into a bar anymore.
You know the land, the true bastions of testosterone, the ones
so thick with blue smoke that the neon beer signs look like UFOs
hovering in a patch of midnight fog. It wasn't for moral or religious reasons, lack of money, or even an alcohol problem that
prompted me to slink out, emasculated, never to return. It was
because I was a phony.

While other guys swapped J.Lo fantasies or nearly came to
blows defending their classic El Caminos, all I could think about
was a commercial-style Viking stove in white enamel. I stared into
the mirror, tawny with nicotine, and dreamed about how perfectly risen my white-chocolate cloud cake would be, thanks to
my baffled-heat convection oven.

The slow disenfranchisement of my manhood, as one friend
likes to call it, began eight years ago when I took my first cooking
class. I walked into the kitchen, and there, lined up against the wall,

were three hulking 48-inch Vikings, gleaming like a row of squat, sweaty sumo wrestlers. I was smitten. Their unqualified size and power thrilled me. Was this what my father felt like when he walked with mouth agape through the lawn-mower department at Sears? Surely it was, because my cooking teacher, a saucy wisp of a thing with a yappy Chihuahua voice, had to nudge me out of my reverie, much as I had to poke my father awake to drag him to the toy aisle.

Chihuahua Lady and I got off to an unfortunate start because I summarily refused to make the requisite lobster à L'américaine (I won't eat anything that can look me in the eye; I always think it's memorizing my face so that it can hunt me down in the afterlife). Miffed, she proceeded to heave a pot of water almost as big as she was on top of the stove and then cranked the burner to high. In no time the water was roiling, and she flung in a couple of stricken-looking lobsters. Trying to drown out the imagined screams of these defenseless creatures, I turned my attention to my work: making a sauce for chicken pot pie. "Wimp work" was the technical term she used. But while I whisked the roux, I was astounded that the same stove that could murder so violently could simmer so gently. I vowed right then and there, amid the barking of Chihuahua Lady to "Get a move on, big boy," to buy all 48 inches of one of these steel babies.

My enthusiasm lasted until I got home. The most my postage-stamp-size kitchen could handle was a Mini Me version of the colossi from class. Not to be outmaneuvered by Manhattan real estate, I opted instead for the still-manly 30-inch model for my weekend house in Connecticut. That bad boy was big enough to come with bragging rights and delicate enough to turn out flaw-less tuiles.

Of course, buying this monster would require some creative accounting, because, thanks to a suicidal economy, the money I had set aside for a rainy day had evaporated long ago. Cashing in my paltry IRA was clearly out of the question, so I looked around for something to sell. My eye landed on my 1987 Mercedes, which I had christened Sadie. My heart sank. That old car had taken me everywhere. And even though the air-conditioning didn't work, the sunroof was broken, and the passenger seat shuddered when adjusted, I adored her. I stood in the kitchen looking at the catalog, chockablock with shiny Vikings, and then at Sadie. Vikings, Sadie. Vikings, Sadie. After some haggling, I got just enough from the Mercedes dealership to buy the stove.

On V-Day I sat at the bottom of my driveway, which is practically a vertical slope worthy of hiking boots, with the phone in one hand and a hazard flag—taken from Sadie's trunk before I abandoned her—in the other. This would be one time that the delivery truck wouldn't pass by. Because the telephone wires swag low overhead, the delivery guys, two men as bulky as the stove, had no choice but to leave the truck in the street and push the range up the driveway on a dolly. After much cursing on the foreman's part, punctuated by colorful hand gestures that compelled him to keep letting go of the stove, I grabbed a hold. In a show of raw physical prowess that would have cowed Mike Tyson, I helped push, lest the last material asset I owned should go tumbling into the street amid a flurry of my own cursing.

Once alone with my coveted Viking, which I immediately nicknamed Thor, I whipped out a batch of cookie dough I had made earlier that morning. I fired up the oven and scooped out nine identical balls of the stuff. I slid them into the inferno and waited precisely ten minutes. When I opened the door, I realized I had a steep learning curve ahead of me. Like my friend Pam's Jaguar, which I almost plowed through the master bedroom of our rental house on Martha's Vineyard, evidently my new stove was far more powerful and terrifying than I had imagined; my cookies had been, for lack of a better descriptive, incinerated.

I was undeterred. It was simply a matter of learning the range's distinctive personality, I told myself. (Of course, the idea of reading the instructions never occurred to me until my friend Alan waved the booklet in my face.) It took ruining a cobbler, two chickens, a lemon tart, and a dozen cookies before I was able to harness Thor's might. But after that, I could roast any fowl my butcher threw my way, sauté the crunchiest sweetbreads, and turn out an almond *financier* with a crumb so fine even Julia Child would be jealous.

Last night, I crept downstairs to look at Thor, not unlike how those men in car commercials tiptoe out to the garage and curl up to sleep inside their new BMWs. I ran my fingers along the sleek, sexy door handle. I revved up each burner to its full 15,000 BTUs. I even cleaned the stove top with Windex. I thought of the guys at the Marble Dale Pub and their raucous one-upmanship. I imagined marching back in there with my towering white-chocolate cake—the killer version with pistachio buttercream frosting. I place it on the bar amid the overflowing ashtrays and empty beer glasses, and watch. Conversation about Heidi Klum sputters to a halt, and the brutes begin to circle. Without waiting for forks, one digs in, then another, and another, caveman-like. As they give themselves over to the pleasures of French butter and imported white chocolate, the machismo vanishes. When the plate is empty, they rush me, offering the keys to their Dodge Ram pickups and to their girlfriends' apartments in exchange for one more impossibly perfect bite of cake. I toss back my head and laugh. I turn and saunter out the door, leaving them despondent. I win. I am victorious.

# Desperate Measures

by Matthew Amster-Burton
from eGullet.com

Amster-Burton's frequent essays on eGullet.com (he's the website's Seattle-based Northwest correspondent) are delightful windows onto an Everyman's culinary preoccupations. Raise your hand if his obsession with getting organized sounds familiar.

The insight hit me Thursday morning as I opened a 5-pound bag of King Arthur bread flour. For years—*years, mind you*—I've been using a 14-cup Le Creuset canister to store my flour. It's a handsome acrylic model with an ingenious airtight closing mechanism. Unfortunately, a 5-pound bag of flour is about 19 cups. I have refilled this canister dozens of times, and each time I somehow convince myself that things will be different—that this time all the flour will fit. Then I die a tiny silent death and shove a not-quite-empty flour bag into the cupboard.

They've been selling flour in 5-pound bags longer than I've been alive, and it suddenly occurred to me that, maybe, they (I'm someone who firmly believes there's a "they" directly responsible for everything) also sell containers designed to hold five pounds of flour. I walked down to the store and returned with a 21-cup Rubbermaid container. It was on sale for four dollars. I whipped out my electronic label maker and printed a "King Arthur Bread

Flour" sticker for the new container. If you don't have an electronic label maker, I recommend the Dymo LetraTag.

I patted myself on the back and got to work making pizza dough; though as I was putting the flour back in the cupboard I saw something shocking and upsetting: another Le Creuset canister, completely filled with two-thirds of a bag of granulated sugar. Something snapped. I'm not the chest-thumping sort of guy, but I think I was having a Tool Time moment. "I can fix this problem," I said, looking at a cupboard strewn with open bags of nuts, pasta, sugars, and grains. "I can fix it with more Rubbermaid."

Last time I had one of these moments, I ended up cleaning out my junk drawer, driving two dozen nails into the kitchen wall, and hanging gadgets from them. It worked out pretty well.

Recently I reread Steven Levy's great book *Hackers: Heroes of the Computer Revolution*. The book was published in 1984, when the Internet was still the ARPAnet and the Apple II ruled. That was the year I got my first computer, an Apple IIc. Levy describes how many of the young hackers were drawn to computers because the computer was a world where they could be in complete control. "Every Man a God" is the title of one chapter. If something goes wrong with the computer and you're smart and meticulous enough, you can fix it, guaranteed.

The real world doesn't work like that. But maybe my cupboard does. Those unsalted peanuts I spent five minutes digging for the other day can go into a 4-cup plastic container labeled "unsalted peanuts." Entropy will decrease.

The coolest dry-goods arrangement around is chef Joachim Splichal's, as seen in the book *Great Kitchens*. Splichal's kitchen island has little drawers on all sides, dozens of them altogether, and each drawer has a window so you can see the ingredient within. Unfortunately, there's no room in my kitchen for an island.

The project needed a guiding principle. I settled on this: no product should remain in its original packaging unless that packaging makes it easier to store and retrieve. Another principle would be: no space-wasting round containers. Catchy, aren't they? This is why I never had a punk rock band; I lack sloganeering skills.

Then, perhaps inspired by Levy's primordial hackers, I put all my dry goods into an Excel spreadsheet. And it told me a lot about why I needed to update my storage strategy. For example, we have nine kinds of sugar. If you had asked me how many kinds of sugar there are in the entire world I might have guessed eight. For the record, our sugars are regular white granulated, fructose, light brown, superfine, palm, powdered, turbinado, muscovado, and demerara. "Turbinado," "muscovado," and "demerara" are all Spanish words that mean "overpriced brown sugar."

For each dry good, I looked up the typical quantity we buy (19 cups of flour, for example) and chose a standard container for it. I took the spreadsheet with me to the store, which happily still had 25 percent off all Rubbermaid, and I spent.

Then, racked with buyer's remorse, I began to doubt the project. Was I guilty of modernist hubris? Was I trying to impose a simplistic order on an inherently complex system? Would I end up with the cupboard equivalent of Le Corbusier's Radiant City, all traffic jams and nowhere to go? Would there be satisfaction at the end of the journey or just a nagging desire to redo the linen closet?

A couple of problems soon became apparent.

Dry goods in plastic bags are impossible to find when you need them, and they tend to leak. But they are compact. Put the same ingredients in plastic containers designed to hold a little more than you need, and suddenly you have *less* cupboard space. I also realized I'd forgotten about the tea shelf. No, organizing teabags and loose tea is not a hard problem, but when the rest of the cupboard is moderately organized, the jumble of PG Tips, Celestial Seasonings, and Stash looks like the start of a spirited game of 52 pickup.

But there were also bursts of cleverness. I took the top off a tall container and stood up all my bags of long pasta in it. I closed the cupboards and saw more wasted space: the white expanse of the cupboard doors. So I taped up some cellophane sheet protectors to slip recipes into when I'm cooking.

It's too early to say whether my project will improve my life or even be worth the cash I spent on Rubbermaid. But it has changed the way I look at the world, or at least the kitchen.

On Saturday I visited my sister-in-law in Sacramento. She hosts Tupperware parties. Naturally, and perhaps foolishly, I brought up my kitchen storage problem with her. She brought out some Tupperware props, and as I started to tell her about my Excel spreadsheet, she flashed a knowing smile. "You mean like this?" she asked, printing off a "Tupperware Custom Kitchen Planning Storage Chart." It was a little slicker than my spreadsheet, but all the elements were there: the dry good, the quantity, the suggested storage device. For decades my idea had been operating as the driving force behind Tupperware parties. What will I think of next?

Cooking? I'll do some of that next week, although, hey, I can never find the shirt I'm looking for. There's probably a fix for that, maybe involving special hangers.

# Stocking the Larder

# Makin' Groceries

by Jessica B. Harris

from *Beyond Gumbo*

> Celebrating the entire gamut of African-American cooking traditions—from soul food to street snacks and every gumbo on the map—Harris' book mixes cultural anthropology with tempting recipes, topped off with warm-hearted anecdotes of people and places she loves.

I first fell in love with markets in Paris, where every Sunday morning my French "father" and I would head off to the *Marché de Neuilly* to *faire le marché*. He'd gather up dew-dappled bunches of leeks and sniff Cavaillon melons, while I'd gaze in wonder at the artfully arranged abundance that changed with the seasons. I honed my market love wandering ankle deep in pig swill; in open-air markets from Guadeloupe to Abidjan to Old Delhi, talking to the vendors, challenging my cast iron stomach, and learning to poke, pick, and bargain with the best of them. Returning to the United States, I missed the everyday ordinariness of the open-air markets. New York's farmer's markets are somehow too Birkenstock precious, and the supermarkets in my Brooklyn neighborhood are filled with double-wide women in stretch pants buying steaks, industrial quantities of potato chips, and grape soda. I contented myself with the city's fancy-food emporia designed for the gastronomically sensitive where each precious plum is swaddled like the baby Jesus.

I rediscovered my fascination in the supermarkets of the South. My first inkling came when a brief stop at an Atlanta Publix transformed me into an aficionada. No provincial purveyors these; not only were there the grits and souse meat, pickled okra and pork rinds, Alaga syrup, and Octagon soap that had punctuated my up-North–down-home childhood, mangoes and jalapeños, coconuts and jerk sauce also lined the bins and shelves in silent witness to a new cultural diversity. Items were available in one shop it would take hours of crisscrossing New York's ethnic neighborhoods to locate. I was hooked.

Subsequent visits and a second home in New Orleans have transformed me into a supermarket sociologist. I've learned that Morton's is to the South what Diamond Crystal is to the North, Hellman's is the *ne plus ultra* of mayonnaise, fifty-pound bags of rice are the norm for the Low Country, grits come without a Quaker on the package, and there are too many types of corn meal to count. I've discovered raw peanuts, Creole tomatoes, and a ginger ale that comes in three strengths.

Each chain has its own personality as well. In Houston, aisles are flagged by country and I can pick up basmati rice and mint chutney mix in one, Pickapeppa and cassava meal in the next, and locate British sugar cubes for tea in a third, all in the same trip. Charleston's Harris Teeter amazes and amuses with its tubs of pimento cheese and benne wafers at a fraction of their souvenir shop tab a few blocks away; I fill my cart and my larder. My friend Ellen Sweet says that she makes her living transporting food across state lines and I certainly try to emulate her, totin' boxes and cartons and brown paper shopping bags on and off planes. The French *faire le marché* that got me started in my love of markets translates into creolized English as makin' groceries in New Orleans, where I am fortunate enough to spend time. There, Dorignac's has turduckens at Thanksgiving, Foodies has picked up some of the slack from the late lamented Spice Inc., and Whole Foods reveals its West Coast origins with more than a hint of California's organic ethos and the fresh produce is just dandy, when I can't find it in season at the farmer's market in the Warehouse District. I've even discovered friends who will ferry me across the river for fresh Creole tomatoes or satsumas in season. As I wander the South, I remind folks that I brake for markets. Winn Dixie still feels a bit politically charged to me as a transplanted Black Yankee, but just saying Piggly Wiggly makes me smile.

# Slow Sausage

by Corby Kummer

from *The Pleasures of Slow Food*

> All you ever wanted to know about the Slow Food movement is in this handsome history/cookbook by Kummer, food editor of *The Atlantic Monthly*. Though his tone is calm and thoughtful, Kummer argues for Slow Food in the surest method possible—by making us hunger for it.

Torsten Kramer is a big man given to big pronouncements, used to commanding without contradiction. He is a ninth-generation butcher, producing a full range of sausages, wursts, and smoked and fresh meats. His recipes and where he makes them are as authentic as is imaginable. Kramer lives and works in Lübeck, a town on the Baltic in the far north of Germany, where people think you can't eat cabbage and kale without sausage, and his products are not an occasional indulgence but an everyday necessity. Kramer is the ideal Slow Food artisan, in using and reviving old recipes for products traditionally made in his region and taking care to make them from animals raised with respect. He is also a careful businessman who insists on quality but does not let the costs of producing it run away with him—another important part of the Slow Food ideal.

Even if his curt courtesy and always-busy demeanor hark back to generations past, Kramer is working in a way very different from both his forebears and his colleagues. He is a butcher in a country that has always cared about the soundness of its food supply, and that has gone through several serious mad-cow disease scares. He is younger, part of the generation that was and remains affected by the social movements of the '60s. And he's a, well, unusual fellow. You never know how he'll greet you when you walk into the 1960s mini-supermarket his father built in front of the butchering workshop. He'll tell you if he thinks you asked a dumb question. But he's also generous (and frequently quite friendly) in explaining why his sausages and cured meats are better—the purity of the organically raised animals, the care and tradition in the preparation—and in giving out tastes.

Not that he tastes much himself. After he married a woman he met in Jordan, Kramer converted from Lutheranism to Islam. He can no longer eat most of the products he makes, because most contain pork. Instead he relies on the smell and touch that guided him through many years of apprenticeship—skills that have made him as busy and sought after as he is ornery.

It's a shame he can't enjoy his dozens of sausages and hams. They're homemade and genuine and use impeccable ingredients, which is reassuring news to anyone who grew up being told not to inquire too closely as to what went into the sausage. They're also extremely good. One bite of a wiener, for instance, shows why children who visit his store clamor for half a frank, the way their American counterparts insist their mothers buy a Tootsie Roll. The precooked sausages, moist and soft and only lightly seasoned, are made from fresh, organically raised pork, in contrast to beefy American hot dogs, which are laced with additives and soy flour and, although also precooked, good only when warmed up. Kramer's roast pork shoulder is a similar revelation—pure and sweet and barely salted, just grainy enough to give interest, and a beautiful light pink. His home-smoked ham shows you why *schinken* is sacred to all of Germany. Its rich mahogany makes prosciutto look pallid, and the flavor of the resilient meat seems to stay forever in the mouth, the husky smokiness lingering long after you swallow. Then there's the salami, cured for months and authoritatively seasoned: one with paprika, garlic, and red wine; one with cardamom and rum; one with just salt and white pepper; one with nutmeg and caraway seeds. All are light pink flecked with ivory-colored circles of fat, like red Italian marble. All taste only of the honest ingredients in them—and the history and skill behind them.

The medieval city of Lübeck, with its corbel-roofed brick warehouses out of a Vermeer cityscape, happens to be a Slow Food redoubt. One of the first founders of a chapter outside Italy was Lothar Tubbesing, a charismatic and dedicated local restaurateur. With his wife, Heike, Tubbesing cooks and serves meals at Lachswehr, their elegant restaurant in a mansion on a city canal. Tubbesing has become a point of reference for many Europeans looking to understand how they can fit into the Slow Food movement. He has inspired other Germans and friends from Nordic countries to begin Slow Food chapters. Tubbesing has also become something of a legend at Slow Food headquarters in Italy for his exuberant dedication and for being a wellspring of ideas.

Lothar tells any Slow-minded visitor to Lübeck, which draws many tourists for its beauty and its marzipan, that it's essential to visit his friend Torsten to see an artisan with real passion for preserving local history and food. Tubbesing is as outgoing as Kramer is recalcitrant, and when he directs people to what might be the best sausage shop in a sausage-crazed country, he makes sure to prepare them for a character.

Humanity seems to come as a vague disappointment to Kramer, who works so hard to bring it the very best and most healthful foods he can. He speaks with scorn of people who "buy with their eyes, not their brain." Take the salami he worked years to perfect without saltpeter, the nitrate that makes sausages red or rosy pink. Saltpeter makes salami attractive to the eye, and nearly every maker—certainly industrial meatpackers but most artisans, too—uses large amounts of preservatives. So reliant on saltpeter are butchers today that the art of making sausage without it has practically been lost. The trouble is the color. Kramer always gives customers who ask for salami a taste of each kind: the admittedly grayish brown one made without saltpeter, and the bright reddish orange one made with it. People don't taste or buy with their eyes shut, though, and a large number of customers automatically choose the red one.

Customers come from thirty miles away to buy Kramer's meats and sausages, because they know they can trust his products. Long before health concerns roused the German public into demanding to know the source of its meat, Kramer decided to use only animals from local farms, most of them organically raised. During the mad-cow and foot-and-mouth scares in November 2000 and the summer of 2001 he was nearly overwhelmed by the stampede of customers to his shop—one of the few places in the united country where people could safely satisfy their cravings for sausage, a national staple. In the weeks after the first cases of mad-cow disease were discovered in Germany, his number of customers nearly tripled.

Kramer was ready for them, but not for so many. The huge increase in demand would please most businessmen, but Kramer didn't have a way of obtaining enough organically raised animals from the several farms who supplied him. And even if he could get the meat, he didn't have room to expand his production. He waited for the rush to subside, and made plans to enlarge his workrooms.

The solution, he thinks, is for there to be more artisans like him. In the kind of collaboration that happens when like-minded people find one another through Slow Food, Kramer and Tubbesing and a woman nearby who raises organic cattle have started thinking of how to sell organic food direct to customers rather than having to deal with middlemen. Tubbesing is also trying to start an outdoor, year-round market for organic farmers and artisanal producers.

Another encouraging development has taken form just a few miles from Kramer's shop: the opening in 2001 of a government-funded research center on a beautiful farm built by a local aristocrat as a hunting retreat. Its mandate is to conduct long-term studies on organically raised produce and animals. The center's establishment owes much to Renate Kunast, who was appointed Germany's minister of agriculture in the same year. Upon her appointment, Kunast called for 20 percent of the country's land to be farmed organically by the year 2010—an ambitious goal, given that perhaps 2 percent of the land and 1 percent of the farms in the entire European Union were farmed organically at the time. The rest of Europe took note.

The first task the center faced when it opened was to persuade the neighbors—that is, local politicians—that organic food doesn't mean old, wilted, gnarled, unappealing food. This perception dogs the organic movement worldwide, and the best way to counter it anywhere is to give people good organic food. For the new research station's first event, it looked for the local artisan whose products could win people over.

That artisan was Torsten Kramer. He set up a barbecue to grill a few sausages and serve some organic potato salad, another sacred national dish. Children, naturally, and skeptical local politicians too lined up in the courtyard of the picturesque former stables, at a daylong festival that brought together Lübeck Slow Food members, local farmers, and people who never thought they'd want anything organic. They came back for seconds. It helped that there was an organic version on tap of perhaps the single most-loved German food after sausage: beer. With foods like this, Germany and its neighbors might convert to organic farming sooner than anyone dared hope.

# Travels with Captain Bacon

by Pete Wells

from *Food & Wine*

A senior editor at *Details*, Wells takes us on a classic road-movie jaunt along the blue highways of Kentucky and Tennessee, all in pursuit of what may be the premier Guy Food: prime artisanal smokehouse bacon.

Throughout most of my twenties, for reasons that would probably make me laugh today if I could remember them, I was a vegetarian. For nearly a decade, I wouldn't go near a porterhouse or a lamb chop or a sparerib. I always made an exception for bacon, though. People thought I was kidding when I explained that bacon wasn't a meat, it was a condiment. But I was serious: Bacon seemed to me like pure flavor—not animal, vegetable or mineral but some intensified, distilled essence of sweetness, salt and smoke. I'm not sure I was wrong, either. A recent cookbook was titled *Everything Tastes Better with Bacon,* and it's true. Everything *is* better with bacon. Even vegetarianism.

It stands to reason, then, that Dan Philips is one of my few heroes. A contributing editor to FOOD & WINE, Philips is the founder of the Grateful Palate, a wine importer and mail-order epicurean-foods company perhaps best known as the perpetrator of the Bacon of the Month Club. The Bacon of the Month Club works like the Book of the Month Club, except that the book club mails you some fat best-seller that sits on a shelf until your next yard sale, while a pound of bacon from the Grateful Palate usually finds itself in a hot skillet before the mailman can say goodbye. One customer wrote Philips to say that each time a new shipment arrives, her husband dances around the box.

The Grateful Palate now offers more than thirty artisanal bacons from all over the United States, and collectively they outsell everything else in the catalog, including stunning bottles of Australian Shiraz and more esoteric treats, like crimson pumpkin-seed oil from Austria. Philips, a native Californian, grew up eating bacon almost every day and still does, but he was nonetheless surprised by the size and excitability of the audience for it. He knew something powerful was at work, but he wasn't sure what. "I don't know much about bacon, other than how it tastes," he told me recently. Then he said that he was thinking of calling on some of his favorite producers to see if he could learn why their bacons are so different from one another. Western Kentucky and Tennessee are particularly rich in makers of country bacon—pork bellies that are cured with salt and sugar, hung to dry and then saturated with hickory smoke. This suggested to Philips a road trip, starting in Louisville and meandering south-by-southwest down country roads in search of knowledge, wisdom and pork products.

I didn't beg. Perhaps I did drop a few dark warnings about the dangers facing the solitary hunter of breakfast meats in isolated rural areas.

A few days later, Philips sent an e-mail inviting me to ride shotgun on his bacon safari. "I have a few stipulations," he wrote. "1. I must always be addressed as Captain Bacon. 2. No stopping for cheap hookers. 3. You must bathe at least once every day. Other than that, I'm easy to travel with."

I met Captain Bacon at 6 A.M. in front of the Seelbach hotel in Louisville. With full cups of coffee and empty stomachs, we charted a course for Bremen, Kentucky, where Charlie Gatton makes a product he calls Father's Country Bacon. As we crawled along a two-lane blacktop past cornfields and convenience stores (MARL-BORO'S $2.10!!!), I mentioned a legendary country-ham producer I'd heard of down in Trigg County, hinting strongly that I might go on a bathing strike unless I was promised I'd leave the state with a ham in my suitcase. "Don't worry," he said. "All the bacon guys we're going to see also make hams." The two meats are cured and smoked in essentially the same way, he explained, but then hams are aged for months while bacon is ready in a couple of weeks.

"If the same people make both things," I asked, "then how come country ham gets talked about as an artisanal product, while bacon is just . . . bacon?"

The Captain thought it over. "I don't really know," he said. "I think it's because people buy hams for Christmas, for Easter. A ham is an event. Bacon is more of an everyday thing." But toothpaste is an everyday thing, and so are socks. Neither could lure me to the back roads of Kentucky before sunrise. Bacon is an everyday thing, but a mystery, too—an everyday mystery.

About three hours out of Louisville, we turned at a sign that read GATTON FARMS. HOME OF FAMOUS COUNTRY HAMS, BACON & SMOKED SAUSAGE. On our left was a white shingle farmhouse planted in the shade of a 100-year-old cypress tree. To our right was a white fence whose pickets were topped by miniature silhouettes of hams. The door of a low-slung redbrick structure swung open, and Charlie Gatton, Jr., stepped out to welcome us.

A born salesman, Gatton took over his family's cured-meats business two years ago, after his father died. Since then, he has experimented with new products, like smoked rib-eyes, and new ways of reaching customers, including a Web site and appearances on the Home Shopping Network. "Bacon is good for you," he tells viewers. "When you cook it, most of the calories melt away." The Home Shopping phone operator who hopes for a relaxing day at work is in for a bitter disappointment when Charlie Gatton gets in front of the cameras.

Gatton told us cheerfully that we'd come on a good day. Just that morning, he'd received more than a ton of fresh bacon from his packer in Missouri. "Dan, would you like to help us cure some?" he asked.

Clearly, Philips couldn't refuse and still call himself Captain Bacon, so he followed Gatton to a fluorescent-lit back room where half a dozen men worked while Hank Williams, Jr., sang "Family Tradition" on the radio. The sides of bacon, cut from the bellies of freshly slaughtered hogs only the day before, were piled up in rubber bins on the floor. Another bin was filled with Gallon's curing rub: salt, brown sugar, white sugar and tiny amounts of nitrite, a preservative that helps the meat keep its alluringly rosy complexion.

"You just rub the cure all over with your hands," Gallon said. "No, don't brush off the extra. You want to leave some on there." Philips coated a slab with the sand-colored rub until it looked like a boogie board after a day at the beach. Then Gatton laid it down in an empty bin so the salt could begin sinking into the meat and drawing out the water. As the meat dries, its flavor gets more concentrated, giving country bacon the depth and intensity that sets it apart from its gentler, brine-cured cousins.

"Our bacon loses about 12 percent of its weight in water when we cure it," Gatton said. "Supermarket bacon has water *added,* with needles that pump it full of brine. When I go on Home Shopping, I'll cook a strip of supermarket bacon. It shrinks to half the size of ours."

Back out front in a small retail shop decorated with fourteen blue ribbons from the Kentucky State Fair, the Captain had a private word with Gatton while I chatted with Gatton's wife, Lori. She doesn't have her husband's polished spiel, but she is a steadfast believer in the mystery of bacon. Whenever she leaves Kentucky, she packs a little plastic bag of Father's Country Pepper Bacon, cooked and crumbled, because she has discovered that some restaurants of otherwise high quality "don't put any bacon on their salad at all," she told me. "And if I can't have bacon on my salad, I just don't care about it."

We said our good-byes and started for Owensboro to spend the night; nobody has yet thought to build a hotel in Bremen, Kentucky. In fact, nobody has built much of anything in Bremen except barns and grain silos and squat brick houses and places of worship. One church we passed had the kind of sign on its front lawn that you see outside car lots and flea markets. TO GO NOWHERE FAST, it read, FOLLOW THE CROWD.

"This area reminds me of where my mother grew up," the Captain said. "She was from Eastern Kentucky. Appalachia. Her grandfather made bacon, and she used to cook it for me every morning. We went back a few years ago to find her house. It's mountainous there, but somehow it looks a lot like this—kind of bleak."

"Where was your father from?" I asked.

"Hungary. He was an Orthodox Jew. He's the reason I got into wine and food. He was a doctor, and he thought he needed to cultivate an interest in the finer things, so we always had expensive wines at dinner. When I was fourteen, I took a wine-tasting class, just so I could know more about it than he did. I was always very competitive with him." That this rivalry with his Jewish father set young Dan Philips on a path that has now brought him to his mother's home state in search of the flesh of the swine struck me as material that would keep a psychoanalyst busy for years.

We set out early the next morning for Greenville, Kentucky, home of the Scott family. As we glided south past soybean fields and horse pastures, Captain Bacon phoned for directions.

"She said we look for the turn where it used to say Scott Road until someone stole the sign," he said.

Scott Road, when we finally found it, led us straight to Scott Hams, and to Leslie and June Scott. Like most small smokehouses, the Scotts' operation grew out of a family farm; Les's grandfather cured hams and bacon at hog-slaughtering time each winter. Les, a talkative man in a cap from the American Cured Meat Championship, raises bulls now as a hobby. "Kept pigs once," Les said. "We had 'em down on the other side of that hill there. The guy who built the pen for us said, 'Don't worry, the smell will never reach you all the way up here.' Well, the very first day we had those pigs, the wind was blowing straight toward the house. It was a real hot day, so we had all the windows open. . . ."

The Scotts showed us the parts of the process we'd missed at Gatton Farms. We saw the refrigerated lockers where the bacon ages for two weeks after it's rubbed with the dry cure, and then the smokehouse where it hangs on wood scaffolds for another week in the company of smoldering hickory logs and sawdust. Les Scott's cure is as simple as they come: brown sugar and salt. His bacon can shade in color from pink to nut brown, since Scott uses no nitrites. The Captain asked him why.

"My people didn't do it," Les said flatly. "My dad never did it back on the farm. So I don't do it."

I had now sampled the two smokiest bacons the Grateful Palate sells, and there was no mistaking one for the other. Gatton Farms' was complex and "gnarly" (the Captain's word); and its flavor lingered and developed like a Polaroid coming into focus. Scott's was more straightforward, lucid: If it were a painting it would have been called "Still Life with Smoke, Salt and Pork."

Les Scott's bacon is cured about ten days longer than Charlie Gatton's and gets a little less smoke. It doesn't have the white sugar Gatton's has, either. But I wasn't sure that the cure and the smoking technique were the whole story. Les said he believed there's more going on, that bacon is changed by the age and the shape and the smell of the rooms where it's made. "I think each smokehouse has its own personality," he said.

Tripp country hams is about an hour north of Memphis in Brownsville, Tennessee, one of those small Southern towns centered around a courthouse square. Charlie Tripp works out of a cavernous facility built by his grandfather, who hauled the sand for the building's mortar in a mule cart. The building started life as a meat locker, where, in the days before electric refrigeration, farmers could store what they'd butchered. Somewhere along the line, Tripp's father "started curing a few hams," Charlie said. Today, Tripp's bacon is a favorite among Grateful Palate customers— perhaps because Tripp puts cinnamon and cayenne pepper in his dry cure. Philips asked if his family has always had the recipe.

Tripp shook his head. "No. We were doing it one way, and it made . . . a good bacon," he said. Good, not great. "But there was this old man who used to have a stand on the side of Highway 70, and he did a little curing. He said, 'I've got a recipe that makes a delicious bacon.' So eventually he gave it to me, and that's the one I've been using ever since." The genius of this mystery man's secret formula became clear a few minutes later, when Charlie Tripp invited us back to his house, an antebellum mansion across the square. His wife, Judy, had baked biscuits and fried some ham and bacon. In the bubbling oil, the spices floated free of the bacon's edges and coated the entire slice. The low burn of cayenne, as many snack companies know, has the effect of making you want to eat more and more, and that's just what we did.

Our bacon safari over, we turned back down Highway 70 toward Memphis. The Tripps had warned us not to drive so much as one mile above the speed limit unless we yearned for an extended vacation in Fayette County, so we had time to soak up the roadside scenery. The far western end of Tennessee begins to look and feel like the Mississippi Delta. Trees are smothered in kudzu, cotton fields flat as a concrete floor extend to the horizon, and tilting frame shacks promise cold beer in roughly painted letters. This is the landscape that bred the blues.

The blues and bacon: both born of poverty, both looked down on by people who feel it's worth drawing a distinction between high culture and low. "When Charlie was talking about that old man by the side of the road, I started thinking about Robert Johnson," Captain Bacon said. "The way Johnson said he'd met the devil on the highway, and the devil showed him how to play guitar."

Johnson is the great Mississippi bluesman who turned up in Delta juke joints in the 30s with a fluid, dextrous guitar style no one had seen before. According to legend, he summoned the devil at midnight at an intersection about 100 miles south of here, and traded his soul for guitar lessons. There is, naturally, a rival theory, which holds that Johnson simply went away for a year and practiced. This is the theory I subscribe to, and in fact I believe it's condescension of the worst kind to suggest that a poor black refugee from the Mississippi cottonfields could make himself into a towering musical figure only through the intervention of sorcery. But then I listen to "Me and the Devil Blues" or "Crossroads" and even the rationalist in me is tempted to say that the song, if not the singer, is in communication with the supernatural.

I'm inclined to be a rationalist about bacon, too, attributing everything to techniques of curing and smoking. But when I eat a slice of great country bacon, I wonder if Scott might be right about the personality of the smokehouse, not to mention the man in the smokehouse, and maybe even the figure by the side of the road who whispered into the ear of the man in the smokehouse. Somewhere in these streaky bands of pig meat is a powerful sorcery that can make a grown man dance around a cardboard box, corrupt a pure-minded young vegetarian and transform the son of an Orthodox Jew into Captain Bacon.

Dan Philips phoned me a few weeks after our trip to say he'd been listening to a lot of blues and eating even more bacon than usual. He'd just received a package in the mail: first-run samples of Grateful Palate private-label bacon, cured and smoked by Charlie Gatton following a recipe that Philips had whispered in his ear on our visit.

Philips said he thought it turned out "pretty damn good" and offered to send me a pound. But no matter how many times I asked, he wouldn't tell me exactly how it was made.

That, he said, would have to remain a mystery.

# Sustaining Vision

by Michael Pollan
from *Gourmet*

As in his recent best-seller *The Botany of Desire*, journalist Pollan explores the delicate interplay between biology and our human food supply system. As in Corby Kummer's preceding piece, Pollan's seeming dispassion makes him a effective proponent of a new way of farming.

O n the second day of spring, Joel Salatin is down on his belly getting the ant's-eye view of his farm. He invites me to join him, to have a look at the auspicious piles of worm castings, the clover leaves just breaking, and the two inches of fresh growth that one particular blade of grass has put on in the five days since this paddock was last grazed. Down here among the fescues is where Salatin makes some of his most important decisions, working out the intricate, multispecies grazing rotations that have made Polyface one of the most productive, sustainable, and influential family farms in America.

This morning's inspection tells Salatin that he'll be able to move cattle into this pasture in a few days' time. They'll then get a single day to feast on its lush salad bar of grasses before being replaced by the "eggmobile," a Salatin-designed-and-built portable chicken coop housing several hundred laying hens. They will fan out to nibble at the short grass they prefer and pick the grubs and fly larvae out of the cowpats—in the process spreading the manure and eliminating parasites. (Salatin calls them his sanitation crew.) While they're at it, the chickens will apply a few thousand pounds of nitrogen to the pasture and produce several hundred uncommonly rich and tasty eggs. A few weeks later, the sheep will take their turn here, further improving the pasture by weeding it of the nettles and nightshade the cows won't eat.

To its 400 or so customers—an intensely loyal clientele that includes dozens of chefs from nearby Charlottesville, Virginia, and Washington, D.C.—Polyface Farm sells beef, chicken, pork, lamb, rabbits, turkeys, and eggs, but if you ask Salatin what he does for a living, he'll tell you he's a "grass farmer." That's because healthy grass is the key to everything that happens at Polyface, where a half-dozen animal species are raised together in a kind of concentrated ecological dance on the theme of symbiosis. Salatin is the choreographer, and these 100 acres of springy Shenandoah Valley pasture comprise his verdant stage. By the end of the year, his corps de ballet will have transformed that grass into 30,000 pounds of beef, 60,000 pounds of pork, 12,000 broilers, 50,000 dozen eggs, 1,000 rabbits, and 600 turkeys—a truly astonishing cornucopia of food from such a modest plot of land. What's more, that land itself will be improved by the process.

Who says there's no free lunch?

"Sustainable" is a word you hear a lot from farmers these days, but it's an ideal that's honored mostly in the breach. Even organic farmers find themselves buying pricey inputs—cow manure, Chilean nitrate, fish emulsion, biological insect controls—to replace declining fertility of the soil or to manage pest outbreaks. Polyface Farm isn't even technically organic, yet it is more nearly sustainable than any I've visited. Thanks to Salatin's deft, interspecies management of manure, his land is wholly self-sufficient in nitrogen. Apart from the chicken feed and some mineral supplements he applies to the meadows to replace calcium, Polyface supplies its own needs, year after year.

Salatin takes the goal of sustainability so seriously, in fact, that he won't ship his food—customers have to come to the farm and pick it up, a gorgeous adventure over a sequence of roads too obscure for my road atlas to recognize. Salatin's no-shipping policy is what brought me here to Swoope, Virginia, a 45-minute drive over the Blue Ridge from Charlottesville. I'd heard rumors of Polyface's succulent grass-fed beef, "chickenier" chicken, and the super-rich eggs to which pastry chefs attribute quasimagical properties—but Salatin refused on principle to FedEx me a single steak. For him, "organic" is much more than a matter of avoiding chemicals: It extends to everything the farmer does, and Salatin doesn't believe food shipped cross-country deserves to be called organic. Not that he has any use for that label now that the USDA controls its meaning. Salatin prefers to call what he grows "clean food," and the way he farms "beyond organic."

That it certainly is. The fact that Salatin doesn't spray any pesticides or medicate his animals unless they are ill is, for him, not so much the goal of his farming as proof that he's doing it right. And "doing it right" for Salatin means simulating an ecosystem in all its diversity and interdependence, and allowing the species in it "to fully express their physiological distinctiveness." Which means that the cows, being herbivores, eat nothing but grass and move to fresh ground every day; and that chickens live in flocks of about 800, as they would in nature, and turkeys in groups of 100. And, as in nature, birds follow and clean up after the herbivores—for in nature there is no "waste problem," since one species' waste becomes another's lunch. When a farmer observes these rules, he has no sanitation problems and none of the diseases that result from raising a single species in tight quarters and feeding it things evolution hasn't designed it to eat. All of which means he can skip the entire menu of heavy-duty chemicals.

You might think every organic farm does this sort of thing as a matter of course, but in recent years the movement has grown into a full-fledged industry, and along the way the bigger players have adopted industrial methods—raising chickens in factory farms, feeding grain to cattle on feedlots, and falling back on monocultures of all kinds. "Industrial organic" might sound like an oxymoron, but it is a reality, and to Joel Salatin industrial anything is the enemy. He contends that the problems of modern agriculture—from pollution to chemical dependence to foodborne illness—flow from an inherent conflict between, on one hand, an industrial mind-set based on specialization and simplification, and, on the other, the intrinsic nature of biological systems, whose health depends on diversity and complexity.

On a farm, complexity sounds an awful lot like work, and some of Salatin's neighbors think he's out of his mind, moving his cows every day and towing chicken coops hither and yon. "When they hear 'moving the cattle,' they picture a miserable day of hollering, pickup trucks, and cans of Skoal," Salatin told me as we prepared to do just that. "But when I open the gate, the cows come running because they know there's ice cream waiting for them on the other side." Looking more like a maitre d' than a rancher, Salatin holds open a section of electric fencing, and eighty exceptionally amiable cows—they nuzzle him like big cats—saunter into the next pasture, looking for their favorite grasses: bovine ice cream.

For labor—in addition to his six-foot, square-jawed, and red-suspendered self—the farm has Salatin's wife, Teresa (who helps run their retail shop and does the bookkeeping), children Rachel and Daniel, and a pair of paid interns. (Polyface has become such a mecca for aspiring farmers that the waiting list for an internship is two years long.) Salatin, whose ever-present straw hat says "I'm having fun" in a way that the standard monogrammed feed cap never could, insists, however, that "the animals do all the real work around here." So the chickens fertilize the cow pasture, the sheep weed it, the turkeys mow the grass in the orchard and eat the bugs that would otherwise molest the grapes, and the pigs—well, the pigs have the sweetest job of all.

After we moved the cows, Salatin showed me the barn, a ramshackle, open-sided structure where 100 head of cattle spend the winter, every day consuming 25 pounds of hay and producing 50 pounds of waste. Every few days, Salatin adds another layer of wood chips or straw or leaves to the bedding, building a manure layer cake that's three feet thick by winter's end. Each layer he lards with a little corn. All winter the cake composts, producing heat to warm the barn and fermenting the corn. Why corn? There's nothing a pig likes more than 40-proof corn, and nothing he's better equipped to do than root it out with his powerful snout. So as soon as the cows go out to pasture in March, the "pigerators," as Salatin calls them, are let loose in the barn, where they proceed systematically to turn and aerate the compost in their quest for an alcoholic morsel.

"That's the sort of farm machinery I like—never needs its oil changed, appreciates over time, and when you're done with it, you eat it." Buried clear to their butts in compost, a bobbing sea of hams and corkscrew tails, these are the happiest pigs you'll ever meet. Salatin reached down and brought a handful of the compost to my nose; it smelled as sweet and warm as the forest floor in summertime, a miracle of transubstantiation. After the pigs have completed their alchemy, Salatin spreads the compost on the pastures. There, it will feed the grasses so that the grasses might again feed the cows, the cows the chickens, and so on until the snow falls, in one long, beautiful, and utterly convincing proof that, in a world where grass can eat sunlight and food animals can eat grass, there is indeed a free lunch.

Did I mention that this lunch also happens to be delicious?

# Earthy

## by Margo True
from *Saveur*

In this installment of *Saveur*'s wonderful series celebrating under-appreciated vegetables, staff editor True pays tribute in elegant prose to the much-maligned beet root. Even a confirmed beet hater might be inspired to rethink.

I must've been six or seven when I first faced a beet. Until then, I had happily eaten everything my parents set in front of me: sardines and squid, liver, broccoli. But then came the beet, slices of it slithering from a can. They were mushy and dead-looking, with the sickly-sweet smell of a bog, and I rejected them mentally, emotionally, and physically. My parents, out of compassion, did not press them on me; but from then on my heart would actually hammer at the sight or smell of beets. I'd worry whenever I'd go to eat at friends' houses, for fear their mothers would serve beets or empurple our hard-boiled eggs with beet juice. At restaurants, beets lurked in salads, staining the crisp lettuce and innocent cucumbers with their malevolent, lurid ooze.

Then, several years ago, while in a particularly questing mood that had led me to love, among other things, sea urchin and quinoa, I happened to be at the home of a friend whose cooking I liked and trusted. She had just roasted some fresh beets, and I caught a whiff as they were cooling on the counter. To my surprise, my pulse stayed calm. So I took a bite—and they tasted fresh and heady, the way rich black dirt smells after a rain, with a deep but not cloying sweetness. They were smooth, firm, and slightly crunchy and glistened appealingly in their dish. Fresh beets, I realized, bear no relation to the processed kind, and I have loved them ever since.

The beet, *Beta vulgaris,* emerged thousands of years ago somewhere along the Mediterranean coasts, and the primordial plant— a leafy green with a puny white or yellowish root—now grows wild on beaches from Europe to India to Australia. Over the centuries, it begat swiss chard, also known as leaf beet; the mangold or mangel-wurzel, a foot-long beet grown for livestock feed; the white sugar beet, which yields 40 percent of the world's refined sugar (and nearly half the refined sugar in the United States); and, of course, the table beet, for which we should thank the early Romans, who were probably the first to develop the root— including its red varieties—for food.

Beets are still sold, at least in this country, mostly in cans or jars (twice as many beets are grown for processing as for selling fresh). But fresh beets are far more flavorful and versatile: they can be sliced raw into crunchy, paper-thin wafers and tossed with a mustardy vinaigrette; roasted or boiled or sautéed until tender; even pickled, with horseradish and onion. In India, beets are simmered with spices like turmeric and black mustard seed. The Germans make a red sauerkraut with beets, bacon, and green cabbage; and the Lebanese like to slather steamed beets with a thick, garlicky yogurt sauce sprinkled with mint. In eastern Europe, where the beet is venerated, tables teem with beet dishes—such as Russia's vinegret, a salad of beets, potatoes, carrots, brined cucumbers, and raw onion; ćwikła z chrzanem, the horseradish-beet condiment of Poland; and, of course, beet soup, eaten all across the region in countless guises, from the sturdy Ukrainian borscht to a clear, brilliant Polish version in which mushroom dumplings bob.

Gold beets are okay, and chioggias—spiraled red and white

inside like lollipops—are charming, but to me the plain round red beet is the fascinating one. Part of the pleasure lies in the cooking of it. While it's still warm, you can slip its skin off easily with your fingers, and there in your hand—sticky and sanguine with juice— is a glossy, heavy globe that looks like a gigantic ruby. Its glorious purplishness comes from betacyanin, a substance that also tints bougainvillea and perhaps, in times past, human cheeks (it's said that Russian women once used beet juice as rouge). And no other vegetable is so alluringly earthy. What makes it taste that way are infinitesimal amounts of a compound called geosmin also found in farm-raised catfish and blue-green algae. Microorganisms in soil produce this compound, and for some reason the beet absorbs more geosmin than does any other root vegetable—so it truly is the earthiest of them all.

I suppose I could be sad about my years of missing out on beets. But why? To discover that something I once considered so loath-some can inspire in me such unmixed delight—well, that is yet one more small proof that life is worth living.

# Buttering Up

by Jeffrey Steingarten
from *Vogue*

Steingarten's monthly mini-epics in *Vogue* (recently collected in *It Must Have Been Something I Ate*) dive headlong into one food enthusiasm after another, guided by his analytical palate, exhaustive research skills, and sly humor.

It is one of the great tragedies of human existence, which the old-time Greek playwrights handled poorly, if at all, that butter is very bad for human beings, yet incomparably delicious. Did you know that dogs are not harmed by fat and cholesterol? It is a burden we humans have been uniquely chosen to bear. (Butterfat is 62 percent saturated—the bad kind of fat; despite its greasy image, pig's lard is just 40 percent.) That's why the food world has, over the past two decades, learned to use butter sparingly in cooking—if not in baking—as a scrumptious flavoring instead of a main ingredient. Some will tell you that if you eat only the finest butter, you'll be so satisfied that you will consume less of it. This is incorrect. You will want to eat much more of it, a half-pound at a sitting, on very good bread, nicely chilled, sliced into slabs. No, the true point is that it makes no sense to use up your bad-food points on mediocre butter.

"It's like standing in front of a fireworks stand," my friend from

Texas exclaimed, amazed at the profusion of fancy butters in the average New York City grocery. Never having seen a fireworks stand, I was unable to get into my friend's homespun simile, but his excitement was contagious. Today you can buy butters from France and from Italy, from England and Ireland and Denmark, from Catalonia in Spain, and from every dairy state in this country. And we've just discovered a butter from the Czech Republic, less expensive than any other and quite good-tasting.

My favorite butter is Burro Occelli, or at least it used to be. It comes in thick, pale, rounded rectangles, imprinted with wooden stamps of cows or mountains, and wrapped in stiff, wonderfully crinkly sheets of parchment paper closed at both ends with little round metal fasteners. It is made in the sub-Alpine foothills of the Italian region of Piemonte, with milk collected from cows that graze in high meadows thick with flowers and herbs of the most vivid colors and intense aromas—forget-me-nots, buttercups, Turk's cap (a lily), daisies, and gentian (if you believe in both Beppino Occelli's story and my ability to translate it). This Edenic milk is quickly centrifuged into cream and skim milk. The cream is then gently pasteurized, lightly fermented, and churned into the freshest, most aromatic butter you can imagine.

The awful problem is that every time I have bought costly Burro Occelli in the past year or so, it has tasted rancid; I keep on buying it, hoping that this time it will be fresh and aromatic. And each time my hopes are dashed. That fabulous, crinkly Italian parchment paper and the butter's low temperature prevent me from detecting the rancidity as I sniff for it in the shop. My subsequent depression is so powerful that I never bother to return the defective Occelli.

What is rancidity? My dictionary says it is "the rank unpleasant taste or smell characteristic of oils and fats when no longer fresh," which I guess is largely circular. A powerful bitterness is always my first impression of a rancid fat. In liquid oils, rancidity is easy to anticipate by a fishy odor that precedes by several days a fully bitter taste and repulsive odor. It appears to be caused by exposure to the air (which gives rise to the production of compounds with names like alcohols, aldehydes, ketones, esters, and hydrocarbons, some of which are truly unpleasant) and, in butter, also by the action of water—butter is about 15 percent water—which releases various disagreeable acids, especially butyric acid. Rancidity is encouraged by heat and light, which is why expensive olive oils are always bottled in dark glass and why some people keep their valuable cooking oils in the refrigerator. I know the way fresh Occelli butter can taste because I've eaten it in Italy on bread, straight off the knife, and licked from the fabulous parchment paper, most recently two years ago at a Slow Food exposition in Turin—fresh and aromatic for sure, but much more than that. I lack the words.

Could it be my fault? I keep my Occelli wrapped up tight in the dark refrigerator; besides, how can oxygen get to the most deeply buried molecules at the center of the patty? It must happen long before I buy it. So I sent off for a bottle of butyric acid, which I would sniff to diagnose the problem. I was informed that if the acid was completely pure, I would need a Hazmat suit, and so I settled for a dilute solution, a fortunate decision. The odor was very unpleasant in amazingly diverse ways. I had been told it would smell cheesy, but I would call it locker room, which is just one aspect of rancidity. Butyric acid is surely only part of the Occelli problem.

It was time to telephone Mr. Beppino Occelli in Farigliano, in the Langhe region near Cuneo and the Maritime Alps, where I had once tasted Burro Occelli at its absolute freshest. I have hired a new assistant named Elizabeth, who on her résumé claimed fluency in Italian. Young women have duped and deceived me before. Now we would discover the truth. Almost as soon as Elizabeth dialed the number, she was bubbling away in what sounded to me very much like the Italian language. What a relief. But her skillful conversation revealed only that Mr. Occelli was attending a festival in Parma and would be unreachable for some time. Neither of the two chief importers of Burro Occelli would take responsibility for the flavor of what they are selling.

A few weeks ago, I found myself in such an unaccountably fine mood that I decided to stop grumbling and do something about it—in short, to light just one little candle rather than curse the darkness. I pondered the idea of making my very own most perfect butter, in the privacy of my home. I will admit to wondering if this was a crackpot scheme that would wreck both my kitchen and my wardrobe. Neither had fully recovered from a recent and entirely unsuccessful attempt to inch just a bit closer to solving the great Southern-fried-chicken problem. Nonetheless, I began reading about butter. It's fun to read about butter.

It is amazing how easily one can turn cream into butter. Both are pretty simple substances—at least for our purposes. Rich cream contains about 40 percent butterfat in the form of tiny little microscopic globules. (Globules are diminutive globes.) When cream is churned or agitated, the globules are forced together into a mass of nearly pure, continuous butterfat with other things trapped inside—water droplets (maybe 15 percent), milk proteins and sugar (2 percent), and crystalline fat (a little). When you try to whip unchilled heavy cream or make ice cream from an insufficiently chilled mixture you often end up making butter by mistake. At least I do. Fifty-five to 65 degrees F. is ideal for the butterfat globules to be nice and soft and nearly liquid.

So, I simply poured a pint of good heavy cream into the electric-mixer bowl, attached the whisk, and let her rip. Cream sprayed everywhere. I cleaned up the largest blobs, except the ones on the ceiling, and began again but at the slowest speed, watching the cream pass through all its usual stages. First it thickened, then it foamed, and finally it mounted, expanding into a fluffy cloud of nicely whipped cream. This is normally one's stopping point, but I kept the mixer whirling, now at the highest speed. Nothing happened for the longest while, except that the cream got increasingly less airy. And then, almost from one moment to the next, the bubbly cream transmogrified into a bunch of yellowish clumps sloshing around in a pale, watery white liquid. I poured the white stuff into a glass and pressed the clumps together.

I was astounded, and very, very proud. I had invented butter!

I tasted the liquid and found it sweet and cool and very delicious. I had also invented buttermilk!

This is all almost true. As I soon discovered by reading a written recipe or two, the buttermilk was surely buttermilk, but the yellow clumps were not quite butter. After decanting the buttermilk, you must wash the butter—yes, actually rinse it in ice water as you continue to whirl it around—to remove any buttermilk and milk solids that stick to the yellow clumps, after which you are supposed to press and knead and beat the butter with a potato masher or pastry cutter or whatever to expel some of the remaining water. Then you squish the butter into a neat and compact shape and wrap it up.

I took another pint of rich, heavy cream and produced nearly a half-pound of washed and kneaded golden butter. Yes, somehow, somewhere along the way it actually becomes golden. It took about twelve minutes.

What hath God wrought, I exclaimed in hushed tones as I fell contentedly into my easy chair, a toasted baguette spread thickly with handmade *Vogue* butter in one hand and a cool glass of true, sweet buttermilk in the other.

Yet even as a sense of complete satisfaction penetrated to my very core, a seed of doubt had already begun sprouting in my brain. Was my butter bland? What are we searching for in butter, anyway? I turned to the USDA, whose Agricultural Marketing Service is responsible for grading the quality of butter. (Just as with beef, there are mandatory inspections for hygiene and optional inspections for quality—which the meatpacker or butter maker must pay for. The butter grades are AA, A, and B, and you find them printed on the package, set in the middle of a shield-shaped symbol.) The grades are determined primarily by flavor, with deductions for flaws in body, color, and salt, if any.

I got hold of the USDA butter scorecard. The flavor criteria are not qualities such as "heavenly," "amazing," "fresh 'n' creamy," or other terms we food critics use. Instead there is a long list of unpleasant tastes and aromas that butter makers must avoid at all costs: cooked, acid, aged, bitter, feed, coarse, flat, smothered, storage, malty, musty, neutralizer, scorched, utensil, weed, whey, and old cream. (Each of these is carefully defined, and a probable cause suggested. The USDA criteria and their descriptions are in themselves a high-level course in butter tasting.) Your butter is graded according to its worst flavor deficits, then "disrated" by defects in body (from crumbly through ragged boring, which sounds totally awful), color (mottled through wavy), and salt (sharp or gritty).

Sure, I may be prejudiced, but apart from the possibility that our *Vogue* butter might be called "flat," I would have to award it the coveted AA rating. Still, something was missing. The USDA quality grades are clearly meant to protect us from defects. They do not guarantee epiphanies.

I turned to Jonathan White, who from 1993 to 2000 ran the Egg Farm Dairy in Peekskill, an hour north of New York City, in partnership with Charlie Palmer, chef and owner of several distinguished restaurants, including Aureole in New York City and Las Vegas. Their motto was "Setting the Dairy Industry Back 100 Years," and their most universally admired product was a cultured butter—frequently judged the best butter in America. It was high in butterfat (86 percent, compared with the legal minimum of 80 percent) and therefore low in water, more plastic when cold (the good kind of plastic—pliant and even taffy-like in texture), and it had a higher melting point—important in baking puff pastry and other flaky treats. Cultured butter is made from cream that has first been ripened or fermented or soured so that the final product takes on a memorable, interesting tang—a very mild acidity—and perhaps other complex flavors, while retaining a fresh, whole cream flavor. Most butters made in Europe are cultured.

Jonathan's formula for homemade cultured butter has you softly re-pasteurize the cream and stir in a "starter" culture to spark the fermentation (you can use sour cream, yogurt, buttermilk). You let it develop for twelve hours as bacteria in the starter culture convert lactose—the sugar in milk—into lactic acid. Then you cool it down and churn it up in a food processor until the butter "comes"—just as I had done before. (Jonathan has posted his discursive recipe on his own Web site, www.cowsoutside.com.) Gentle pasteurization is accomplished by heating the cream to 165 degrees F. in a pot on the stove, removing it from the heat, covering, and leaving it for a half-hour. Commercial pasteurization uses very high temperatures for very short time periods, which does no good to the taste of the cream.

On my first try, I let the cream sour too far, and the resulting butter was as tart as any I have tasted, and not very pleasant. I went out and bought a pH meter, and searched in vain for my high school chemistry book. On my second try, the result was close to perfect, truly deserving of the name "*Vogue* butter." Or so I thought at first. Yes, it was fresh and sweet, with a nicely acidic edge. But the flavor did not linger in the mouth. My butter had a weak and puny finish.

After reading a little more about the flavor of butter, I realized that fine-tasting butter has a variety of attractive flavors. A compound called diacetyl, for example, contributes a caramel-butterscotch-toffee note. Aha, I reflected, that's just what the *Vogue* butter needs—diacetyl.

But which bacteria would do the trick, and where would I find them? Each species has its own favorite foods and produces its own special flavors. I located a company called Dairy Connection that sells dairy cultures, and soon I had three small envelopes of freeze-dried bacterial colonies—one that generates a strong lactic flavor and only a little diacetyl, one that does the reverse, and one said to be a fine compromise between the two. Elizabeth and I pasteurized a big pot of cream, divided it in three, stirred in the cultures, and let them ferment. Each envelope was meant to culture 50 gallons of cream, so our one-pint batches required only 1/400th of the entire dose, not an easy thing to measure out. I asked Jonathan White for advice. If your fermentation goes too far overnight, he counseled, just add more sweet cream the next morning.

How did the three latest *Vogue* butters turn out? We won't know until tomorrow afternoon. I have the highest hopes.

A few weeks ago at midnight, I stood in deep contemplation before the refrigerator, sampling some of the treats I had stored there and aimlessly reading, by the dim light of the refrigerator bulb, the labels on the various jars and packets. When I came to the Land O Lakes butter carton, I gasped. Land O Lakes is the only national brand of butter and always scores well in competitive tastings. And there it was in the three-word list of ingredients: "Cream, natural flavoring." Could it be? Could this proud butter maker adulterate its cream? I telephoned the number on the end of the box and received a friendly, straightforward answer. "We add lactic acid to our unsalted, sweet-cream butter," I was told, "to improve its flavor."

Two degrees of separation later, I had entered a world whose very existence I had not even suspected, the world of "starter distillates" and a company called DairyChem. "Most manufacturers of *unsalted* butter find that the production process itself does not give them the distinctive 'butter flavor' they are seeking," the DairyChem materials explain. But the large butter producers are not willing to ripen and ferment their own cream. Instead, DairyChem and a few smaller firms prepare a variety of starters using a range of bacteria and then distill the starters' essential flavors. (European producers favor a strong dose of caprylic acid, characteristic of goat's milk.) The butter companies buy starter distillates specially designed for them, and pour these flavorings into their cream; the FDA considers them natural as long as the bacteria belong to these species: *Streptococcus lactis, S. cremoris, S. lactis* subspecies *diacetylactis, Leuconostoc citrovorum,* and *L. dextranicum,* all of which can presumably be found in milk. DairyChem's list of clients is long and impressive. Nearly all commercial unsalted butter these days appears to be flavored with starter distillates. Producers of handmade butter are skeptical that added flavors have the complexity and depth of those produced by flourishing colonies of bacteria. And as one scientific paper concedes, ". . . the complexities of the flavour of sweet-cream butter are still obscure." DairyChem says that flavors from these two sources are indistinguishable.

In hopes of adding the *Vogue* butter account to their roster of satisfied customers, I suppose, the people at DairyChem are sending me several butter flavors, including their favorite bouquet. (Pure diacetyl itself smells like movie-theater popcorn.) I feel that it is only a matter of time before *Vogue* becomes the butter of choice at your finer homes and restaurants.

In the meantime, I'll continue to collect and sample butters from the astounding proliferation in my local shops. (We have just recently discovered another source for Burro Occelli and several Irish butters, only a few blocks away.) The American Cheese Society and the Wisconsin Cheese Makers Association both run yearly competitions, and I have tasted several unsalted-butter winners. Unfortunately, one recent champion is now serving five years in prison and is unavailable for buttermaking. But a fresh and delicious butter arrived just yesterday in a FedEx package from Batavia, New York. We've tasted maybe thirty unsalted butters in the past week, and while you await the ultimate perfection of the *Vogue* butter brand, these butters should make you very happy:

- VERMONT CULTURED BUTTER,
VERMONT BUTTER & CHEESE COMPANY,

WEBSTERVILLE. VERMONT. Naturally fermented, very lightly salted. Wonderfully fresh, tangy, and nutty. Widely available.
• **GOLD COW UNSALTED BUTTER, 0-AT-KA MILK PRODUCTS COOPERATIVE,** BATAVIA, NEW YORK. The butter makers attribute the incredibly fresh bloom of their product to their use of extremely fresh local cream. (I also detect diacetyl.) Available as Gold Cow at the plant also sold at Pathmark as whipped butter under the Pathmark name.
• **CADÌ,** CATALONIA, SPAIN. Bought in New York City at Whole Foods.
• **BEURRE ECHIRÉ,** DEUX-SÈVRES, FRANCE. Considered the best commercial butter in France. Widely available, too acidic for some.
• **CELLES SUR BELLE,** CHARENTES-POITOU. FRANCE.

We also tasted these butters, some of which were excellent but not, to our taste (and in the condition in which they were kept in local stores), as fine as those above: Beurre de Baratte, Normandy, France. Domaine de Provence Goat Milk Butter, Canada. Fall Creek, Wisconsin. Farmhouse Irish Country Butter, Ireland. Grasslands, Wisconsin. Isigny Ste. Mère, Normandy, France. Isigny Ste. Mère' Beurre Cru, Normandy, France. Jana Valley, Czech Republic. Kate's Homemade Butter, Maine. Kerrygold Pure Irish Butter, Ireland. Land O Lakes, Minnesota. Lescure, Charentes-Poitou, France. Lurpak, Denmark. Michigan Milk Producers Association Unsalted Butter, Michigan. Burro Occelli, Italy. Organic Valley, Wisconsin. Organic Valley European Style, Wisconsin. Plugrá, Pennsylvania. Président, Normandy, France. Ronnybrook, New York. Somerdale English Butter, England. Straus Family Creamery, California. Wuthrich, Wisconsin.

# Looking for the Lard

by Elmer R. Grossman

from *Saveur*

Professional foodies have nothing over someone like physician Elmer R. Grossman, whose dogged pursuit of the perfect pie crust led him on a quixotic quest—equal parts medical, social-economic, and religious in nature—for the ultimate shortening.

Like most of the women in our family, my mother was a talented baker. She would have been the first to admit that her pastries were perhaps not as delicate as Aunt Ella's, and her sour-cream cookies were widely acknowledged to be slightly less rich than Aunt Emma's—but when it came to pie, the basic foundation of family desserts, she had no equal.

Because her Orthodox Jewish grandparents lived in the house she grew up in, she learned to bake with Crisco, a fat with three virtues: it was not butter, so baked goods made with it could be served at the same meal with meat dishes; it wasn't lard from that brazenly nonkosher animal the pig; and it produced dependably tender, flaky pastry. When I started baking myself, I followed the family tradition. After my first dozen or so pies, though, I decided that tender and flaky wasn't enough; if I was going to go to the trouble of making a pie, the crust had to be worth eating in its own right—which couldn't be said of the Crisco-based version. Anyway, recent studies have shown that hydrogenated fats, like Crisco, are among the worst substances you can legally put into your mouth; the process of hydrogenation produces trans fats, and the more trans fats in our diets, the more likely we are to get coronary artery disease. For reasons of both taste and health, then, it was time for me to look for an alternative shortening.

The choice offered by most classic cookbooks was clear: lard. So, ignoring muffled stirrings from the grave of my great-grandfather, I started baking with this rendered pig fat. The books were right: lard-based pastry is wonderfully flaky—and the mixture of lard for texture and butter for flavor yields even better results. I was happy, and my family and friends left no slice uneaten.

Then one day I read the label on a package of the lard I was using. It said, "Contents: lard and hydrogenated lard." Well, of course; the stuff was sold from an unrefrigerated grocery shelf. If it had not been hydrogenated, it would have spoiled in a matter of days. If I wanted to avoid trans fats, I realized, I would have to find old-fashioned fresh lard, the kind that old-fashioned butchers always sold from their refrigerated cases.

By this time, my reading had revealed that all lard is not created equal. While any old pig fat can be rendered into lard, the best kind for baking is leaf lard, which comes from the collection of fat around the animal's kidneys—nearly all of which is purchased by commercial bakers, who call it leaf fat. If I was going to use lard, then leaf lard it had to be, and I set out one morning to find some.

The butcher at my neighborhood supermarket in Berkeley, California, was too young to be helpful; he had never heard of any lard that did not come in a package. The butchers at a fancier market not far away were a little puzzled. Two of them conferred briefly and reported that they recalled having sold fresh refrigerated lard some years back, but it was no longer available. They agreed that if I wanted lard, it was the package or nothing. Their African-American colleague was more optimistic. He suggested a meat market specializing in pork in Emeryville, a nearby town with a less affluent but pork-eating population.

The Emeryville store was one of those emporiums of pork that sell every part of the hog. I walked slowly down the length of the long meat counter admiring the snouts, ears, tails, and trays of pig blood. Surely they would have fresh lard? Surely not, as it turned out. The butchers advised a visit to the Housewives Market, down the road in Oakland, and there I went. It was a cavernous building with dozens of stands selling bulk foods, grains, truly obscure ethnic delicacies, fish, smoked meats, and lots of pork. They didn't have any lard, either—but butchers at two separate establishments assured me that the Mexican markets a mile away would have lots of lard since they prepared their own lard-fried foods. My hopes grew when I entered the first of these. No, they had no lard, but the market-restaurant just two blocks away was awash with the stuff. At that richly fragrant store, the owner asked only how much I wanted and whether I had brought a container. They bought the fat by the barrel and rendered it in their own kitchen. Ah, but did they have leaf lard? Well, no, replied the owner; that all went to the bakers.

By this time, it was early evening, and I went home to reconsider the problem. My wife had been somewhat concerned when I had failed to return promptly from what I'd expected to be a brief trip to the grocer. My explanation for my four-hour absence was met with relief and then a certain amount of incredulity that anyone would have spent so much time in pursuit of fat.

The next day, I went off to look for leaf lard in the pork stores on Stockton Street in San Francisco's Chinatown, across the bay. If you like food and don't mind crowds, Stockton Street is a great place: Chinese produce markets, fish markets with every kind of local and exotic sea creature, dim sum houses, restaurants—and at least a dozen Chinese meat markets. These are generally small stores, staffed by Chinese butchers, most of whom have only limited familiarity with the English language and none of whom seem to want to deal with a puzzled-looking non-Chinese man. Leaf lard? Did I want to buy pig kidney? Perhaps pig blood? Some other part of the pig? At one shop a young Chinese-American appeared at last to understand what I was looking for. "You want the fat from around the kidneys," he said. "But we don't have any! When we get the pigs, the kidneys come in a little plastic bag, and the fat has already been taken away." He pointed to a fresh side of pork lying on a long table like a body in a morgue awaiting an autopsy. "You can see the space where the kidney should be, and it's empty," he said, and, sure enough, the cavity was clean as a whistle, the fat nearly dissected away. "But, no problem," he continued. "Hop Sang, the meat market on the next corner, sells the fat."

And indeed it did. "You want kidney fat to make leaf lard?" asked the shop's owner. "How much, and when do you want it?" He told me it had to be ordered a day in advance and that I could pick some up the next day. I returned to Hop Sang the following morning. After false starts with three butchers who had no idea what I had come for, I was sent to wait in a large, dank room for a few minutes until a husky man carrying an enormous sack of pig fat appeared. Somehow I had expected kidney fat, that precious and hard-to-find material, to be presentable, if not actually handsome. It turned out to be a stringy, shapeless, slightly blood-tinged mess. Putting esthetic considerations aside, I paid for five pounds and hurried home.

My wife looked with interest and only a little dismay at the fat lying limply on the kitchen table. "What do you do with it now that you've got it?" "I'll look it up in Larousse," I replied. The process turned out to be a lengthy version of the one my mother used for rendering chicken fat. You cut the fat into small chunks and cook it slowly in a large pot with a little water. After several hours, the connective tissue turns crisp and tan (you stop before it becomes brown) and the fat is clear and transparent, ready to be poured through a fine sieve into jars and cooled overnight. (Stored in the freezer, it will last for a year or more.)

The next morning I started baking—and I can report that my search for leaf lard was worth the effort. My crust was beautifully flaky, more so even than Crisco crust, and very flavorful—and I can only assume that my arteries appreciate the effort I have made to keep them free from trans fats. (Hop Sang has closed since my visit, but I've recently discovered mail-order sources for both leaf fat and leaf lard on the Internet; see below. Or render ordinary pork fat or fatback, available from any butcher; it's not leaf lard, it still makes great pie crusts.)

## Not My Mother's Pie Crust

*Makes two 9" pie crusts*

According to Grossman, "a pie crust made with all-purpose flour is strong and firm. One made with pastry flour is tender and delicate. Using a mixture of the two is a good compromise."

2 tsp. white vinegar
1½ cups all-purpose flour
¾ cup pastry flour
2 tbsp. sugar
½ tsp. salt
⅛ tsp. baking powder
12 tbsp. chilled unsalted butter, cut into small pieces
6 tbsp. leaf lard, chilled

1. Combine vinegar and ¼ cup ice water in a small bowl. Combine flours, sugar, salt, and baking powder in a large bowl. Put both bowls into the freezer until well chilled, about 20 minutes.

2. Using a pastry cutter or 2 table knives, cut butter and lard into chilled flour mixture until it resembles coarse meal flecked with pea-size pieces of butter and lard. Sprinkle in water-vinegar mixture, stirring dough with a fork until it begins to hold together.

Press dough into a rough ball, then transfer to a lightly floured surface. Give dough several quick kneads until it becomes smooth.
Divide dough in half, gently shape into 2 balls, and flatten each ball
slightly to make a fat disk. Wrap disks individually in plastic wrap.
Refrigerate for at least 30 minutes and up to 8 hours before using.

**NOTE:**

Many quality pork stores and butchers will special-order leaf fat.
If you can't find a local source, call **D'Angelo Bros. Products**
(215/923-5637; www.dangelobros.com) to order some ($2.49 per
pound; there's a 2-pound minimum order).

# from *Sugar*

## by Fran Gage
from *A Sweet Quartet*

Though Gage's beloved San Francisco bakery Pâtisserie Française has closed, in her books she passes on her sweet secrets. The premise of *A Sweet Quartet* is basic: to examine in depth each of the baker's four essential ingredients—sugar, butter, almonds, and eggs.

When I was growing up, my entire family went grocery shopping on Friday evenings. While my parents frugally mapped out dinners for the coming week, my brother and I raided the aisles for snacks; most, but not all, of our selections were rejected by the two with the purchasing power. If I pleaded hard, I was usually allowed a bag of my favorite candy—orange bulbous forms shaped like peanuts. I don't know why they were peanut-shaped; they certainly didn't taste like peanuts, or nuts of any kind. Nor do I know, especially today, what attracted me to them.

At home, while my parents unpacked cans, boxes of frozen vegetables, quarts of milk, and plastic-wrapped packages of meat, I sat on a stool next to the built-in cupboard and methodically ate one piece of candy after another, sometimes coming close to finishing the entire bag. I remember the texture of those ersatz nuts—thick and rubbery, but breaking down quickly after a few chews, like dense marshmallows. Just as distinct in my memory was the flavor, a chemically perfumed sweetness. And if I'm not mistaken, the orange color permeated my tongue, remaining long after I had swallowed the last bite. I haven't eaten one in decades. I thought they were gone from the market, but recently I saw bags of them in a grocery store. How the power of sugar endures!

My mother's favorite candy was more sophisticated. She loved Almond Joy candy bars. Peter Paul Candy Company introduced them—their first bar to contain almonds—in 1948, with the snappy slogan, "Oh Boy! Almond Joy!" For ten cents, my mother bought not one but two bars wrapped in the same package, two for the price of one being a sound marketing ploy in the inflated postwar market. Under a milk-chocolate coating, two roasted almonds sat on top of a coconut filling. I often pestered my mother for a bite and was rewarded with a mouthful of creamy coconut, a crunchy almond, and a whisper of chocolate. It was an education for my orange-tinged taste buds.

Until the mid-nineteenth century, candy making in the United States was a laborious process. Candy was either made at home or an expensive luxury, because it was so time-consuming to produce commercially. Then, in 1847, Oliver Chase, a Boston candy maker overwhelmed by orders for his handmade lozenges—rounds of sugar and peppermint oil, held together with gum arabic—rigged up a contraption that resembled a small clothes-wringer with holes cut in the rollers. Instead of stamping out rounds from a sheet of candy, he could roll the sheet through his invention, dramatically increasing his production capacity. A few years later, he patented a mill for powdering sugar, which increased the quality of his confections. These innovations were the nascence of what would become the New England Confectionary Company, which still makes Necco wafers today.

Another pair of clever candy makers invented a revolving steam pan, thus eliminating the constant stirring that had been required to make boiled confections. Another decided to use a native sweetener, maple syrup, rather than expensive imported West

Indian sugar, to glue together the popcorn balls he sold from a cart. He also stumbled upon a confection made by immigrants from Syria called Turkish delight. It was delicious, but he couldn't decipher the source of its haunting taste until a missionary who had been to Syria provided him with a detailed recipe for the candy, including the elusive ingredient, oil of roses. He added Turkish delight to his list of confections.

Confectioners searched out other new flavors, crushing herbs and other plants for their oil, stripping sassafras bark from the tree, gathering wild gingerroot. Other flavors came from abroad—vanilla from Mexico, cloves from the Spice Islands, licorice root from Europe. Gum arabic, from acacia trees growing on Mediterranean islands, held many of these confections together. But the unit of sale was still the individual piece of candy, attractively wrapped in cellophane.

All that changed when Milton Hershey made the first milk-chocolate bar in 1900, kicking off a candy-bar revolution. The next year, he added almonds, and combination bars featuring mixtures of nuts and nougat covered with chocolate weren't far behind. Initially, people didn't flock to the stores to buy these new bars, though; loose candy was more economical. World War I changed the picture. The U.S. government commissioned Hershey's to supply soldiers with candy during the war, and, given the conditions at the front, the rations couldn't be dainty bonbons. Hershey's chemists concocted a bar containing six hundred dense calories, which could withstand temperatures of up to 120 degrees Fahrenheit without melting, and packaged it in a waterproof box.

After the war, the market for wrapped bars took off, and over the ensuing decades, candy bars with every imaginable combination of ingredients appeared—coconut, caramel, toffee, crisped rice, fudge, nuts, and especially all-American peanuts. Most were covered with chocolate, either milk or bittersweet. And what fanciful names! Charleston Chew, Butterfinger, Powerhouse, Black Cow, Slo Poke, Milky Way, Munch, Oh! Henry, Mary Jane, and Baby Ruth.

In 1923, the owner of the Curtiss Candy Company chartered a plane and dropped Baby Ruth bars by parachute over Pittsburgh, Pennsylvania. Too bad he didn't wait thirty more years, when I could have profited from his largesse.

Many of the candy-bar companies started small, then grew. But the competition was fierce. Bigger players bought out the small enterprises; some companies changed hands many times. Now Hershey owns Peter Paul, and they still make Almond Joy. Today, two giants, Mars and Hershey, control 75 percent of the candy sales in the United States, a market that totals a staggering fourteen billion dollars per year. The two are arch-rivals, with a history of sparring that spans the last century.

More recently, a unique marketing scheme that pairs snack foods with education has been developing. In 1982, a Massachusetts nursery-school teacher composed a poem about M & Ms to teach her charges to count. She developed the concept into a book, but it took twelve more years to convince a publisher that this would sell. Now, with more than a million copies of *The M & M Brand Counting Book* sold, other publishers have joined the frenzy with brand-name books aimed at children, and many more are on the way. Not everyone is happy with this trend. Some pediatricians, parents, and publishers dismiss these books as pure advertisement and are aghast at their proliferation, even if some promote "healthy" snacks.

Still, a Web site that encourages children to do their own science experiments gives a cut candy bar as an example of a cross-section and challenges the viewer to identify a whole page of candy-bar cross-sections by brand name. I was glad to see that the first example was an Almond Joy.

Although Hershey and Mars are the giants of today's candy industry, small companies with a hands-on philosophy survive, even thrive. One is Charlotte's Confections, housed in a nondescript building on a suburban street not far from the San Francisco airport. I went there one morning to witness the making of old-fashioned peppermint twist-end chews, and to pay homage to the machine that works its magic to produce them.

The chief confectioner is José Chávez, and he is a man who loves his work. He never sits down; he regularly lifts heavy loads; he repeats the same task many times. Ah, but he's a candy maker. The heavy loads are bubbling cauldrons of sugar. Or fat cylinders of white nougat, some striped like a barber's pole, others containing a tiny green Christmas tree, also made from nougat, hidden in the center. Or blocks of chocolate wrapped in foil that he breaks up with a hammer, then deposits in a heated tub to melt.

José has worked for almost twenty years at Charlotte's Confections. "Charlotte" no longer owns the company, but the operation is little different from when it started sixty-five years ago; it continues to make candy the old-fashioned way. The most new-fangled addition is an expensive wrapping machine, and it's temperamental.

The ingredients José uses are those every candy maker knows well—sugar, corn syrup, egg whites, fat, and flavoring. But the proportions of the components and how long they are cooked, then mixed together, are crucial details.

"Of course, every candy maker has his secrets," I hinted.

"The secret is in the heart," he responded. "If you don't love what you do, it shows in the candy."

When José was only eight years old, his father, a candy maker in Mexico, introduced him to the craft. Jose embraced it with enthusiasm and made it his life's work. His face glowed when I told him I had seen the Louisiana sugarcane harvest. Here is a man with a soul connection to sugar.

José and his apprentice, Javier, white bib aprons over their clothes, started another batch of peppermint chews. Reconstituted powdered egg whites whipped in the bowl of a 120-quart mixer. A propane-fired ring stood on the floor, cradling a copper kettle bigger than a baby bath. Sugar, corn syrup, and water bubbled inside. Nearby, a wooden pallet supported brown paper sacks, each filled with fifty pounds of granulated sugar. A white tank that looked like a small silo stood ready to dispense corn syrup. Although nuts weren't used that day, a roaster that looked like a pot-bellied stove sat next to the silo. It hasn't broken down during José's tenure.

When the temperature of the syrup reached the desired level, Jose and his helper picked up the kettle, moved it a few steps, then slowly poured the contents into the mixer bowl. The egg whites thickened and turned glossy. The candy makers mixed up another batch of syrup in the copper kettle and set it to heat. Just before it was hot enough, José added fat and a shot of peppermint oil to the beating mass in the mixer. The aroma of mint instantly wafted through the air. Then they added more sugar syrup, until the bowl was almost overflowing, and after a few more revolutions stopped the mixer.

A long table with a metal top waited, rigged with a special cooling system that sends cold water under the surface. The candy makers removed the bowl from the mixer, attached it to the chains of a hoist, and ratcheted it higher than the table. They rolled the apparatus to the end of the table, then tilted the bowl and slowly dragged the hoist down the length of it, as most of the warm white candy ribboned from the bowl. They pushed the candy to the upright extensions that boxed in the table's edge and smoothed the surface.

As the candy cooled, they mixed the small amount they'd reserved in the bowl with red coloring made from beet concentrate. Javier held a ball of the red candy in one hand and pulled with the other to make nine stripes at one end of the rectangle of cooling white candy. While it was still pliable, the men flipped it over, all one hundred pounds. They folded the end opposite the stripes onto itself, then folded again. Then they rolled the rectangle onto itself, so that the red stripes were on the outside. Next they cradled it in their arms as they moved it to a special machine, the "former," where it was massaged like a sore muscle. The machine turned it and pushed it toward three rollers, one on top of the other two—the same configuration as the rollers in the sugar mill. The nougat was slowly pushed through, its diameter shrinking dramatically. One more set of rollers thinned it even more. As it reached the end of the line, a cutter chopped off bite-size pieces—*ka-chunk, ka-chunk*—then two whirligig arms twisted cellophane around each one. Dressed up in their shiny coverings, the candies rolled down a chute and showered into a waiting bin. José gave me a handful of the soft pieces, which I slipped into my pocket.

The two candy makers can make eight batches of chews in one day. The flavor and look vary with the season and the holiday. In October, the nougat is orange, with chocolate Halloween faces in the middle of the rounds. For springtime, a lemon with a leaf announces the flavor. It takes an artist to make these fanciful images. Forms are available, but José uses only a V-shaped trough and works free-hand.

At another table, a worker was trimming rocky-road Easter eggs, a fusion of bittersweet chocolate and marshmallows. They were utterly unlike my memories of the bouncy rounds I roasted over fires as a kid, and certainly unlike the rubbery orange "peanuts" of my childhood. These were soft, sweet pillows just barely held together with gelatin and suspended in chocolate. Jose and his crew make them here—beating the ingredients in the mixers, pouring the mass on the cooling tables, cutting it with special rollers, then dusting the pieces with finely powdered sugar.

I collected more samples from the different production rooms—chews of different flavors, a new candy called Tidbits that combined squares of nougat with nuts. My pockets filled. I felt like a squirrel just before winter. I'm glad I chose the right jacket.

# Treat or Treat

by Dara Moskowitz

from *City Pages*

Readers of this Minneapolis weekly rely on Moscowitz as a spirited guide through the local corridors of restaurants, bakeries, and other food sources. Opinionated and colloquial, her pieces are always fun to read and insightful, even if you don't live in the Twin Cities.

Both Halloween and Thanksgiving are upon us, and so it is the time of year to give thanks, above all, that we are adults and can buy our own damn chocolate. I got to thinking this the other day, when I was busy mining the single American natural resource that will forever remain unexhausted: niggling childhood dissatisfactions.

For example, in my own hippie girlhood, refined sugar was strictly outlawed. This created a general atmosphere in which candy was regarded the same way British tabloids imagine Madonna and Guy Ritchie's relationship: What goes on in there? It must be heaven! Or, alternately, quite likely, hell! But anyway it is a completely restricted area and thus clearly holds the key to human happiness. Of course, it being America in the 1970s, my brother and I still managed to get the stuff occasionally, by, for example, trading homemade macramé planters to Abbie Hoffman for Charleston Chews. By reciting bits of the Watergate tapes on street corners in exchange for Tootsie Rolls. Or, of course, by dressing in ways designed to convey support for renewable energy resources on Halloween. Oh, Halloween, when candy finally runs free, liberated from the oppressive rules of parents.

Yet every single solitary time we finally got hold of some sweet, sweet candy, adults—when they weren't telling you about the sugar-plantation-associated oppression of children in far-off lands—would try to put some kind of overarching philosophical frame on the experience. Appreciate it now, for you'll never be as carefree and happy as you are when you're a child with candy. Adult life is a vale of worry and tears. So you'd best enjoy this unpolluted innocence, because it's going downhill fast.

I believed this until three weeks ago!

When suddenly, it hit me: Wait a minute. Adults have nothing but unfettered, 365-day-a-year, 24-hour-a-day access to candy. And, more important, to chocolate. And much more important, to the really good stuff. While kids, kids are busy designing costumes so they can battle it out for 3 Musketeers bars!

Suckers!

Sometimes I think we forget how good we have it because how good we have it is ubiquitous: Did you know that what is probably the most watched and celebrated artisan chocolate company in America right now is based in Minneapolis? And their chocolate and toffee is available right here, everywhere? In nearly every local Lunds, Byerly's, most of the co-ops, and most of the specialty food stores, like Turtle Bread and Surdyk's.

I am talking about B.T. McElrath, whom I first wrote about back in 1998, when the company was just two people. Just Brian McElrath, a former cook at places like the New French and Cocolezzone, working alone in a basement laboratory, and Brian's wife Christine, who worked there after working her other full-time job. Well, they worked and they worked and they worked, and then suddenly, last year, as they say, they blew up.

First, in the summer of 2001 they won the tippity-top prize at the show for the NASFT—the National Association for the Specialty Food Trade, which everyone calls the Fancy Food show. This show is the most important thing that happens all year in gourmet foodstuffs. The first year they entered, Brian and Christine McElrath couldn't even afford to get a booth at the show, but they could afford the entry fee for the new-product contest, where their chocolates went head to head with 1,600 other entries. When they won, it was one of those industry-rocking, rookie-pitches-no-hitter moments that left everyone who knew about it amazed. They got on the cover of the trade show magazine, they got sales reps, they got employees who weren't obligated to show up by the whole till-death-do-us-part thing. Then, this summer, they went back to the show, and won the top prize for best confection. Now B.T. McElrath chocolates and toffees are placed in many of the most prestigious places that chocolates can be sold—in the chain Dean & DeLuca, in New York City's Zabar's, in Napa Valley's Oakville Grocery, in the West Coast coffee chain Tully's, in one of the Martha Stewart catalogs, on the pillows at the $800-a-night Salish Lodge in Washington (called the Great Northern Lodge in the television series *Twin Peaks*), and many other places. I think it's also safe to speculate that they're represented by the caseload in the research kitchens and focus groups of major chocolate companies. So when Cadbury launches its zinfandel-balsamic chocolate bar next year, you know where it came from.

Yes, I said zinfandel-balsamic. The McElraths have made their fortune concocting adult chocolates for adult tastes: A lavender-black-peppercorn truffle that tastes floral, sharp, and dark in the most intriguing way; a green-tea truffle with the high-tannic tang and young fruity-chocolate quality that I associate with certain Spanish wines; a cinnamon-star-anise chocolate that brings to mind eating licorice in a meadow at night. I don't fear too much that big corporations will be able to pull off chocolates this good—Brian uses small kitchen techniques that can't be, as they say, blown up. For the star-anise chocolate, he simmers whole star anise in local Hope Creamery cream; for the pillow chocolates at Salish Lodge he hand-stencils each one with a picture of a waterfall.

I don't fear replication, but I do fear locals overlooking the stuff because it is local. To me it's old news, to the other food writers it's old news, too: Yes, the McElraths make the most amazing, bedazzling, show-stopping chocolates in town, and the sky is blue and the earth is cold, and which of these facts deserves a headline? To you it might be old news, too. Or it might be impossible to imagine doing your holiday shopping at Lunds, because what then? Why not just give your secretary a box of Ritz crackers? They're in the same aisle, after all . . . Since the smallest box of two costs less than $4, the nine-piece assortment around $11, and the 18-piece around $23, they're inexpensive enough to factor into normal celebrations, so why do we forget about them?

We forget about Sonny's ice cream, too, and their spumoni. Ever had it? It's one of those things that I feel like I write about too much, sometimes, and too little when I find someone who hasn't had it. What their spumoni is, is four kinds of ice cream, tumbled together like dreams on a good night: The splendid vanilla (made, like all their ice cream, from local, fresh cream from a single organic farm, and some of the world's finest vanilla, which costs them hundreds of dollars a gallon), here doctored with rum; then, a ghostly and rich chocolate-cinnamon ice cream that tastes spicy and lively; green, full, nutty pistachio that tastes inexplicably like custard; and then a dark-cherry, dark-rum ice cream that's all resonant and sweet. It costs somewhere between $4 and $5 a pint, depending on the store, and it's fantastic, and in practically any other town we'd have parades to celebrate it and Sonny's Spumoni Days, and such. But do we even know it's there? I met another group of people recently who called themselves passionate about food and had spent hours on the Internet hunting for the best truffle oil, and they had never heard of it.

How tight are the circles we run in, from job to gym to home, how great the constraints on our time, that these treasures—even in our grocery stores—don't pierce our consciousness? We finally got the mobility, the taste, and the cash we needed to appreciate all this great chocolate. Let's not take it for granted because it's local, or because we're too adult and doing that adult thing of taking the myriad small treasures around us for granted, or transferring all the possibilities for pleasure to children, or any of that.

Oh well. I guess I should apologize here: This has run out of steam as a Halloween column. Maybe it's just as well, because even if you don't end up getting yourself something grown-up and chocolaty for Halloween (like maybe the Chocolate Kiss martini at the Imperial Room—two kinds of Godiva liqueur and vodka in a chocolate-rimmed glass?), sometime before Thanksgiving we will see the debut of B.T. McElrath's ginger toffee. So you can appreciate the miracles of adulthood anytime this holiday season. I got to try this stuff pre-release: it's a dark-chocolate-robed square of brittle, real-butter toffee made with ginger and spice in such a way that you really only notice the ginger in a bit of burn and fragrance on the finish. Sophisticated stuff.

I got the advance ginger toffee by stopping by McElrath's chocolate shop, which you get to through a Maxwell Smart-style path, starting with a door that looks like it leads to an air vent, snaking through a series of underground passages, and braving more forbidding doors. At the end of this trek I found Brian, looking about as exhausted as an adult can look, surrounded by his Fancy Food show statuettes, which look like Oscars who have been pressed into food service and forced to carry platters and wear toques. Brian said that on winning again last summer, fancy-food big shots kept coming by their booth and advising, in mock-threatening jokes, that the McElraths take care, because the heads of their food Oscars are easily snapped off. And how have things been since they got back from the show? "It's mania, it's mayhem, it's madness," says Brian. "It's like trying to push the Mississippi through a drinking straw."

And that's how it is, I thought, when you're a success, and an adult: All our lives are more and more like reined-in, and thus more quickly rushing, rivers. When they could be meandering streams dotted with bucolic chocolate islands.

# Home Cooking

# What Einstein Told His Cook

## by Robert L. Wolke
from *What Einstein Told His Cook*

Longtime University of Pittsburgh chemistry professor Wolke found a new audience with his wryly witty *Washington Post* column, Cooking 101, a forum for demystifying the little scientific miracles that take place in a kitchen every day. Here are a few intriguing tidbits from the collection.

### FASTA PASTA

*Why do we have to put salt in the water before boiling
pasta in it? Does it make the pasta cook faster?*

Virtually every cookbook instructs us to salt the water in which we cook pasta or potatoes, and we dutifully comply without asking any questions.

There is a very simple reason for adding the salt: It boosts the flavor of the food, just as it does when used in any other kind of cooking. And that's all there is to it.

At this point, every reader who has ever paid the slightest attention in chemistry class will object. "But adding salt to the water raises its boiling point, so the water will boil hotter and cook the food faster."

To these readers I award an A in chemistry but a D in Food 101. It's true that dissolving salt—or really anything else, for that matter

(I'll explain)—in water will indeed make it boil at a higher temperature than 212°F at sea level. But in cooking, the rise is nowhere near enough to make any difference, unless you throw in so much salt that you could use the water to melt ice on your driveway.

As any chemist will be happy to calculate for you, adding a tablespoon (30 grams) of table salt to five quarts of boiling water for cooking a pound of pasta will raise the boiling point by seven hundredths of 1°F. That might shorten the cooking time by half a second or so. Anyone who is in that much of a hurry to get the spaghetti onto the table may also want to consider rollerblading it from the kitchen to the dining room.

Of course, you know that as an incorrigible professor I now feel obliged to tell you *why* salt raises the boiling point of water, small as the effect may be. Give me one paragraph.

In order to boil off, that is, in order to become vapor or steam, water molecules must escape from the ties that bind them to their liquid fellows. Wresting themselves loose with the aid of heat is tough enough because water molecules stick together quite strongly, but if there happen to be any alien particles cluttering up the liquid, it's even tougher, because the particles of salt (Techspeak: the sodium and chloride ions) or other dissolved substances simply get in the way. The water molecules therefore require some extra oomph, in the form of a higher temperature, in order to make good their escape to airborne freedom. (For more, ask your friendly neighborhood chemist about "activity coefficients.")

Now back to the kitchen.

Unfortunately, there is even more mumbo jumbo surrounding the addition of salt to cooking water than the fallacy about boiling temperature. The most frequently cited fables, even in the most respected cookbooks, tell us precisely *when* we must add the salt to the water.

One recent pasta cookbook observes that "it is customary to add salt to the boiling water prior to adding the pasta." It goes on to warn that "adding the salt before the water boils may cause an unpleasant aftertaste." Thus, the recommended routine is (l) boil, (2) add salt, (3) add pasta.

Meanwhile, another pasta cookbook counsels us to "bring the water to the boil before adding salt or pasta," but leaves open the momentous question of salt-first or pasta-first.

The fact is that as long as the pasta cooks in salted water, it makes no difference whether or not the water had already been boiling when the salt was added. Salt dissolves quite easily in water, whether hot or merely lukewarm. And even if it didn't, the roiling of boiling would dissolve it immediately. Once dissolved, the salt has no memory of time or temperature—of precisely when it entered the water or of whether it took the plunge at 212°F or 100°F. It cannot, therefore, affect the pasta differently.

One theory I have heard from a chef is that when salt dissolves in water it releases heat, and that if you add the salt when the pot is already boiling the extra heat can make it boil over. Sorry, Chef, but salt doesn't release heat when it dissolves; it actually absorbs a little bit of heat. What you undoubtedly observed is that when you added the salt, the water suddenly erupted into livelier bubbling. That happened because the salt—or almost any other added solid particles—gives the budding bubbles many new places (Techspeak: nucleation sites) upon which to grow to full size.

Another theory (everybody has one, it seems; is boiling pasta such an Earth-shaking challenge?) is that the salt is added for more than flavor, that it toughens the pasta and keeps it from getting too mushy. I have heard some plausible but quite technical reasons for that, but I won't trouble you with them. Let's just add the salt whenever and for whatever reason we wish. Just make sure we add it or the pasta will taste blah.

### WHEN IS AN OIL NOT AN OIL?

*How do those nonstick cooking sprays work? Their labels say the contents are nonfat and low calorie, but when I spray it on the pan it sure looks like oil to me. Is there such a*

*thing as a nonfat oil? Or does it contain some kind of*
*chemical substitute for oil?*

No, there is no such thing as a nonfat edible oil. Fats are a family of specific chemical compounds, and an oil is just a liquid fat. Nor do the sprays have to contain a substitute for oil, because—are you ready?—they *are* oil.

Those handy little cans, so great for coating baking pans and muffin tins instead of greasing them, contain primarily a vegetable oil, usually with some lecithin and alcohol added. Lecithin is a fat-like substance (Techspeak: a phospholipid) found in egg yolks and soy beans, among other places, and helps to keep food from sticking. But the sprays are still almost entirely oil.

Their main virtue is that they put you more in control of your calories and fat usage. Instead of pouring a heavy-handed glug of oil into your skillet, you just give the pan a quick spritz from the can. The alcohol evaporates and the oil and lecithin remain behind, coating the pan. You'll still be cooking on a layer of oil, but it's a very thin and therefore low-calorie one.

In the manufacturers' effort to earn that highly profitable "nonfat" claim, the cooking spray labels can engage in some pretty bizarre arithmetic. The label on a can of Pam, for example, boasts that it contains "only two calories per serving." But what is a "serving"? The label defines it as a one-third-of-a-second spray which, the label advises, is just long enough to cover one-third of a 10-inch skillet. (Just right, we must presume, for making one-third of an omelet.) In the race to claim even fewer calories, the label of one oil spray advises that a "serving" is a spritz that lasts for only one-quarter of a second.

If you don't have the finely calibrated trigger finger of Billy the Kid, or even if you throw caution to the winds and defiantly spray your pan for an entire second, you'll still be getting by with fewer than six calories. But even so, a little bit of fat isn't no fat. So how small must an amount of fat be before a label can legally call it "none?"

According to the FDA, any product that contains less than 0.5 gram of fat per serving may be labeled as containing "zero grams of fat." A one-third-of-a-second "serving" of cooking spray contains around 0.3 gram of fat; hence, it is legally "nonfat." If they had defined a serving as a whole second's worth of spritz, they'd be over the 0.5-gram limit and couldn't call it nonfat. Cute dodge, eh?

By the way, if you're a belt-and-suspenders type, spritz a little nonstick spray onto your nonstick frying pan. The food will brown better than it would without the fat. Excuse me—I mean without the nonfat.

## THE WHITE POWDER TWINS
*Some recipes call for baking soda, some for baking powder,*
*and some even call for both. What's the difference?*

It's all in the chemicals.

Baking soda (aka bicarbonate of soda) is a single chemical: pure sodium bicarbonate, whereas baking powder is baking soda combined with one or more acid salts, such as monocalcium phosphate monohydrate, dicalcium phosphate dihydrate, sodium aluminum sulfate, or sodium aluminum phosphate.

Now that I've warmed the hearts of chemistry fans and confounded the rest of my readers, let me try to win the latter back.

Both baking soda and baking powder are used for leavening (from the Latin *levere,* meaning to raise or make light): making baked goods rise by producing millions of tiny bubbles of carbon dioxide gas. The gas bubbles are released within the wet batter, after which the heat of the oven expands them until the heat firms up the batter and traps them in place. The result is (hopefully) a light, spongy cake instead of a dense, gummy mess.

Here's how these two confusingly named leavening agents work.

Baking *soda* releases carbon dioxide gas as soon as it comes in contact with any acidic liquid, such as buttermilk, sour cream, or, for that matter, sulfuric acid (not recommended). All carbonates and bicarbonates do that.

Baking *powder,* on the other hand, is baking soda with a dry acid already mixed in. It is used when a recipe contains no other acid ingredients. As soon as the powder gets wet, the two chemicals begin to dissolve and react with each other to produce carbon dioxide. To keep them from "going off" prematurely, they have to be protected zealously from atmospheric moisture by being kept in a tightly closed container.

In most cases, we don't want our baking powder to release all its gas as soon as we mix the batter—before it has been baked enough to trap the bubbles in place. So we buy a "double-acting" baking powder (and most of them are, these days, whether the label says so or not), which releases only a portion of its gas when it gets wet and releases the rest only after reaching a high temperature in the oven. Generally, two different chemicals in the powder are responsible for the two reactions.

But why would a recipe call for *both* baking soda and baking powder? In this case the cake or cookie is actually being leavened by the baking powder, which contains exactly the right proportions of bicarbonate and acid to react completely with each other. But if there happens to be an acid ingredient such as buttermilk present that would upset that balance, some extra bicarbonate in the form of baking soda is used to neutralize the excess acid. (Ask any chemist about this, but walk briskly away if he or she utters the word *titration.*)

Commercial bakers mix up their own witch's brews of leavening chemicals, designed to release just the right amounts of gas at just the right times and temperatures during the baking process. At home, the safest course is simply not to tamper with a well-tested recipe; use the prescribed amount(s) of whatever leavening agent(s) it calls for.

### How Now, Brown Cowburger?

*The ground beef in my supermarket is bright red on the out-side and dull-looking on the inside. Are they spraying it with some sort of dye to make it look fresh?*

No, they're probably not playing games.

A freshly cut meat surface isn't bright red; it's naturally purplish because it contains the purplish-red muscle protein, myoglobin. But when myoglobin is exposed to oxygen in the air, it quickly turns into bright, cherry-red oxymyoglobin. That's why only the outer surface of your ground beef is that nice, bright red color that we generally associate with freshness; the inner parts haven't been exposed to enough air.

Freshly cut, purplish beef is shipped from the packing house to the markets in airtight containers. After being ground at the market, it is usually wrapped in a plastic film that permits the passage of oxygen, and the surface of the meat then "blooms" with the red color of oxymyoglobin. But on longer exposure to oxygen, the red oxymyoglobin gradually oxidizes to brownish metamyoglobin, which not only looks bad but gives the meat an "off" flavor. It's this metamyoglobin-brown color that signals over-the-hill meat. In reality, however, this transformation happens long before the meat becomes actually unwholesome.

Retail markets use plastic packaging materials (either low-density polyethylene or polyvinyl chloride) that allow just enough oxygen to penetrate to keep the surface of the meat at the bright red oxymyoglobin stage.

To sum it up: If your beef, whether cut or ground, is a dull purple, it's really very fresh. But even if it has gone brown with metamyoglobin, it can still be good for several days. Your nose, not your eyes, is ultimately your best sense organ for determining whether your hamburger is *too* brown.

### LOOKY, LOOKY, LOOKY. AIN'T THAT OOKY?

*After I roast a chicken, there are all these ooky drippings in
the pan. Can I use them for anything?*

No. If you have to ask, you don't deserve them. Pour off the fat, scrape the rest of the "ook" into a jar, and ship it to me by overnight express.

Seriously, this stuff is composed of marvelously flavorful juices and gels, and it would be a crime to feed it to your dishwashing machine. I have often thought that if I were a king or an emperor, I would order my cooks to roast a hundred chickens, throw them to the peasants, and serve the combined drippings to me on a silver platter along with several loaves of crusty French bread.

Or else I would soon have a barrel of the best gravy ever made, because all those wonderful fats, chicken juices, protien gels, and browned bits are the flavor foundations of great gravies.

# With Pancakes, Every Day Is Sunday

by Lucian K. Truscott IV
from the *New York Times*

Like many novelist-turned-food-writers, Truscott comes armed with a sharp eye for character, setting, and family dynamics. Here he meditates on an age-old question—how do parents transmit their food values to their children?

The whole pancake thing began on a Monday morning. I was standing in the kitchen, running through the everyday duties necessary to launch an eight-year-old on a week in third grade. Daughter awake, check. Rolling backpack blocking exit through front door in cannot-forget-to-take-to-school position, check. Car pool today, check. Hot lunch today, check. Piano lesson, negative. Brownie meeting, negative. Morning snack: Juice box, check. Apple, check. Ritz Bits, check.

It was only 7:10, and already I was beginning to feel woozy with exhaustion, when suddenly the swinging door flew open and Lilly sprang into the kitchen wearing an oversize Richard Griffin sprint-car T-shirt and one of those glowing smiles only eight-year-old girls seem able to conjure.

"Daddy, may I have pancakes for breakfast?" she chirped, bouncing excitedly.

"It's a school morning," I replied absently. "How does Cheerios and orange juice and half a bagel sound?"

"Please, Daddy; I *really* need pancakes," she said, and shot me a plaintive look before turning on her heel to go back upstairs. As I listened to the soft thunder of her bare feet pounding away, I wondered where I got the idea that you didn't make pancakes for kids on a school morning. I had opened the cabinet and was reaching for the box of Cheerios when it came to me: from my parents, of course.

My mother and father adhered to an unwritten dictum that pancakes belonged in that pantheon of dishes defined as so delicious that they couldn't be good for you, so they were automatically relegated to the rarefied status of Sunday morning treat, and not every Sunday, either. In those days before the International House of Pancakes and the Waffle Hut exploded into a new culinary subgenus, pancakes to our family fell into the yawning gap between availability and desire, which is to say, we didn't have them a fraction as often as we younger members of the clan would have liked.

Now here I was, reacting to Lilly's desire for pancakes in the way every enlightened boomer parent swore on a lid he or she would never behave: just like my parents.

I put down the Cheerios and reached for the Bisquick. I checked my watch: forty minutes until we had to be car-pooling to school. I figured we'd make it if I hurried.

I whipped the ingredients together in a large stainless mixing bowl with a wire whisk and let the batter rest. We had recently bought a new nonstick skillet to replace a battle-weary veteran that was approaching mandatory retirement age. I gave it a wipe with a towel and placed it over a burner on medium. By the time I'd set a place for Lilly on the kitchen table, the skillet was hot, so I ladled three dollops of batter onto its gleaming, agate-black surface and called to her from the bottom of the stairs.

"Daddy, I'm not ready yet; I'm doing my *hair*," came her

impassioned reply. I turned to the stove, flipped the pancakes, and checked my watch. To my abject amazement, there were still thity minutes before we had to leave for school. When the first three pancakes were done, I ladled three more dollops of batter into the skillet: two more for Lilly, one for her younger brother, Five. I was removing the last three from the skillet when Lilly bounded into the kitchen in her school uniform. I poured heated syrup from the microwave over her stack of pancakes and cut them: She sat down at the table and took a bite, smiling with her mouth full. "*Yum-mmmm*," she said, chewing happily.

My wife, Carolyn, walked in carrying Five and put him in his high chair. I cut up his pancake and put a few pieces on his tray. He grabbed one and shoved it in his mouth, kicking his feet with excitement. He managed to emit a muffled squeal as he reached for another bite. Just about then, Lilly polished off the last of her stack and took a long swig of juice. "May I have some more, Daddy?" she asked. "These were good!"

It gave us such pleasure to watch the kids devour their pancakes that Carolyn and I began nibbling at them in the morning. Lilly was right. They were good. We knew if the pancakes from the box were that good, there had to be a from-scratch recipe that was better. So we dug through our cookbook collection and started to experiment. We tried a recipe called "fly off the plate" pancakes from an old Virginia cookbook I inherited from my grandmother. It was basic batter made with flour, a little salt, sugar, baking powder, egg and milk, with some sour cream and butter added. The batter was creamy, but none of us could taste much difference between "fly off the plate" and "fly out of the box."

One morning Carolyn had an inspiration. Why didn't we try putting bananas on them? When Lilly was born, our housekeeper, Haydee, taught us how to microwave an overripe banana with a little brown sugar, butter and cinnamon. Stirred with a spoon, it turns into a kind of instant pudding that became a staple for Lilly when she was a baby, and now it's Five's turn. We made Haydee's bananas and left out the stirring step, leaving the banana slices whole and put them on Lilly's pancakes. Another hit.

Carolyn got ambitious one night and found a recipe for yeast griddle cakes in the *Beard on Bread* cookbook. She made the starter of yeast, water, sugar and a cup of flour the night before and left it covered to rise. The next morning, we finished the batter by adding more sugar and flour, an egg, butter and a little salt to the starter. James Beard wrote that the batter would be a little thicker than normal, and it was. Lilly made an effort, working her way through a couple of very chewy bites before giving up and asking for cereal. I didn't blame her.

We went back to the box for a couple of days, and then one afternoon, Carolyn was looking through one of several binders full of recipes we have collected over the years and came across the handwritten recipe for pancakes that had been passed down to her from her mother, who had received it from her mother. The next morning, we whisked together the ingredients and noticed that the batter was far more velvety than any we had made. The resulting pancakes were thick, airy and light, and tasted truly homemade, like fresh baked bread or biscuits. Lilly made short work of a stack and pronounced them the best she had ever had. After Carolyn and I tried a couple we had to agree. There was a real difference between Mississippi pancakes, as the recipe became known, and the others we had tried.

Five woke up at his usual six-thirty one Sunday morning, so I let the girls sleep and stuck him in his stroller and walked down to the Hollywood Farmers Market, which is only a few blocks from our house. The peach and nectarine harvest was at a peak. We found a stand where they had a bunch of ripe fruit, and we picked up a box of strawberries from Oxnard, which because of the coastal climate are always in season here.

When Lilly woke up, she wanted pancakes—surprise, surprise—so we whipped up some Mississippi batter. When Carolyn checked out our booty from the market, she decided she could come up with a compote. The result—the chopped fruit mixed and warmed with sugar and orange juice—exceeded our expectations. As we spooned the compote over three plates of pancakes, Carolyn went one step further. If we thinned out the Mississippi batter, she said, we could make crepes for dessert. We could serve the regular compote to the kids and flame the remainder with a quarter cup of rum for us.

One night we tried it using batter left over from the morning. Maybe my parents' instinct about pancakes was right after all.

## Mississippi Pancakes

*About 20 medium pancakes*

*Time: 20 minutes*

2 eggs
1 cup milk
2 tablespoons vegetable oil
3 tablespoons butter, melted
1¼ cup all-purpose flour
3 teaspoons baking powder
3 teaspoons sugar
½ teaspoon salt

1. Place a nonstick griddle or a skillet over medium heat. In a large bowl, beat eggs until light and foamy. Add milk, oil and butter. In another bowl, sift together dry ingredients, then beat them into the liquid ingredients with a wire whisk.

2. When skillet is hot, pour in about ¼ cup batter for each pancake, leaving space between. Flip when batter bubbles. Continue cooking for about a minute. Serve immediately.

## Haydee's Microwave Bananas

*4 servings.*

*Time: 2 minutes*

2 very ripe soft bananas, peeled and sliced lengthwise
2 tablespoons unsalted butter
2 heaping tablespoons brown sugar
¼ teaspoon cinnamon.

Place bananas in a ceramic bowl with all other ingredients. Do not mix. Microwave on high for 1 to 2 minutes. Spoon on top of pancakes.

# Fried Chicken and Grits

**by Damon Lee Fowler**

from *Damon Lee Fowler's New Southern Kitchen*

Perhaps no foods emblemize Southern cooking more than grits and fried chicken —but start dictating recipes, and you're bound to start a fight. If anyone can settle the disputes, though, it's Fowler, cookbook author and *Savannah Morning News* food columnist.

Now, here is a curious thing. Everybody talks about grits. Nearly everyone will agree that they are as Southern as a magnolia. Yet, not all Southerners eat grits: there are even places in the South where grits are almost unheard of—well, except for the few lonely packets of instant grits on the hot cereal shelf of the supermarket. I am not talking about ethnic communities in large cities, or the enclaves of retired snowbirds in Florida either.

The truth is, this so-called icon is anything but. Efforts to explain why usually fall short. One social historian once boldly drew a "grits line" across the center of the country, still another tried to place such a line in a loop that hugged the Gulf of Mexico, cutting off the tip of Florida, Arkansas, half of Texas, and most of Kentucky. Brave men: they are both wrong. There is no such thing as a neat little grits Maginot Line. This is more true today as the urban centers of the Deep South become increasingly cosmopolitan, but historically, it has always been true. A "grits map" that accurately showed where grits were and still are eaten in the South would more closely resemble the way a map would look if you slung a pot of grits at it and let them splatter.

But that is neither here nor there. Where grits are eaten, they are deeply loved and staunchly defended—and are as deeply Southern as it gets.

## Breakfast Grits

*Serves 4*

*This is actually the basic method for preparing grits for any occasion and for any of the recipes that follow. Exact proportions of grits to water are a little tricky; a lot depends on the humidity of the day, the amount of moisture in the grits before they are cooked, and, sometimes, I think, the way you are holding your mouth. The usual proportion is 4 parts water to 1 part grits, but this can and does vary. Start with that proportion and keep a teakettle of water simmering close at hand in case the grits need more water before they are done. You never want to add cold water to the pot; the grits just get terribly confused and seem to take that much longer before they get tender.*

*One is always learning: I have been cooking grits since I was four years old and it was only lately that the secret to really creamy grits came my way through my friend and fellow cookbook author Kathy Starr. She never adds salt while the grits are cooking. Salting prevents the grits from properly absorbing moisture while releasing enough starch to make for the fine, creamy texture that many a Southerner lives for. Kathy is a great traditional Southern cook and has cooked more grits than most of us have even seen. Trust her on this one.*

*The best pot for cooking grits is one that has a porcelain-enamel or stainless-steel interior and a heavy bottom. An ideal alternative to such a pot is a ceramic-lined slow cooker (such as a Crock-Pot). This type of cooker is especially ideal for cooking grits in large quantities. The longer grits cook—even the quick-cooking variety—the better, so choose a pot that will allow a slow, steady simmer.*

1 quart (4 cups) water
1 cup raw corn grits (preferably whole corn grits)
Salt ·

1. Bring the water to a boil in a stainless-steel or enameled pot. Slowly stir in the grits, pouring them in a thin, steady stream. Bring the liquid back to a boil, stirring constantly.

2. Reduce the heat to the slowest simmer your cooktop will manage and loosely cover the pot. Cook, stirring frequently at first and then occasionally as the grits begin to thicken, until the grits absorb all the moisture and are thick and creamy, about one hour. Add a couple of pinches of salt, and let the grits simmer for a few minutes to absorb the flavoring. Taste and adjust the seasoning, and serve hot.

## GUSSIED GRITS

Although home cooks have long made use of leftover grits in casseroles or even in the frying pan, and would sometimes serve company what my grandmother would have called "gussied up" grits, few of those old-style cooks would recognize some of the stuff that is being served in these nouvelle Southern establishments around the country. Sometimes it's enough to make traditionalists like me lie down with a bottle of bourbon—particularly when I see both the ingredient list and how many pots it takes to make a little timbale of grits in a pool of something like hoisin-spiked red-eye gravy.

But that's not to say that some of those new dishes aren't ingenious and absolutely delicious; only that many of them are impractical for home cooks to manage. The recipes that follow are a few simple homestyle preparations that don't require a battery of equipment and a specialty grocery in your pantry. Feel free to experiment with them and make them your own, but do try to remember that this is basic soul food.

**Cheese Grits**

Before adding the salt to Breakfast Grits in step 2, stir in 1 cup sharp Cheddar, Gruyère, or Parmesan cheese (or a combination). Stir until the cheese is melted, taste and add salt, if needed. Allow the grits to simmer for a couple of minutes so that the seasoning is absorbed. You may make Cheese Grits ahead and bake them: pour them into a 2-quart casserole and sprinkle another ¼ cup grated cheese over the top. Cover and refrigerate the pan if you are making Cheese Grits more than an hour ahead, then bake them at 350 degrees F. in the center of the oven until they are hot and bubbly, about 30 minutes.

**Fried Grits**

*Serves 4*

*In spite of their plebeian-sounding name, these little cakes of golden-fried grits are an elegant and delicious way to recycle leftover grits, and make a spectacular carrier for creamed seafood, chicken, or ham. Grits are full of natural gelatins, and when cold they set up into a jellied cake that can then be sliced and broiled, baked, or, in this case, fried. Since they are seldom served on their own, but usually as a carrier for other food, they are simply seasoned—most of the time with nothing more than salt—but if you like, you may flavor them by stirring in a couple of tablespoons of minced onion, ham, herbs, or cheese while the grits are hot.*

2 cups hot Breakfast Grits
¼ cup all-purpose flour
1 large egg, lightly beaten
1 cup cracker crumbs or matzoh meal
Lard or peanut oil, for frying

1. Rinse a 9 x 9-inch glass casserole or two 8-ounce tumblers with cool water. Pour the hot grits into the casserole or tumblers, cool,

and then refrigerate until the grits are chilled. Unmold the grits onto a cutting board and using a sharp knife dipped in cool water, cut them into 3-inch squares or into round cakes about ½ inch thick.

2. Lightly roll the grits cakes in the flour, then dip them in the egg, allowing the excess egg to flow back into the bowl. Roll them in the cracker crumbs and lay them on a clean, dry platter. Allow them to sit for at least 10 and up to 30 minutes.

3. Put enough lard or oil in a large, heavy-bottomed skillet or sauté pan to cover the bottom by half an inch. Turn on the heat to medium-high. When the fat is hot, but not quite smoking (about 375 degrees F.), put in enough grits cakes to fill the pan without crowding. Fry, turning once, until they are golden brown and heated through, about 3 to 4 minutes per side.

4. Lift them from the fat with a slotted spatula, holding it over the pan to allow all the fat to drain back into the pan. Blot briefly on absorbent paper (butcher paper, brown grocery bags, or paper towels). Transfer them to a serving plate and serve at once.

## Baked Grits and Greens

*Serves 6 to 8*

*Every March 17, Savannah is host to what is said to be the third-largest St. Patrick's Day celebration in the country. For three days the whole town—from the fountains in the South Side's suburban malls all the way to (and including) the Savannah River—is awash with green. Pre-parade breakfasts and brunches are commonplace and a frequent centerpiece of these meals is, of course, grits—dyed as green as the river. It looks as frightening as it sounds. Here are green grits that come by the color more naturally, and in a combination that is a lot more traditional—not to mention appealing.*

1 pound fresh spinach, poke sallet, or Swiss chard greens, or one 10-ounce package frozen whole leaf spinach, thawed, squeezed dry, and roughly chopped
2 tablespoons unsalted butter
4 medium green onions, such as scallions, thinly sliced
1 recipe Breakfast Grits
½ cup heavy cream (minimum 36 percent milk fat)
1½ cups freshly grated extra-sharp white Cheddar (preferably Canadian or English Farmhouse) or Parmesan cheese (preferably Parmigiano-Reggiano)
Salt and whole white pepper in a peppermill
2 large eggs, well beaten

1. Position a rack in the center of the oven and preheat the oven to 350 degrees F. If you are using frozen spinach, skip to step 2. Wash the greens in a basin of cold water, changing the water if necessary, until all the sand and soil are removed from them. Drain briefly, but not thoroughly—there should still be plenty of water clinging to the leaves. Put the wet greens into a large lidded frying pan or Dutch oven. Cover and cook over medium-high heat until the greens are wilted, about 3 to 5 minutes. Immediately drain and refresh the greens in cold water. Drain well, gently squeezing the greens dry. Roughly chop them and set them aside.

2. Wipe out the frying pan or Dutch oven in which the greens have cooked and put in the butter. Turn on the heat to medium. When the butter is melted, add the green onions and sauté until they are wilted, about 4 minutes. Add the greens and heat them through, about 2 minutes more. Turn off the heat.

3. Combine the cooked grits with the cream and stir until smooth. Stir in the greens and 1 cup of the cheese. Taste the mixture and add a pinch or so of salt, if needed, and a few liberal grindings of pepper. Beat in the eggs. Lightly grease a 9-inch-square or

10-inch-round casserole and pour the grits and greens into it. Sprinkle the top with the remaining cheese, place the casserole in the center of the oven, and bake until the eggs are set and the top is browned, about 35 to 40 minutes. Serve hot.

## THE SOUTH'S GOLDEN ICON

There is nothing in all the world's cooking that is as fraught with emotion as chicken is in the South. You wouldn't think it to look at one of these birds. They are rather unimpressive creatures. Chickens cannot fly very well and are notoriously stupid. However, butcher one and cut it up, roll it in flour, and drop it into hot fat, and you have created a cause célèbre.

I once delivered an academic paper on the European roots of the signature dishes of the South, using fried chicken's evidently European pedigree as an example.

Though it didn't discount the expertise that African-American cooks had brought to the skillet, it caused a tempest that may never settle down. Well, I still stand behind the research. But it was also—in a way—wrong, because fried chicken is much more than its purely academic history. It is a complex and fiercely defended symbol, deeply rooted in people's hearts and consciousness. I used to resist the whole business of fried chicken as an icon of Southern culture and even thought, briefly, of omitting it from this book. There were, after all, many other sides to Southern culture and food, fried chicken was so impossible to neatly define, and I had already written an entire book on the subject. But nothing in Southern culture can be neatly defined—so as icons go, why not the golden perfection of a Southern fried bird? Could there ever be an icon nearly as delicious?

## Buttermilk Fried Chicken

*Serves 4*

*Nowhere is the eclectic nature of my cooking (and of Southern food in general) given away than in the way I fry chicken these days. In it are combined both sides of my family's traditions, two years of research into a book on fried chicken from all over the world, and a lifelong love affair with Italy. The saltwater soak (from my paternal grandmother) makes for tender, juicy chicken; the buttermilk bath (from my maternal grandmother and mother) further enhances tenderness, gives the chicken a lovely flavor, and ensures a crackling-crisp crust that will stay that way even after the chicken is cold; and the garlic whispers of the Mediterranean.*

*Yet everything—including that garlic—is consistent with deep Southern traditions.*

*Before you begin, here are some basic notes on successfully frying chicken:*

- *The pan does not (here come the letters) have to be cast-iron, but it must have a very heavy bottom—and for that, of course, cast-iron is the best.*
- *The most important draining step occurs as you remove the chicken from the pan: hold it over the pan until it no longer drips, then let it finish draining on a rack.*
- *If you must use absorbent paper to briefly blot the chicken,* briefly *is the operative word. Don't allow the chicken to remain on paper for more than a minute. Otherwise, that paper will absorb what it absorbs best—the moisture from inside the chicken, resulting in a soggy bottom crust and dry chicken.*
- *Though modern health regulations preach against it, the chicken should be allowed to lose the deep cold from the refrigerator or it will not cook evenly—which invites salmonella poisoning more readily than leaving it sitting out. Allow it to*

*sit, covered, for 15 to 30 minutes and make sure that you cook
it thoroughly.*

1 frying chicken (2½ to 3 pounds), washed and disjointed for frying
Salt
2 cups whole milk buttermilk or plain whole milk yogurt
5 to 6 large cloves garlic, crushed and peeled
Hot pepper sauce, such as Tabasco
3 cups all-purpose flour
1 tablespoon freshly ground black pepper
½ teaspoon ground cayenne pepper (optional)
Lard or peanut oil, for frying

1. Put the chicken pieces in a glass or nonreactive stainless-steel
bowl. Sprinkle a handful of salt over the chicken and cover it
completely with cold water. Toss gently until the salt is dissolved
in the water. Let soak, refrigerated, for at least 2 hours or as long
as overnight.

2. Drain the chicken and pat it dry. Pour the buttermilk over the
chicken (or if you are using yogurt, stir it until it is smooth and
creamy and pour it over the chicken). Turn the pieces until all are
coated. Add the garlic and a generous sprinkling of the hot sauce.
Toss until the sauce is mixed into the buttermilk. Let marinate for
30 minutes to an hour.

3. Combine the flour, a small handful of salt, and the pepper in a
large paper or Ziploc plastic bag. Fold over the top to close it
tightly and shake until well mixed.

4. If you plan to serve the chicken hot, position a rack in the center
of the oven and preheat the oven to 150 degrees F. Place a wire
cooling rack on a cookie sheet and set it aside. Put enough lard or
oil in a 14-inch-diameter, deep, cast-iron skillet to come halfway
up the sides. Turn on the heat to medium-high and heat until the

fat is very hot but not quite smoking—370 to 375 degrees F. Beginning with the thighs and drumsticks, lift the chicken pieces out of the marinade, allowing the excess to flow back into the bowl, and drop them into the bag with the seasoned flour. Fold over the top and shake until the chicken is well coated. Lift the pieces out, shaking off the excess, and slip them into the pan.

5. Fry until the outside is well sealed and beginning to brown, turning the chicken once. Reduce the heat to medium and continue frying, maintaining the fat temperature at 325 degrees F., until the chicken is just cooked through and golden brown, about 25 minutes for the thighs and drumsticks, 20 minutes for the breast meat and wings, turning it halfway. Remove the pieces as they are done, drain them well, and lay them on a wire rack set in a cookie sheet. If you want to serve it hot, keep the finished chicken in the warm oven.

Notes: You can deep-fry the chicken if you prefer; the chicken will be crispier and will take a little less time. Put enough fat in the deep fryer to come a *little less* than halfway up the sides (never fill the fryer more than half full of fat) and maintain a steady temperature of around 350 to 365 degrees F. throughout the frying, about 15 minutes for breast meat, 10 minutes for wings, and about 20 minutes for the legs and thighs.

Feel free to doctor the seasonings, adding herbs (sage and thyme are traditional with chicken in the South—but chives, rosemary, oregano, and tarragon would all be compatible) and/or spices (ginger, nutmeg, cumin, and paprika all complement chicken nicely) as the spirit moves you. But don't overwhelm the chicken with too much: there is nothing worse than the overblown taste of too many herbs and spices.

# Pepper Pot Hot

by John Thorne

from *Simple Cooking*

Reading John Thorne's newsletter is like spending the afternoon cooking with an old friend; you digress, you tinker, you browse through old cookbooks, you taste and tinker again, and eventually you produce something die-and-go-to-heaven delicious.

To tell this story properly, I have to take you back about thirty years to the time when, just out of college, I spent a while teaching at a tiny progressive private school near Stockbridge, Massachusetts. The faculty there was a motley crew of the very young and the very old—either just starting their careers as teachers or at the very end of the line ... and in either case not in a position to be too choosy about who hired them. I was one of the young ones; the math teacher, Steve Stephens, was one of the old ones, in years if not in spirit. Scrappy and full of contrarian opinions, Steve had led an adventurously checkered life during which he had made and lost a couple of fortunes, and was very enjoyable company.

Unlike most of the faculty, Steve lived off campus, in a house that while not of his own devising had certainly been adapted to his tastes. When, for instance, he decided to put a glass-surrounded fireplace in the center of his living room, he designed it himself using window safety glass from junked automobiles, thus saving thousands of dollars. He was also a gourmet cook, and on one of the occasions he had some of us other faculty over to dinner, he served his version of Philadelphia pepper pot, which I found so delicious I couldn't get it out of my mind.

Thirty years ago, recipes for Philadelphia pepper pot were still relatively common in American cookbooks, so I must have come across one, including the various bits of lore as to why it is attached to Philadelphia—some of it spurious,* some of it interesting and perhaps even true.** It's also easy to see why these never caught my eye. The traditional version is a rather complicatedly old-fashioned, flour-thickened, stock-based soup made with beef tripe and an assortment of vegetables, topped with dumplings and pepped up with the addition of what to today's taste would seem a rather skimpy number of peppercorns.

Steve's version, on the other hand, was suavely smooth and rich, the creamy broth speckled with black pepper—i.e., less like the original than the one given by George Rector in *Dine at Home with Rector: A Book on What Men Like, Why They Like It, And How*

---

* That it was created by George Washington's cook at Valley Forge, who found he had only some tripe and peppercorns at hand one evening and was forced to improvise, concocting a dish that won him—and his home town—instant acclaim. If true, he was a lucky chef to have *any* peppercorns in his larder, let alone a sufficient supply to season enough soup for an army. In any case, I have yet to find a reference to the dish connecting it to Philadelphia that dates back further than the early twentieth century . . . which makes the whole story sound more like fakelore than folklore to me.

** That into the last century black women sold it out of pushcarts in the streets of Philadelphia. The food historian Karen Hess told me that West Indian blacks made up a large part of the catering trade in that city, and there's little doubt regarding the African origins of the dish, as the versions in early American cookbooks make clear. In fact, Sarah Rutledge's recipe for "Pepper Pot" In *The Carolina Housewife* (1847) is at least kissing cousin to contemporary Jamaican recipes for the same dish. The Philadelphia version, however, replaces hot bird peppers with black peppercorns, Northern root vegetables for the yams and plantains, and perhaps most significantly, tripe for the traditional mélange of salt meats.

*To Cook It* (1937), a cookbook so much on Steve's wavelength that I can easily believe he owned it. Here's how Rector does it:

> You start by dicing up a couple of slices of bacon a good quarter-inch thick and frying them golden brown. An onion and a green pepper, both chopped fine, are cooked with the bacon for five minutes. Then you introduce three pints of good veal or chicken stock and three quarters of a pound of honeycomb tripe, washed and drastically shredded. Here the mixture gets seasoned with a bay leaf well crumbled, a pinch of thyme, say half a teaspoon of salt and a teaspoon of whole black pepper well crushed. Bring it to a boil and put in a cupful of diced potatoes, then simmer it gently for about an hour. Thicken it with two tablespoons each of butter and flour well creamed together and just before serving, add a half cup of cream.

Unfortunately, I didn't come across this recipe until I was writing this piece—helpful for it but only incidentally to me. Because, before I had a chance to wheedle the recipe out of Steve, he was killed in a head-on automobile collision late one night in the middle of a blizzard (he was never one to do things by half measures), and years of subsequent searching failed to come up with anything like his recipe. I was entirely on my own—which meant, practically speaking, that for decades nothing happened at all.[*]

This lack of initiative is partially explained by the fact that, offal-lover though I am, tripe is something I have always been more willing to eat than to cook. You would think that someone

---

[*] Of course, the Rector volume had been sitting in plain view on the shelf for years—ever since Matt moved in and brought her cookbooks with her. But the book has no index, the recipes are all in prose, and, perversely, the chapter on soup is second to last in the book. It's a miracle that I ever stumbled upon the recipe at all.

who handles brains and kidneys without qualm would have little problem dealing with stomach lining, but there it is. Raw tripe—rubbery, webby, squeaky—reminds me less of an animal organ than something sliced from an old Playtex girdle.

Of course, the prepared version is not all that different, except in one important way. Cooking tripe makes it deliciously succulent. If you've never eaten tripe, it's hard to explain what it's like. Fried oysters come to mind, but they're too soft. A tender piece of gristle is closer still—but most people don't eat gristle, however toothsome, and would consider anyone who attached the phrase "deliciously succulent" to it to be a barefaced liar. Don't even get me started on cow hoof.

In any case, it isn't the texture that many people find off-putting about tripe, it's the taste, and, to an even greater extent, the smell. In raw tripe, especially, this can quickly turn my stomach . . . although it's not easy to explain why. The phrase that most immediately comes to mind—although it's been some time since I last smelled it—is "cow breath." It isn't exactly a *bad* odor, but there's something oppressively intimate about it, a sense of getting a little too close to a very large animal's maw.

However, once tripe is cooked, that aspect pretty much fades away. What is left tastes like gristle seasoned with a spritz of stomach acid—chewy, tasty, and with the vaguest whisper of the abattoir. There's nothing quite like it for provoking a visceral response. Probably the line that separates those who love tripe from those who hate it has to do with the strength of that reaction . . . or how our particular psychology deals with it—just the way a loud explosion outside on the street sends some of us straight under the bed and others bursting out the door with our video recorder already rolling.

As long as I wouldn't cook tripe, my only dependable fix came when I would go back to Maine (about twice a year) and get the chance to order fried tripe at Moody's Diner. It's always on the menu, and it's almost always very good—a crispy, deep-fried coating wrapped abound chunks of tangy chewy juiciness. Apart from that, my only other recourse—and a not very satisfactory one—was to reach for a can of menudo, the classic Mexican tripe soup. When we lived in Maine, I had to persuade my pal and occasional contributor to these pages Bill Bridges to send me some from Texas, but here in central Massachusetts I can find it for myself. That there might be a canned version of pepper pot, however, never even crossed my mind.

Then, a few months ago, wandering past the Campbell's Soup section in an aisle of the local supermarket, there one was, flagging me down from the top shelf—just above eye level, where grocers put items that rarely generate impulse sales, since shoppers don't tend to see them unless they're intentionally looking for them. At our supermarket, all the canned soups with gourmet pretensions are up there in one long row.

There are a good number of Campbell's soups—tomato, chicken noodle, cream of mushroom—that can be found without fail in any supermarket, whatever its size, but there are other varieties that appear only because of local interest or a whim of the grocery buyer. In one store, it might be oyster stew or cream of onion, in another Scotch broth or shrimp bisque. Strangely, the supermarket we frequented in Maine was partial to chicken wonton (a real loser). But here at the local Stop & Shop, by gum, was Campbell's pepper pot.

I took down a can and examined it. The ingredient list was promising, despite the fact that three of the first four ingredients were actually three different ways of saying water. It began as so—

> INGREDIENTS: beef tripe stock, water, cooked beef tripe, beef stock, potatoes, enriched macaroni product, carrots, flour, tomato paste, salt, lard, vegetable oil, sweet red peppers, green peppers, etc.

—with "etc." marking the point where such things as BEEF FAT

SPICE (that's just *one* ingredient, by the way) begin to make their appearance. Still, your heart has to warm to a canned soup these days with a touch of lard in the formula—which perhaps can be explained by another encouraging sign: this Campbell's variety is made in Canada, a country that still takes humble, hearty soups very seriously. (Appropriately enough, they produce Campbell's Scotch broth as well.) I bought two cans of pepper pot, a container of milk, and headed for home.

Let me say straight off that this stuff is wicked good, even more so if you dilute the contents of the can with milk instead of water and stir in a generous dose of Tabasco as you heat it up. (Astute readers may have already noticed the mystifying absence of peppercorns or hot peppers from the list of ingredients.) There's only a minimal amount of tripe, but it makes its presence felt; the soup's flavor has just enough animal edge to balance off the blandness of the potatoes, carrots, and tiny plump inner tubes of macaroni. This is one of those dishes that works not by harmonious agreement (think chicken noodle soup) but because of the attraction of opposites—neither of which Campbell's allows to get the upper hand.

A can of Campbell's pepper pot became a regular midnight snack for me, even an occasional breakfast. And there things would have remained quite happily if it were not for one aspect that kept sticking in my craw: the price. $1.79 seemed just too damned much to pay for a can of condensed soup. (Campbell's Scotch broth costs $2.49 a can: you can imagine how often I buy *that*.)

This is one of the unexpected pains of growing old: your sense of what things should cost gets more and more out of whack with what things *do* cost. For decades you keep your equilibrium as prices creep up and up; then, for some reason, you just lose it. A few weeks ago I went to our local newspaper stand to see if they had a special issue of a computer magazine devoted to the new Macintosh operating system, OSX. I was sure that (a) I wouldn't find it and (b) it would be priced at something ridiculous, like $7.95. Well, they did have it, and it cost $12.95.

I was not only incredulous but simultaneously angry and *mortified*—all but imagining that the help was snickering at me as I slunk out of the store. It isn't as though I can't afford that much money or that, looking back on it, the amount seems all that out-rageous. No, what it's like is going down a flight of stairs and dis-covering too late that the last step is a few inches deeper than the ones that came before. The shock is out of all proportion to the physical jolt. You feel at once stupid and betrayed.

I relate this not because I imagine it to be all that fascinating but because it illustrates something that *does* intrigue me: the com-plex strands of motivation that make us decide when and what to cook. I can leaf through cookbooks all day, engrossed by the recipes and the color photographs of the finished dishes . . . and then put them down and go open a can of soup, a can of soup that reminds me of a dish I ate once decades ago and that I can now only vaguely remember. Then, because that can of soup costs fifty cents more than I think it ought to, I plunge into unknown waters, setting out to prepare a dish from a piece of offal that, in its raw state, I have so far in my life pretty much managed to avoid having any contact with at all.

Furthermore—remember I have yet to see George Rector's recipe—I immediately begin to compose a version of pepper pot that, mostly by dint of creative misremembering, is almost entirely my own. First, I confuse the macaroni for barley and track down a bag of that. I seem to recall the Campbell's version containing corn and grab a can of Niblets. Finally, I decide to replace the potatoes with something with a little more presence—a can of hominy. By the time I throw in a can of beef stock, I've already spent—what?—at least the price of a can of pepper pot, and this before I've even factored in the tripe.

By now, this just doesn't matter. Appetite has commandeered the steering wheel and told me to sit back and enjoy the ride. Culinary correctness is also left in the dust. Because what I'm set-ting out to replicate came out of a can, half of what I've assembled in my cart is also canned, even though such goods rarely intrude into my serious cooking efforts. Here is what resulted.

**Pepper Pot Not**

*serves 4 to 6*

1 pound beef tripe, honeycomb by preference
1 carrot
1 onion
1 stick of celery
2 or 3 tablespoons unsalted butter
1 teaspoon hot pepper sauce (or to taste)
1 or 2 large garlic cloves, minced
1 tablespoon tomato paste
scant ¼ cup barley
1 14½-ounce can low-sodium beef or chicken broth
1 15-ounce can white or yellow hominy
1 15¼-ounce can whole kernel corn
1 cup half & half (or milk, if preferred)
salt and black pepper to taste
minced parsley to garnish

• Rinse the tripe under cold running water and pat dry with a paper towel. Use a sharp knife to cut it into bite-size pieces.

• Chop the carrot, onion, and celery into medium dice. Melt the butter in a large soup pot over medium heat. When it is bubbling season it with the hot pepper sauce, then add the chopped vegetables and the minced garlic. Cook, stirring, until the onions are translucent. Add the cut-up tripe and the tomato paste. Stir some more, letting the tripe absorb a little of the color and flavor of the seasonings.

• Mix in the barley, the can of broth, and the entire contents (including the liquid) of the cans of hominy and whole kernel corn. Bring up to a gentle simmer, cover, and let cook until the tripe is tender but still chewy, about an hour to an hour and a half.

• Finally, mix in the half and half or milk. Let this heat up while you season the soup to taste with salt and grindings of black pepper. Serve garnished with minced parsley.

It is one of the clichés of cooking that homemade soups are better than canned soups, but this is not always true. Yes, a really good homemade soup is usually better than a canned one, and, conversely, even a pretty bad homemade soup can outmatch certain canned varieties—beef noodle, for instance—if only by default. However, Campbell's black bean soup, modestly enhanced with a tablespoon of sherry, is about as good as a soup can get. And since I already thought pretty highly of their pepper pot, I wasn't all that confident that my own efforts would produce something any better.

But it was better. My version took everything I liked about the canned soup and stroked it until it purred. The barley had more flavor and more texture than the macaroni; the hominy outclassed the potatoes; the corn kernels added a gentle sweetness; the quantity of tripe gave the soup more savor, more punch, more chew. It reminded me of the day I replaced my portable monophonic record player with a real stereo system and put one of my favorite recordings on the turntable. It was the same music, sure, but now the sound had gained palpable richness and depth.

# Grilling, Short and Sweet

by John Kessler

from *The Atlanta Journal-Constitution*

Kessler's range makes him indispensable to the Atlanta food scene; experienced cook, restaurant reviewer, and essayist, he does it all. Readers feel they can trust his advice, won over by his unpretentious writing style, self-deprecating persona, and clear-eyed sensibility.

The Satay Club in Singapore was razed long ago, a victim to development. But I'll never forget it. To one side was the harbor, and to the other the city's futurama skyscrapers. And, in between, on an open lot dimly lit by strings of bulbs, were vendors squatting by low grills and madly fanning rows and rows of skewered meat. The satays sizzled and popped, the charcoal embers glowed and the smoke smelled like caramel.

It was perhaps a tiny bit scary from a health perspective. You chose a vendor by sitting at his table, which he promptly loaded with dipping sauces, rice cakes, cucumber salad and scores of satays. When you had your fill, he'd count the sticks. The leftovers went, um, back on the grill.

I visited the Satay Club on my way home to America, seventeen years ago, after having lived in Japan. I had been traveling in Asia for a couple of months, and the food had stopped scaring me. I went to Japanese yakitori joints and ate unimaginable chicken bits brushed with treacly black tare sauce and grilled behind a counter. I dined in small, fluorescent-lighted and perfectly unventilated Korean restaurants where we cooked meat ourselves over charcoal hibachis. I sampled delicious mysteries grilled streetside in Thailand—flat pieces of meat that curled and buckled from the heat of the fire—while my girlfriend watched with alarm.

And then I went home to my life as a quasi-adult, with a Weber on the back porch and cold beer in the fridge. But after that time in Asia, I knew I'd never be the kind of backyard chef who would be happy brushing chicken pieces with barbecue sauce and rotating hot dogs. No, I developed an idiosyncratic relationship with my grill—one that takes to heart the techniques of Asian grilling without any attempt at authenticity.

Whatever it is I do, I usually ignore the commandments of American barbecue—the ones written in K.C. Masterpiece and followed like liturgy. I do not build an even, softly glowing fire on one side of the kettle and place the meat on the other. I don't cover the grill with a lid; I pay no attention to wood or smoke.

These are the hallmarks of the indirect method of grilling that the folks at Weber have done their darnedest to promote. It works wonders for roasts and turkeys, for chicken legs, for ribs that need to expel their grease (don't forget that drip pan underneath), for fat burgers that plump and stay juicy inside. If the flavor of wood smoke is of paramount importance, there is no other method.

Me, I'll have none of it. I'll build a fire that's one-Miss-iss-ouch hot from one side of the grill to the other. I cut the meat thinly, steep it in a thick marinade that jumps with flavor and let it char and sizzle with abandon over a direct flame. I never need the lid and can't be bothered with a drip pan. When I have company over, I don't even consider firing up the pork or chicken until everyone is ready to eat.

Why should I? Dinner's ready in three minutes flat.

And as I've experimented with this kind of grilling, I've developed a set of guidelines for everything from cutting the meat to rounding out the menu. My grilling is not a set of recipes. It's a way.

First, I choose or cut meat so that it's thin but not too uniform in texture. I'll sliver pieces of pork shoulder from a Boston butt, butterfly boneless chicken thighs or go to a Korean butcher to get the thin sliced beef short ribs called "kalbi." If I am faced with a terminally boring cut of meat, such as a boneless/skinless chicken breast, I'll cut it haphazardly through the center, pound it with a mallet and make sure to leave the bits of yellow fat attached. In short, anything to make sure it cooks unevenly, that it crisps on the edges and curls on the thin side. That the juiciness of the thickest part strikes your palate like a gift.

Next I'll devise a marinade that American barbecue mavens consider all but illegal—one that is thick with sugar. They tell you not to use sugar because it smokes and burns, that it creates an ungodly mess on the grill. (And then they go to Vietnamese restaurants and wonder why the pork is so delicious.)

Sugar in a marinade performs wonders. It concentrates the flavor of chiles and spices, it keeps soy sauce from becoming heavy murk. It crisps fat into candy. It accentuates grill marks and gives meat surfaces a glossy, appetizing sheen. And when it is used in a marinade rather than applied afterward (as in cheap-o teriyaki sauce) it doesn't taste too sweet. Those people who complain about clean up have obviously never used a grill brush. Carbonized sugar not only flakes right off, it leaves the grill bars cleaner than before because it pulls the fat and grime with it.

I like to use dark brown sugar for its caramel undertones that segue so nicely into the flavor of browned meat. Or, better yet, I'll chip a piece from the solid brown spools of palm sugar available in Asian markets. But I've also found that juice concentrates, hoisin sauce and Coca-Cola do the trick.

A marinade should also contain something salty like soy sauce, fish sauce or just plain salt. And it should have plenty of aromatic ingredients—chopped fresh chiles, ginger, garlic, coarsely chopped rosemary, curls of orange zest, slivered shallots. I like to see these ingredients stick to the surface of the meat and burn a bit on the grill. The smell is an invitation, the flavors add lip-tingling imprints and nobody minds picking off a burnt herb sprig.

And a marinade needs something sour. I now see why denizens of the tropical world reach instinctively for tamarind, but citrus juice and vinegar work as well. One of my favorite two-ingredient marinades is equal parts balsamic vinegar and Chinese oyster sauce.

As I said, these kind of grill creations are ready in three minutes if the grill is burning hot but not flaming (which is why my favorite fuel is real wood charcoal, available at Whole Foods Market). Also, the meat should not be refrigerator-cold; I usually take it out of the fridge when the first guest arrives.

The only way to eat this kind of meat is hot off the grill—with a squeeze of lemon or lime—when it is still has some juice and gloss. (Alas, chicken satays and pork slivers that look like carnivore's heaven the moment they're plucked from the fire turn dry and gray after twenty minutes.)

These grilled meats show well with only a fresh, bright salad and a plain starch alongside. Satays are traditionally accompanied by cucumber salad and soft rice cakes (sometimes amended to white toast in restaurants). Korean barbecue needs its lettuce wraps and plain rice. Vietnamese grilled pork usually finds its way onto a rice noodle bowl loaded with carrots and lettuce. I find that plain jasmine rice and a salad or slaw with tart dressing is all I want for my grilling adventure, though a relish or dipping sauce is always welcome. But the complex flavors of the meat come through best amid the trappings of a simple meal.

And, in that way, my pseudo-Asian grilling is a lot like good ol' American barbecue.

# Cajun Pig Party

by Kathleen Brennan

from *Saveur*

Senior editor Brennan pulled a plum assignment: show up at a backcountry Louisiana reunion and let the local characters display their moves. Capturing the rhythms of a regional culture that's all about food, family, and music, she brings her readers to the table.

Short and stout, with streaks of mud on her bristly pink skin, Sue stands calmly in her cage on the banks of the murky bayou, unaware of what awaits. Nearby, a black cauldron full of water bubbles and steams, its lid clanking ominously. One man attaches a pulley system to a barren pecan tree, while another pulls a hose over to a tilted wooden platform covering a patch of spent March grass. "How you do? How you do?" asks Andy Reaux, as he greets some latecomers in the backyard of his low-slung pine home on the outskirts of New Iberia, Louisiana, 130 miles west of New Orleans, in the heart of Cajun country. Reaux and a group of his childhood friends, along with a smattering of guests, are about to perform a generations-old Cajun rite, the boucherie, or pig butchering, and Sue is the 200-pound sacrificial sow.

Once the preparations are complete, Lewis Pitman, a quick-witted local attorney and the unofficial master of ceremonies, calls for the participants to gather around Sue's cage. There's plenty of snickering as Pitman hands out paper cups of Old South Miss Scarlett, a muscadine wine from Natchez, Mississippi ("It's cheap," he explains), but he eventually quiets everyone down enough to make a brief toast: "Sue, you do not know what you are getting ready to do, but for those of us who do, we salute you, Sue." After the group raises its cups, Preston Boudreaux—who with his buff physique, thick mustache, camouflage gear, and white rubber boots calls to mind a Cajun version of G.I. Joe—reaches into the cage and ceremoniously drapes strands of Mardi Gras beads around Sue's neck. Then, on cue, sets of fast-moving hands swing open the door, tie Sue's back legs together so that she can't run, and half drag, half carry the fiercely struggling animal out of the cage and onto the platform. Until now, Sue has been surprisingly quiet, but as soon as the men try to immobilize her with their knees, hands, even torsos, the squealing begins—a heart-rending, desperate cry. At this point, Reaux, a second-generation veterinarian, ducks into the house. Boudreaux, the only member of the group who grew up taking part in boucheries, is the designated executioner. Pulling a long-handled knife out of his back pocket, he remarks, "I don't feel any emotion right now. I've been doing this since I was a little boy. My main focus is to cut the jugular so she doesn't suffer and she bleeds right." The moment Sue's head is steadied, he swoops in toward her throat, and with one deft motion the noise stops.

Few animals have served man better than the pig, which was introduced to North America in 1539. A low-maintenance creature, easy to raise and house, it has long been a staple of the Occidental and the Oriental diets. Pigs have been particularly important to the Cajuns, descendants of French Acadians who were expelled from Nova Scotia in the 1750s by the British for refusing to swear allegiance to the crown and who found refuge on the uninhabited flatlands of south Louisiana, an area subsequently known as Acadiana (*Cajun* is a corruption of *Acadian*). The exiles quickly adapted to their new surroundings, foraging the area's many swamps and forests; it was during this period that the Cajuns became known for eating all manner of exotica, a reputation that lingers to this day. (There's an old joke that in a Cajun zoo, the cage labels list the animal's popular and scientific names, its habitat, and a recipe.) In time, however, the Cajuns began to cultivate rice and breed cattle and swine. Lacking electricity and refrigeration, they embraced the European practice of killing the family pig at the onset of winter and then curing or smoking the meat—or cooking and storing it in lard—to assure a steady supply of food during the less bountiful months of the year.

In the hands of the tight-knit and spirited Cajuns, what began as a household ritual quickly became a communal one. Neighbors helped neighbors with the time-consuming work, each family receiving a portion of the meat in return. Nothing was wasted: cuts that weren't preserved or cooked fresh were used in pâtés or sausages, including the classic Cajun rice-and-pork links called boudin. The intestines served as sausage casings. The blood was used to make "red" boudin. The stomach, or *chaudin,* was stuffed and baked, the feet pickled, the head turned into hogshead cheese, the fat rendered into lard. A boucherie typically lasted a day, at the end of which all the men, women, and children would sit down to a rollicking feast.

Although electricity arrived in Acadiana in the 1940s, paving the way for commercial food shops, boucheries were still prevalent as recently as the 1970s, in part because many Cajuns couldn't afford to buy meat. A quarter century on, the region is no longer so impoverished, and like the Cajun-French language, communal butchering has become all but obsolete. The only boucheries taking place nowadays are held mainly for social purposes.

It was the promise of a good party that led Reaux and his friends Pitman, Boudreaux, Brian Breaux, Matt Crochet, Steve Miguez, Mike Peltier, Byron Price, Clark Romero, and Travis Segura—they call themselves the James Gang, after the 1970s rock band—to hold their first boucherie, in 1982. That was the year

Reaux graduated from veterinary school and Pitman earned his law degree, and it was around this time that career and family responsibilities were beginning to pull the James Gang apart. Then Reaux was given a pig by a client. When he asked his friends what to do with it, one of them suggested putting on a boucherie as a way of reconnecting with one another and with their Cajun roots. Thus was born the annual reunion, which has grown over the years into something of a community-wide bash. In fact, the porcine bacchanalia is now too large for Reaux's backyard; it instead takes place at Lake Fausse Pointe State Park in nearby St. Martinville. But because it's illegal to kill animals in the park, the core group gathers for the actual slaughter at Reaux's on a Friday, then overnights en famille at the park. The rest of the attendees— sometimes upwards of 400 people—join them the next day to participate in the butchering, cooking, and revelry.

As soon as Boudreaux pulls back from Sue's neck, Matt Crochet, Reaux's partner at the local animal clinic his father established in 1947 and the boucherie's main cook, puts a saucepan under the incision to catch the blood for the red boudin. Everyone has fallen silent with the pig, and it isn't until Reaux saunters back over that the mood lightens. "Not my good pan!" he yelps, half in jest, drawing laughter all around. Brian Breaux proceeds to hose off the pig, and scarlet water runs off the platform, angled for this very reason. Next comes the most arduous step, scraping the hair off the pig. Kerman LeBlanc Jr., a "fringe" James Gang member, pours some of the boiling water onto the animal (which is covered with burlap to help trap the steam), and people begin running sharp knives across the skin.

Sitting in a portable chair taking it all in is 94-year-old Dewey Patin, a veteran of countless boucheries and something of a local legend (in 1986 this former commercial fisherman caught a 128-pound catfish, breaking the world record; he's also an ace alligator hunter). The éminence grise of the gathering, Patin is gleefully holding court, recounting boucheries past as he taps his cane against his gleaming brogues: "We *had* to kill the pig. Beef didn't conserve too well, and there were no stores then. We needed grease, too. We'd kill three or four at a time."

Reaux is now back in the house, standing at his grandmother's 1950s Chambers stove: the guys are hungry and he's been cajoled into whipping up a batch of his crawfish scrambled eggs topped with a bell pepper cream sauce. Crochet's mom, Joyce, and aunt Ruby Halbert are making a thick, oniony barbecue sauce to take to the park tomorrow, along with a vat of vegetable gumbo (this being a Friday during Lent, many Cajuns—devout Catholics— won't eat meat) for later that day. The talk here, too, revolves around food and pigs and the old days. "I grew up on a farm," says Mrs. Halbert, "and what I remember is that we fed the pig slop, but before slaughter time, it got corn." "Well, I lived in town, and we didn't ever kill pigs," chimes in Mrs. Crochet, as she stirs a caramel-colored roux for the soup. "But one thing's for sure: pork doesn't taste the way it used to—it doesn't have the fat."

"You got that right," Reaux says, as he adds more butter to the eggs. He explains that rich food is the Cajun way, joking, "Every time a healthy restaurant opens around here, it closes. It doesn't matter, though. All of us guys are on heart medicine anyway."

Outside, the pig, now hairless and spotless, is ready to be decapitated. Again, the honors fall to Boudreaux, a special-ed agriculture teacher. His father, Preston Boudreaux Sr., who's been standing on the sidelines all morning, will take the head home to make his specialty, hogshead cheese, a savory, gelatinous concoction commonly eaten with crackers. After the pig's feet are sawed off, several of the guys attach the carcass to the pulley and hoist it in the air so that Boudreaux can remove the innards. To keep from puncturing them, which would let the waste leak out, he proceeds cautiously. "On a cold day, everyone wants this job," he comments, his hands inside the warm cavity. After Boudreaux separates the stomach, kidneys, heart, liver, and intestines, Crochet comes over to collect the makings for his boudin and chaudin. "C'est bon?" Boudreaux asks. "Bon," Crochet replies, glancing at the steaming organs.

All that's left to do is saw the carcass in half, a task that fair-haired, blue-eyed Breaux, the high-school heartthrob of the group, performs while the rest of the crew cleans up. Soon it's time for lunch, and Sue, now just two big slabs of meat hanging from a tree, is left alone in the yard. Some watered-down blood dripping from her front legs is the only reminder that this was, a few hours ago, a living, snorting creature.

By eight the next morning, stations for barbecuing, frying, butchering, and sausage making, as well as a steam table from which to serve food, have been set up around a two-story pavilion in the park. In this remote setting, surrounded by acres of rustling woods and alligator-filled waters, Cajuns are clearly in their element, arriving in pickup trucks stuffed with coolers of beer and soda, boom boxes, camp chairs, all kinds of snacks and desserts, and tiny sealed cups of potent Jell-O shots. Not even the watchful eye of the park ranger—"Every coonass's archnemesis," says Reaux, alluding to the Cajun passion for hunting—can dampen the enthusiasm. (Cajuns habitually call one another "coonass," a controversial term that may derive from the fact that Cajun trappers and woodsmen wore coonskin fur caps with the tail hanging down the back.)

In the James Gang's modern take on the boucherie, everything that is prepared is eaten the same day, and because one pig is not enough to feed a crowd this large, extra pork is purchased from a local butcher shop. Before distributing the coffin-size coolers of meat to the various stations, Pitman makes another wry toast to mark the twentieth anniversary of the event. Then the group disperses. Crochet, a lumbering, gentle sort who learned how to cook from his mom, gathers a bunch of people around a picnic table to take the skin off one of the carcasses and then cut it into rectangles for the cracklins. Some know the drill, others need instruction.

"Hey, is this good?" a young woman asks. "Whoa, you gotta try to get them uniform and a little wider," he answers patiently. With so many hands, the work goes quickly, and soon the team relays several tubs of the creamy-white strips to Boudreaux and his son-in-law, Damon Theriot, who are setting up gas burners under two massive cast-iron pots. Crochet then demonstrates how to remove the leg, shoulder, and neck meat, which will be cubed and ground up for the sausages, as well as the ribs and chops, which will be barbecued. The remaining scraps and bones, as well as the liver, heart, kidneys, and tongue from yesterday, will be boiled for the boudin.

A few feet away, Breaux, in bright-yellow rubber overalls, mans the washup station. Keeping him company is fellow James Gang stalwart Travis Segura, who notes, "I didn't realize 'til today it had been twenty years. Remember that first year when the meat was burnt on the outside and raw on the inside? But we ate it anyway. We've come a long way." "Yeah," adds Breaux. "Coming from Andy's [Reaux] to here, it's almost a little commercialized, but I like that we can do this with more people—especially the kids—'cause it keeps the whole Cajun tradition goin'. My mama loves it, too. She'll be here soon. She's a true Cajun—speakin' Cajun French, livin' the food, the culture. Doesn't matter if it's rain or shinin', if there's a good Cajun band playing, she's out there dancin', in the mud, havin' a good time."

Eventually, the warm, meaty smell of melting animal fat cuts through the damp air. The rain has been holding off so far, but when a drizzle starts to fall, Pitman announces, "Don't worry, this is Louisiana. Wait a minute, and the weather will change." As the morning progresses, people of all ages continue to arrive, including the three-month-old "boucherie baby," the result of a romance kindled at last year's event, consummated that night (or so the story goes), and ended not long thereafter. Most of the guests are connected to one of the James Gang members, but every year there are some welcome interlopers, like the campers from New Jersey in 1997. They had so much fun, they came again the following year.

Back at Crochet's table, seasoned sausage mixture is being tunneled through grinders set up at either end of the table and into casings. Boudreaux stops by and offers pointers on twisting the links: "There's a technique to doin' it. First you twist it one way; then, for the next link, you go the other way." As the group forges ahead, creating many a misshapen sausage, Crochet starts on the boudin (which Cajuns eat by putting it between their teeth and squeezing the filling out of the casings). To tubs of the scraps, now cooked and ground, he adds steamed rice, scallions, parsley, and generous amounts of cayenne and Tabasco. "If it ain't hot, it ain't Cajun," he says.

Over by the barbecue pit, dozens of chops and ribs, basted with the Crochets' barbecue sauce, are starting to caramelize over gray coals. As music blares from a "Cajun radio" (a radio fitted into a cooler punctured with holes in order to rainproof it), men smoke, drink, and trade jokes, while kids play tag.

Once the pieces of pig skin have turned mahogany, Boudreaux strains them out of the pot, then puts sliced sweet potatoes in the rendered fat. These, topped with sugar, are what passes for the day's vegetable. Next into the pots will go the Cajun egg rolls (boudin mixture encased in egg roll skins). Lending a hand is Howard Broussard, a 73-year-old St. Martinville resident who doesn't feel much nostalgia for the Cajun past: "My parents didn't speak English, and my teachers whipped me when I spoke French. I had so much work on our farm, I quit school in the sixth grade. I grew up doing boucheries, most certainly. But there was no propane then—we had to gather wood. And sometimes the pig was a thousand pounds, and we had to hold him down. That's why when people talk about the good old days, I say, 'You got to be crazy. It was hard!' "

Soon the steam table is loaded with red and white boudin, both varieties packing enough heat to be certifiably Cajun; crisp, addictive cracklins; the egg rolls—yet more proof that deep-frying makes everything taste better; tangy ribs and chops. All the food is so good—and so rich—it's hard to save room for Wolla Mae

Broussard's airy, gingerbread-like gâteau de sirop (cane syrup cake), a dish that figures prominently at any Cajun fête. Pitman waits until people are abundantly fed and well lubricated before soliciting contributions; instead of passing around a hat, he passes a piggy bank. First stop: a group of his employees. "They can't say no," he chortles. After lunch, the band Jambalaya starts playing the two-step and people take to the dance floor. As guest singer D. L. Menard, an official "Cajun living legend," warbles in a patois that only the older folk can understand, Brian Breaux's mom is in the thick of the crowd, joyfully and proudly struttin' her Cajun stuff.

## Barbecue Sauce

*Makes 5 cups*

After tinkering with various recipes, the Crochet family created this sauce in the 1970s. Slather it over chops, ribs, chicken, or brisket toward the end of barbecuing. Heat ½ cup vegetable oil in a large heavy-bottomed saucepan over medium heat. Add 1 large finely chopped peeled yellow onion and cook, stirring often with a wooden spoon, until soft, 8-10 minutes. Add 4 finely chopped peeled garlic cloves and cook for 1 minute. Add 2 ½ cups ketchup, ½ cup cider vinegar, ½ cup Worcestershire sauce, ¼ cup yellow mustard, ¼ cup light brown sugar, ½-1 tsp. Tabasco sauce, and 1 tsp. liquid smoke and stir until well combined. Reduce heat to medium-low and gently simmer, stirring occasionally, until sauce thickens, about 30 minutes.

# A Dieter's Dilemma

by Jason Epstein

from the *New York Times Magazine*

New York City publishing executive Epstein went public with this wistful valedictory to all the foods he gave up by adopting the Atkins diet. Necessary footnote: A few months later he wrote ruefully that he'd fallen off the Atkins wagon for good; once a food lover, always a food lover.

In August and September, as the blueberry crop advances northward across Long Island on its way to Canada, I like to bake a blueberry pie, to which I add an entire lemon, including the peel, coarsely chopped. By the time the pie is baked, the peel and its pith caramelize and give the berries a surprising tang. A tablespoon or two of arrowroot doesn't quite absorb all the lemon juice, but I prefer my blueberry pie a little runny, not glutinous and stiff with cornstarch like pies from the bakery. I enjoy the way a scoop of vanilla ice cream melts into the warm juice.

During blueberry season, I usually make a dozen or so of these pies, their top crusts lightly browned with egg wash and accented with little rivers of purple syrup. But this year I'm not making any. And when they ripen, I'm not cutting up plump Golden Delicious or crunchy Mutsu apples from the Milk Pail in Water Mill on Long Island and laying the thick slices out neatly in circles in caramelized sugar and butter on the tarte Tatin pan that I bought from Fred Bridge in the 1960's. Nor will I be topping the apples with a thin sheet of buttery pie dough and sliding the tarte in the oven for fifty minutes at 360 degrees, to keep the apples from sticking to the pan the way they would at a higher temperature. And I won't be adding a tablespoon of flour to thicken the syrupy apple juice, because a tarte Tatin, unlike a blueberry pie, should not be runny at all.

Never again will I make the buttery muffins that I used to bake on Sunday mornings. I am also giving up ketchup, which is mainly corn syrup flavored with tomato and vinegar. Moreover, I'm going to think twice before I buy another Walla Walla onion, laden with sugary carbohydrates, or the wonderful rolls from Amy's Bread. That probably means no more hamburgers either and, for that matter, no more onion marmalade, the perfect accompaniment to *magret de canard* (the breasts of moulard ducks, the kind raised for foie gras), sautéed until warm and pink inside, then sliced and fanned out on the plate accompanied by the marmalade, a silky reduction of a half-dozen large, sweet onions—a critical mass of carbohydrate waiting to turn itself into body fat.

According to Dr. Robert Atkins, 60 percent of the American population is perilously plump, an endangered group from whose condition I have been withdrawing for the past month at the rate of a pound every other day. I am especially wary of pecan pie, of which a single triangular slice contains three times the daily amount of carbohydrate permitted during the two-week initiation phase—Atkins calls it the Induction Phase—of his diet. This is the phase I have recently completed, having lost ten pounds. I am now well into the Ongoing Weight Loss (O.W.L.) phase, with the permission of my wise friend and physician Stanley Mirsky, who for years has been urging me to avoid carbohydrates. But it was to the evangelical pitchman Dr. Atkins, not the stately Dr. Mirsky, that I finally succumbed, goaded by my son, Jacob, who, though not at all plump, lost twenty-seven pounds and reduced his cholesterol in two months on Atkins.

The physiological case against excessive carbohydrates, reported in this magazine seven weeks ago, is fairly straightforward and by now well known. The low-carbohydrate diet, touted originally by Atkins and adopted successfully by millions of his followers, contradicts the widely accepted theory, introduced in the 1980's and later promoted by the Department of Agriculture's Food Guide Pyramid, that carbohydrates should be the basis of the American diet. Most researchers now agree that carbohydrates, especially refined ones like sugar and other vegetable-based sweeteners, white flour and rice, are quickly absorbed as energy by the body, while carbohydrates in excess of the body's immediate needs are stored as fat for future use. A secondary effect of this quick absorption is renewed hunger soon after a high-carbohydrate meal, for example after a Chinatown dinner of noodles, rice, wonton wrappers, egg-roll skins, syrupy ribs and cornstarch thickeners.

A low-carbohydrate diet, on the other hand, not only forces the body to seek energy by consuming its own stored fat but also suppresses appetite, since dietary fat and protein take longer to digest and enter the bloodstream than carbohydrates. Moreover, the body expends more energy burning fat than burning carbohydrates, yielding what Atkins calls "a metabolic advantage." These phenomena explain the quick weight loss, especially during the Induction Phase, which allows only twenty grams of carbohydrates per day, about half the amount in a single bagel.

Even in its rigorous two-week Induction Phase, however, Atkins provides a rich larder of bacon and eggs, steak, lamb, pork and poultry, fish, including most shellfish, cheese, butter, cream (but not whole milk) and green vegetables—except leeks, onions, peas and artichokes. Gin, vodka, whiskey and other spirits, according to Atkins, become "acceptable," as does wine. Excluded forever are pasta, pizza, pastries and so on. No more sushi, congee, cookies, cereals, bagels, croissants, pancakes or waffles; no potatoes or corn, though one or two chips with guacamole is allowed. Above all, no more pretzels, which deliver five times as many carbs as potato chips. Orange juice, alas, is also out. But pecans, almonds and macadamia nuts are in.

Despite these restrictions, you can make a splendid breakfast of eggs scrambled through a strainer and cooked gently in a Teflon pan over simmering water, accompanied by warm prosciutto or its Austrian cousin, speck, with a few spears of asparagus, or a lunch of lobster, shrimp or chicken salad with homemade mayonnaise. (My favorite, Hellmann's, contains sugar.) For dinner you can have a pan-roasted rib-eye steak or striped bass with braised fennel or grilled trevisano radicchio. Most cheeses are acceptable, including blue, cheddar, cottage, cream and mozzarella. Tomatoes are iffy, but Atkins includes a recipe for fried green tomatoes using a noncarbohydrate bake mix. He may be an evangelist, but in his recipes he is not inflexible.

For the moment, at least, I seem to have successfully reversed my compulsions. Not only am I no longer addicted to croissants, hash-brown potatoes, blueberry pies and lobster salad stuffed into hot-dog rolls, but I am also slightly repelled by them. For moderately resourceful cooks, a low-carbohydrate diet offers abundant opportunity, and many of the recipes in *Dr. Atkins's New Diet Revolution* are worth considering. Nevertheless, I include my recipe for blueberry pie. Perhaps one day, when I am beyond Atkins's O.W.L. phase and into Maintenance, I'll make it again.

**Blueberry Pie**

For the pastry:
   4 cups all-purpose flour
   6 ounces unsalted butter, diced
   1 tablespoon sugar
   Pinch salt
   ¾ cup water
   1 egg mixed with 1 tablespoon water

For the filling:
   2 quarts plus a little more firm, fresh blueberries

3 cups sugar
1 cup arrowroot
1 lemon, seeded and coarsely chopped in the food processor
Vanilla ice cream for serving.

1. Preheat the oven to 400 degrees and place a sheet pan lined with aluminum foil beneath the rack where the pie will bake.

2. To make the pastry, place the flour, butter, sugar and salt in a food processor and pulse briefly until the butter has been cut in coarsely. Add half the water and pulse, watching to see if the dough forms a ball. If not, add a little more water until it does. Too much water will make a heavy, gummy pastry. Too little will make a crumbly one. If the dough feels too wet, add a little more flour and pulse. If too dry, add a little more water. Pulse sparingly. On a floured board, cut the dough into two parts, one slightly larger. Roll out the smaller portion and place it neatly in a 9-inch deep-dish pie pan. Refrigerate the larger portion while you prepare the berries.

3. To make the filling, pick over the berries, discarding green or bad ones, and remove any stems. Rinse the berries and drain. In a large bowl, mix the sugar and arrowroot. Add the berries and lemon and mix well. Mound the filling in the pastry shell.

4. Roll out the remaining pastry into a large round. Brush the rim of the bottom shell with some of the egg mixture and carefully lay the large pastry round over the berries. Trim the edges, leaving a ¾-inch overhang. Press the top and bottom pastry halves together to seal well. Fold excess top pastry under and crimp the edges. Cut 4 triangular holes near the top. (Do not cut along the sides or all the juices will leak out.) Brush with more of the egg mixture.

5. Bake for 15 minutes. Reduce the oven temperature to 375 degrees and bake 40 to 50 minutes.

# The Zen of Frosting

by Ann Patchett
from *Gourmet*

Among the many moonlighting novelists that *Gourmet* has lured in recent years, Ann Patchett (author of *Bel Canto*) is one who actually writes about food like a cook. Here she traces her love-hate relationship with the sweetest part of the cake.

Throughout high school, parts of college, and whenever she needed money for years thereafter, my sister decorated cakes at our local Baskin-Robbins. To get an idea of what a waste this was, imagine Matisse painting Elvis's face on black velvet day after day. My sister had talent with her pastry tube, real talent, which she squandered back in the freezer writing "Happy Birthday [your name here]" over and over again, perfect rosebuds springing in endless succession onto slabs of ice cream.

When I decided to marry, on the cheap, at the sophisticated age of twenty-four, my sister volunteered to make our wedding cake—five tapering tiers held aloft by Doric columns. It was a wildly ambitious piece of work, which she drove over to the reception site three hours before the wedding to assemble. It would have been her piece de resistance but for the fact that it was over one hundred degrees that day.

When she opened the trunk of her car, she found nothing but

boiled confection, the hundreds of tiny violets she had so carefully rendered now mere lavender smears in a sea of white gunk. With no time to craft a new cake, she dashed home, whipped up an enormous vat of frosting, slathered it onto the outsides of the empty cake pans, and made it back in time to be my maid of honor. In the wedding pictures, my husband and I gamely hold a knife over that which cannot be cut. Our wedding cake was beautiful and utterly inedible. We were divorced within a year.

So goes the metaphor of frosting and cake. In a perfect world, the two would exist as complements to each other—they would achieve synergy, enabling us to love the balance between them more than we could love either part alone. But most of the time it isn't like that. All too often, the frosting simply isn't good. Frosting is the short skirt, the fast car. Frosting turns our heads from a distance, making promises it cannot keep.

Much of my childhood was spent praying that I would be the lucky one at the birthday party, the one who received the corner piece of cake pinned down by a sugared reenactment of an American Beauty rose. But on those rare occasions when I got what I wanted, it was as gritty as a beach in a gale, greased down with Crisco or maybe something worse. It took forever for that waxy feeling on the roof of my mouth to go away. And still there would be another party, another rose, and I would want that, too, positive that this time it would be different. How could something so beautiful be so misleading?

Over the years, I have found myself turning away from frosting altogether: the seven-minute icing sealing my lips together with its sticky froth; the double fudge frosting stretched over the cake like a leather tarp; the cream cheese frosting so uninspired it might have been a block of Philadelphia brand, unmolested in its foil wrapper. Instead, I choose cakes that are delicious over ones that are beautiful. The recipes I am attracted to sport at best a light glaze. They are tea cakes topped with stewed fruit, jam spread thinly across a sponge cake, something with a dab of crème anglaise on the side.

But we all crave beauty, and long after I had given up on frosting I was still missing it. The reunion happened the way these things usually do, with a birthday cake made for a friend. It was a recipe for a lemon cake with a lemon curd frosting—homemade lemon curd folded into whipped cream. It was delicious because the tang of the lemon kept it from erring on the side of sugar. The recipe yielded enough frosting to generously coat my entire sofa, and so I heaped it onto the poor cake in ridiculous quantities, just for fun. I knew I would have to go back and trim, but for a while I simply gave myself over to the swirling. I smoothed a perfectly flat top, then sculpted it into a series of rough waves. I used the tip of my spatula to score zigzags down the sides. This was delicious frosting, but it was lazy and wet, not the kind that yields a work of art.

And that's when it struck me. Frosting is really about art. Sure, every now and then it's delicious, light and ethereal or creamy and deeply flavored, but most of the time frosting is sculpture. It's about turning a regular dessert into a snowstorm of hyacinth blossoms. It's about jewel colors, pinks and yellows as bright as humming-birds—after all, what takes color as beautifully as a bowl of vanilla frosting? In the same way that we can love the works of Picasso and Gauguin while acknowledging that we wouldn't have wanted them to marry our daughters, we can love frosting for its elo-quence if not for its flavor.

On my birthday this year I decided to forgo the cake. I made myself a batch of pale green frosting and covered my granite coun-tertops with sugary leaves. It's a trick I learned years ago from my sister—that practice can be much more creative when you know the final result will eventually be scraped up and thrown into the trash. I wrote my name beside the sink in a swooping script, and then I wished myself a happy birthday using leaves. Several times I forgot myself, running my finger over the tip of the pastry tube and then touching my finger to my tongue. It wasn't good. But it was beautiful.

# Dining Around

# Josiah & the Giant Onion

## by Dave Gardetta
from *Los Angeles Magazine*

Senior editor Gardetta's cover story for *Los Angeles Magazine*'s August 2002 restaurant issue is as much a business story as a food story; even more, it's a piercing examination of American values, seen through the prism of one chef's master plan.

T he last time I was in Valencia I ate an Awesome Blossom. The town of Valencia, which sits off the Golden State Freeway just north of L.A. and south of Magic Mountain, is a community conceived, designed, built and now tended after by a single company, Newhall Land. The Awesome Blossom—a giant onion sliced into neat tiny quadrants, battered, and then deep-fried—is an appetizer conceived, designed, cooked, and then served with a tangy dipping sauce by a single chain, Chili's. I was not alone eating my Awesome Blossom, but I was 1.5 people short of the average Awesome Blossom consumer party which Chili's has calculated to be 3.5 people. Usually a Chili's employee brings up this fact if you mention that the Awesome Blossom contains roughly 2,900 calories, 222 grams of fat, and is one of the worst things you could possibly ingest, myocardial infarction–wise. At our table in the Valencia Chili's, my lunch companion looked up and asked our waitress, "Did you know these things are pretty bad for you?"

"Well, I've heard that," she smiled. "But an average of 3.5 people eat the Awesome Blossom, so it's not that bad really."

Josiah Citrin looked back to our table, which, in addition to the Awesome Blossom, also supported plates of Chili's boneless buffalo wings, shrimp pasta Alfredo, spinach salad, citrus-fired chicken and shrimp, and two small bowls of enchilada soup. Citrin put a spoon in his soup, then slipped it into his mouth and made a face. "Ughh—terrible," he grimaced, and then, glancing sideways, raised an eyebrow as a waiter tucked in his shirt beside our table. "I probably shouldn't say this," Citrin began slowly, measuring his words while appraising a food server whose hands were down his pants. "But I don't know why people eat here."

There are 816 Chili's restaurants in the world, including 124 in Texas, 63 in California, 5 in the United Arab Emirates, 1 in Lebanon, and 0 in Montana—the only state in the Union yet to host a Chili's. A new Chili's appears virtually every week in America; on the day of our lunch in Valencia the Chili's in Greenwood, South Carolina, was celebrating its grand opening. Until the week he tasted his first Awesome Blossom, Josiah Citrin owned just one restaurant, Mélisse, which along with Patina, L'Orangerie, and Valentino is considered one of the crown jewels of L.A. restaurants. Citrin is regarded as a chef's chef—Mélisse is famously patronized by L.A. chefs on their nights off—and also something of a mensch; other cooks seem impelled to hug him or affectionately cuff him on the shoulder when in his presence. He had yet to visit a Chili's before our lunch, but he is not philosophically opposed to the baser taxonomies of prepared food. One of Citrin's favorite things to do is eat at Fat Burger. While the onions are grilling he sneaks around the counter to admire the kitchen's spotlessly clean floor mats. Perfection in food as well as kitchen mats is Citrin's consuming passion; like Saint Augustine following God, he looks for signs of its presence everywhere. He has almost realized it in Mélisse, which was awarded four of Mobil's five stars, but as often as not he finds perfection absent. I used to think it would be hard being Citrin in the world—you would notice all the dirty silverware, soggy carrots, and waiters with hands down their pants. Then I realized he is actually a reformer, not a cynic. He is not far in theory from Alice Waters at Chez Panisse, who started with the Revolution, then switched to the perfect risotto as an organizing principle for redeeming the state. Replace the state with the world and you have some idea what Citrin is trying to accomplish at Mélisse.

Citrin is thirty-four years old. He has a ruddy face with features set close together and dark hair he wears slicked back. When he cooks in Mélisse's warm kitchen his face flares up and his hair shoots toward the ceiling. Citrin trained as a chef at Wolfgang Puck's Chinois on Main and Joachim Splichal's Patina, yet unlike his former employers, he long held off creating a secondary group of restaurants that featured his name. Then this May, a week before our lunch, Citrin opened Café Mélisse in the Valencia Town Center, across from a T.G.I. Friday's. Café Mélisse is a downsized version of the Santa Monica Mélisse, closer in theme to Splichal's Pinot restaurants than to Puck's cafés; if Café Mélisse proves successful, Citrin plans it to be the first of many.

As it happened, I had dined the night before my lunch with Citrin at Café Mélisse, where among other dishes I tasted Hudson Valley foie gras on poached quince; soft-shell crab balanced atop shaved fennel and blood orange; seared salmon nestled in morels, spring ramps, and truffle emulsion; and a perfectly cooked filet sitting on fingerling potatoes. The dinner was like nothing else served in Valencia; in fact, as a food primer, Citrin's line cooks—whom he hired locally—were tasting foie gras for the first time in their lives during my visit.

Inside Chili's, Citrin popped a piece of Awesome Blossom in his mouth, then rolled it around on his tongue. "Everything has the same flavor here," he said, trying to flag the waitress. "It's like the candy version of food, like Jolly Ranchers."

"How are you guys doing?" our waitress asked. "Hey, you guys aren't from the food police, are you?"

"No," Citrin smiled. "I want to ask you something. What is the Chili's taste?"

"The chili? It comes already mixed in a bag, but it goes on the Awesome Blossom, the mashed potatoes, french fries, a lot of the burgers, and some other things."

"The Awesome Blossom," Citrin repeated, eyeing the giant steaming onion like it was a porcupine that had just crawled onto our table. "It's like Jolly Ranchers, like drugs." Citrin thought about what he had just said, then added, "They start training you to eat this stuff at a very early age."

The Awesome Blossom was created in 1990 inside the Chili's test-kitchen complex at the corporation's Dallas home office, a collection of glass-and-steel buildings that dot some property formerly developed by the Dallas Cowboys quarterback Roger Staubach. The onion, with its signature spice, has become one of Chili's more successful menu items. Four hundred Awesome Blossoms are sold each month at the Valencia Chili's; four million are sold every year worldwide. You can eat an Awesome Blossom in Peru as well as Anchorage. The homogeny of spice flavor in Chili's food—everything pretty much tastes like everything else—is a gastronomical metaphor of the Chili's idea that no matter where you go, if you stumble into a Chili's, the food will taste as it does anywhere else.

The Chili's business model—there are 200 new Chili's planned over the next three years—is in turn a metaphor of how rural America is now commercially developed. No matter where you go, everywhere increasingly looks like anywhere else, especially when it comes to restaurants. The Valencia Chili's, like Valencia itself, sits on former farmland that was once used to grow onions. Exit the front door and you can walk to a Chuck E. Cheese's (one of 469), a Romano's Macaroni Grill (one of 167), a Pick Up Stix (one of 61), a Claim Jumper (one of 29), a Subway, a Noah's Bagels, a Starbucks, and a Wal-Mart McDonald's. Developed by a single corporation, Valencia is dominated by corporate restaurants. You can drive locally to dine out in an Outback, a Sizzler, a Red Lobster, an Olive Garden, a T.G.I. Friday's.

Before Citrin, however, you could count on one finger the restaurants in Valencia owned and run by a single chef. Citrin does not have a test-kitchen complex, a Dallas home office, an Awesome Blossom. Yet the giant onion is what he's up against. Will a community fond of T.G.I. Friday's firecracker crab rolls, Outback's Jackeroo chops, and Claim Jumper's Eureka dessert sampler dine at a Café Mélisse? Citrin realizes it's a fight as portentous in its nature as it is symbolic of his role in the world's perfecting.

"I know what we have to do to succeed in Valencia," Citrin said at the end of our lunch. "We have it broken down into different scenarios. But if we don't make it up here, if Café Mélisse fails, no one will make it up here. It's the small towns like Valencia that should be supporting the little guys, and they're not doing that anymore. This is like the battle for America."

The waitress appeared with the check. "Good luck with your new restaurant," she smiled. "It's tough up here."

"Why?" Citrin asked.

"Well, everyone wants everything quick, a lot of it, and at a cheap price."

An earnest look came into Citrin's eye. He was fighting the battle of America, and he would do so one waitress at a time.

"*You* should come in," he said. "We did 280 people on Saturday night."

"Okay, that's great. All right—we'll come in. You know what would really help you, though?"

"What?"

"A special. Maybe a coupon."

Citrin drives a black Ford Expedition and keeps a brown Suburban parked in its backseat. I discovered this one day when I accompanied Citrin and his Mélisse sous-chef, Luke Johnson, to the Santa Monica farmers' market. Citrin popped open a passenger door and Johnson rolled out a bilevel plastic cart that looks like a lunar rover and is used for hauling produce. "We call this the Suburban," Citrin said. "Everyone has one now, but we were the first to get it."

The Wednesday-morning farmers' market is known as a chefs' market. As Citrin picks through the stone fruits and root vegetables, he stops occasionally to say hi. He greets Evan Kleiman of Angeli Caffé wheeling her own Suburban; Thomas Boyce, Spago's chef de cuisine; Kim Boyce, Thomas's wife and pastry chef at Campanile; Spago's Sherry Yard, who has just returned from New York with a James Beard Award; and Joe of Joe's Restaurant. Mark Peel, who owns Campanile, walks by, quietly confiding to an intense-looking woman, "I can't do anything until I finish my sandwich cookbook."

Chefs at the Santa Monica market are like wild porcini mushrooms: They begin showing up in real numbers in spring. Citrin attends every Wednesday of the year. The winters can be tough—a lot of onions and potatoes. Today he is looking for purple artichokes, white radishes, yellow tomatoes, and lavender. He carries a printed list of needs, yet Citrin's memory being what it is, it's a wonder he writes anything down. The scope of Citrin's recall is terrifying: He can recollect a food course he botched for a diner two years ago, the dessert someone ate at his table a half decade past. My first conversation with Citrin took place a year after my last meal at Mélisse, where Citrin had stopped by the table to casually say hi. In our conversation he remembered the table I'd sat at, a half-dozen courses I'd tasted, and what my date looked like.

List in hand, Citrin buys apricots for a crème fraîche pound cake, fava beans for a soft-shell crab, cherries to cook in caramel and sherry for the seared foie gras. He buys white carrots for a vegetable fricassee, spring onions for the *côte de boeuf*. He buys fenugreek shambalilee to sauté with amaranth for the turbot. Near the summer peaches Citrin runs into Kazuto Matsusaka, Chinois's former executive chef, and his wife, Viki, who is dressed in a cute green Winnie-the-Pooh sweatshirt.

"Hey, Kazuto," says Citrin, looking happy.

"Hey, good-looking," Kazuto smiles, reaching out to squeeze Citrin's belly like it's a ripe cantaloupe.

"We need golden beets," says Viki, looking distracted.

Citrin is not heavy, but he is stout. Onstage he would make a good Falstaff, and in the ocean he would make a great seal, which in fact he resembled recently just off Malibu, when the Food Network filmed Citrin and two other chefs in wet suits surfing and Citrin spent some time on camera floundering. This has not always been the case. When Citrin first met Kazuto he was eighteen and a tournament surfer. His heroes were the surfing and skateboarding legends the Dogtown Z-Boys, and like them, he had spent much of his waking life in the waves near the old Pacific Ocean Park. Unlike the Dogtown Z-Boys, however, he didn't see the life going anywhere in particular. He decided he would become a chef. He walked into Chinois, because among other reasons it was near the ocean, and asked Kazuto, "Should I go to cooking school, or should I go to France?" Kazuto answered, "France."

One of the mysteries of hanging out with Citrin today is figuring how he ascended from surfer to gourmand. Both selves seem present at once in him. He walks and talks like an OG surfer but can suddenly scare you with a recitation on Moroccan tree-bark oils or his own method for curing pork fatback. I once asked Citrin about his transition, and he exploded in laughter: "It doesn't make any sense, does it?"

Citrin cooked for three years in French kitchens, then returned and asked Kazuto for a job. In 1993 he and a childhood surfing buddy, Raphael Lunetta, opened their first restaurant together, Jackson's. Citrin was just twenty-five. Three years later the partners opened JiRaffe in Santa Monica, and on Super Bowl Sunday in 1999 Citrin left the partnership to create Mélisse, which is named after the French word for lemon balm.

Citrin's business partner is his wife, Diane, whom he met at Patina when he was cooking and she was the pastry chef. He remembers the first dinner of their honeymoon: hamburgers.

Diane helped design Café Mélisse, which is meant to suggest a French brasserie and is airy and open with lots of banquettes and brass railing and has windows that look out on the Valencia Town Center. The room is larger than Mélisse, but Citrin is thinking of a smaller restaurant with the food. A pancetta-wrapped John Dory in shellfish broth at Mélisse shows up in the café as pancetta-wrapped trout on spinach. The average ticket price per person in Mélisse is $105; Citrin is aiming for $35 at the café. He is trying to fit the restaurant in between a T.G.I. Friday's that is across the way, the Olive Garden down the street, and an idea of perfection he carries in his head. So far he has not been completely successful. Citrin invested nearly $1 million in Café Mélisse. If diners fail to appear, he knows he can hold out just three months in Valencia before considering closing the venture. On weekends, while he would like to see 400 customers a night, Café Mélisse has not yet topped 280. Every Saturday night in the kitchen at Mélisse, Citrin gets on the phone around 9:30 and calls Mario Perez, Café Mélisse's executive chef, for the night's numbers. It is now a ritual. Two-sixty, Perez tells him, 275. Weeknights are worse yet. On a Tuesday, one week after opening, only four tables were seated at eight o'clock. Two were filled with employees and their families.

At the farmers' market Citrin finds some lemon balm, rubs it between his hands like a stogie, then breathes into his palms. "It's more about the smell than the flavor," he says. Like most chefs, Citrin has a hard time describing his cooking style, but he does call it "going deep into the food." He means he focuses on primary ingredients over spices, a cooking style that dates back to France in the mid '80s. At the moment Citrin is highly regarded, but like the Pacific swells he surfed off Venice as a child, he is riding a wave that will eventually crash. Café Mélisse was created in part as a kind of financial lifesaver for that day, because when Citrin's wave does break, he knows he will be stranded in his moment and soon become obsolete as a chef. There are already younger chefs on the wave behind him.

Citrin stops in front of a raw food stand where a half-dozen tattooed and pierced men and women in their early twenties are busily chopping and piecing together uncooked produce, selling it to a line of customers that stretches down the block. He circles the stand, peers inside at the frantic activity, gauges the wait time, then shakes his head. "These guys are here every week doing all this business," he finally says. "I just don't get it."

Frank Ferry, the mayor of Santa Clarita, is fond of a jambalaya found on a local menu, but his favorite food is everything. "You just have to look at me to know that," says Ferry, a mountain of a man. Like most of his constituents, Ferry is from somewhere else—in his case the San Fernando Valley, which he left ten years ago to start a family and teach high school. At that time the Santa Clarita Valley was well on its way to what it has become today, a once-empty space now filled with endless tracts of coral-stucco housing and identical shopping centers that have, in turn, inspired their own particular kind of emptiness. In 1987 the disparate communities of the valley—Valencia, Newhall, Canyon Country, Saugus—changed their status from unincorporated county to the City of Santa Clarita, which suddenly opened the door for a local teacher who was unhappy enough about the pace of development to run for the city council.

"You're in a community that has grown 40 percent in the last ten years," Ferry told me one afternoon in his office, which sits across the street from the Newhall Land offices and is staffed by a former government student of Ferry's. Valencia, which is still being constructed by Newhall Land based on a master plan now three decades old, makes up a quarter of Santa Clarita and is filled with parks, wandering paseos, public swimming pools, and preserved wildlands. "I was part of that influx that came from somewhere else. Yet when I looked at the city council, the demographics there didn't represent my family. There were people in city government who had lived here for thirty years before I came. Some were into

slowing growth. Other people wanted to spend more money preserving open space and on historical preservation. Who was
fighting for my interests? I'm saying you can't build parks fast
enough, teen centers, skate parks, more roads. The council was
completely out of touch."

That morning I had sat down to breakfast with John Boston, a
local writer who lived in the valley thirty years before Ferry
arrived, and who lately has found himself feeling out of touch. We
met in Newhall on the valley's east side, inside the Way Station
Coffee Shop, which looks much like it must have a half century
ago and is today lorded over by a portrait of its patron saint—John
Wayne in a peacoat drinking a cup of coffee—above the pastry
rack. Boston remembers when the valley switched from operator-
assisted dialing in 1960. He remembers hardly a stop sign in the
valley, much less a stoplight, and all the restaurants he ate in, like
the Backwoods Inn and the Snak Shack, and the day James Dean
finished a piece of apple pie down the street at Tips and then drove
off and killed himself in a wreck. The roads were smaller then, but
in 1967 the Golden State Freeway was put through, and Newhall
Land—which owned a significant amount of the valley and
raised row crops and cattle there—found its property taxes
reassessed upward. Suddenly it was financially infeasible to raise
onions and carrots. Newhall Land decided to raise houses.

"That's when we began the change from rural community to
one of urban development," Boston told me. "In the '60s, the '70s,
and the '80s you had a lot of old-time families selling out hog farms
and dairies, watching their land turned into enclaves of million-
dollar houses set five feet apart from each other. But I'd say up to a
few years ago we still had a balance between the western ranching
areas and growing suburbia. Today, however, we have a Stepford
Wives valley, a smothering mediocrity where the land has been
turned into Disneyland and you get the twinkly lights and an infan-
tile fantasy of what lifestyle is. The city even had a slogan, 'One
Valley, One Vision.' Jiminy Christmas! How Orwellian is that?"

The irony of places like Santa Clarita is that they attract families who have John Boston's valley in their heads—full of open space, small-town values, and an individualism lacking in cities—and then are handed Frank Ferry's valley, one of rampant growth, erased wildlands, and commercial landscapes that appear faxed out from the home office in Dallas. In Santa Clarita, as in the rest of America, it's the once-rural areas of new sprawl that are now dominated by corporations and chains, not the urban areas. This has everything to do with housing construction trends. Where houses were once built one lot at a time, today they are built in groups of 400 or 1,600 or 2,400. Housing tracts, in turn, attract commercial-site developers, who must then woo chain restaurants like Chili's and the Outback to prove their financial solvency before breaking ground. Developers are not interested in a Café Mélisse. It is a national growth pattern that is slowly shifting the American palate from one of regionalism to one of test-kitchen universalism, creating a country of Valencias where instead of finding a café with a winning apple pie, locals know of a quiet side street that has a great little Red Lobster tucked away on it.

This is where Citrin has found himself: the battle for America. At Café Mélisse he told me, "I don't know if they have a corporate palate out here, something they've chosen, or if it's just one that's been imposed on them." Citrin's dilemma is the dilemma of mass production over the last half century. The questions he's asking himself are the same questions that have been asked about movies, music, Broadway, and novels. Why do people choose a deep-fried onion over a pancetta-wrapped trout?

When Citrin cooks at Mélisse, concentric circles of potential surround his station. In the first circle are his cooks, working toward perfection. "They can grow from what they see," he says. "They must always decide, Do I want to be this way, or better?" On a Saturday night at Mélisse, Citrin stands at the kitchen's pass, its apex of activity, calling out orders. His face is the color of a strawberry, and his hair stands straight up. Citrin practices a call-and-response method he learned in French kitchens. There is only one response: "Yes chef."

"Give me two *hamachi* and three pig."

"Yes chef."

"Fire tables 6, 23, 1."

"Yes chef."

"I need two veal, two lobsters, sole, go on 90, four John Dory, fire 53, 61, 70, 13."

"Yes chef, yes chef, yes chef."

In the next circle stand Citrin's waitstaff, ever discovering new ways to polish the silver or expertly crack a soft-boiled egg over lobster at the table. If they slip from perfection, Citrin is there. His temperament in the kitchen is famous. When angry, Citrin punctuates his demands with select words whose pitch resonates in your sternum if you're standing too close: "Why are you waiting there with the ASPARAGUS!" "I need a soft-shell CRAB right now!"

In the final circle sit Mélisse's diners, who, like pilgrims in a medieval church, are presented nightly a world vision that wraps their progress around a perfectly seared foie gras supported by a bed of sautéed cherries. Now Citrin has extended a fourth circle, enclosing Valencia. He does not view himself as a missionary, but Citrin may still find himself rejected by the valley's lost tribes.

At 9:30 Citrin turns away from a côte de boeuf the size of a stuffed Fendi purse and calls Café Mélisse on a phone that hangs above the pass. So far, Café Mélisse has still not topped 280 guests on a Saturday night, far off from the 400 Citrin needs to survive. After a few minutes on the phone with Perez, Citrin turns back to the beef dish.

They did 265, he says quietly, arranging the plate. "That's it. People are coming in later, which is better, but I need 400."

The côte de boeuf goes out to the floor. There are two salmons, a veal, and a mushroom soup making their way to the pass for Citrin's final touch.

"God—I don't know if they're going to come in," he says.

# Guess Who's Coming to Dinner

by Gabrielle Hamilton

from *Food & Wine*

Cooking skills and writing skills come hand-in-hand with Hamilton, the presiding chef and owner of New York City's Prune. Who better, then, to explain the starry-eyed impulse that lures chef after chef into opening such a risky business as a restaurant?

When I opened my restaurant, Prune, I had a few ideas about what *neighborhood* meant.

The space I found was actually in my neighborhood in Manhattan's East Village, on the block where I have lived for the past twenty years. I felt I knew my territory. I wanted an unassuming way to slip into the shallow end of the pool of New York City restaurants and not drown, since I knew that 70 percent of restaurants in New York City go under or change hands in the first five years. I thought, if I open a small, modestly ambitious neighborhood restaurant, I'll have less stuff to auction off when we fold.

I hoped that opening a neighborhood joint would mean that people would have lower expectations of it. Generally, when people think of a neighborhood restaurant, they relax their standards. They don't have Saturday-night-box-seats-at-Dustin-Hoffman-as-Willy-Loman-in-*Death-of-a-Salesman* expectations. They're thinking more like they're watching their daughter's Off Off Broadway debut in some young playwright's new oeuvre. I didn't want William Grimes or any other restaurant critic to come anywhere near me and mistake my ambitions. I knew they would be much happier up the street where the chef has turned on the marquee lights and is just dying to recite his latest poem. I also wanted to reclaim my neighborhood. There was a lot of limousine action on my block and twelve dollars cosmopolitans being spilled onto zinc-topped bars. I saw women in Chanel suits and pearl earrings step out of cabs looking for the new slick spot serving ostrich carpaccio with sesame-lime emulsion. I'm not making this up. I wanted to open a restaurant that would save me from everything I didn't want to do anymore. Everything I didn't want to read on a menu ever again. Everything I didn't ever want to cook again. Everything I didn't want to have happen to my part of town. I had spent too many years training under chefs making veal demiglace and torchons of foie gras and countless roulades of anything the chef could think of to pound out, stuff with julienned red pepper and roll up in Saran Wrap—and I just couldn't do it anymore.

But most importantly, I wanted to cook for my neighbors. My physical neighbors. I had spent years as a private chef and caterer for uptowners who argue over the comparative merits of their Ecuadorian and Bahamian nannies, who don't know where to put the recycling in their building, who have kitchens equipped with thousands of dollars' worth of copper pots that they have never even used to boil water.

I wanted to cook for the woman upstairs in my building who sells pot, and the half-naked performers around the corner at P.S. 122 who use Barbie dolls and ripe fruit in their "work," and all the gay kids from ACT UP. I thought we all wanted to eat monkfish liver with warm buttered toast and sea salt. I thought we would all hang out at Prune with our tattoos and scare off the pearl-earring ladies from uptown. Together, I dreamed naively, my hardworking, artsy neighbors and I—the aging, slightly tired and softening counterculture—would abolish fennel-crusted tuna with orange-ginger vinaigrette and red pepper brunoise and break bread over a plate of sweetbreads and a wooden bowl of salad and a juice tumbler of decent Côtes-du-Rhône. We would plan the revolution over a succulent roast capon, I thought. Why not?

So yes, a neighborhood restaurant it would be. I thought of everything I wanted: the pastrami duck breast with small rye omelet, the butter-and-sugar sandwiches, the tarnished silverware and discontinued-pattern wedding china, the Velvet Underground CD, the naked-girl glasses. I wanted to serve the canned sardines I ate as a starving student, the marrow bones my mother made us eat as kids that I grew to crave as an adult. We would have brown butcher paper on the tables, not linen tablecloths. Jelly jars for wineglasses. We would put a rubber band around the middle of the wine bottle so if you only wanted half, you could just pay for what you drank, down to the line. There would be nothing stacked tall on the plate, no crab cocktail served in a martini glass with its claw hanging over the rim. We would never serve anything but a martini in a martini glass. Preferably gin. There would be no foam and no foie gras, nothing to seek the attention of the denizens of other ZIP codes.

But I would not be sloppy, either. I didn't want to be amateur, or merely adequate. Didn't have any interest in making "prole-tariat" food, or kitschy, ironic Mama's meat loaf with ketchup and Lipton onion soup mix. This would not be the neighborhood place that paints rainbow murals on its walls and cranks out grated-raw-carrot salads. I have a lot of experience, and I wasn't going to throw all that out just to open a neighborhood restaurant. I chilled the wine, unlocked the doors and waited for my neighbors to walk in. Imagine my astonishment, then, in the first few weeks, to see a chauffeured black Lincoln Town Car pull up outside our door, promptly at 6 P.M. Gingerly, two 80-year-old gentlemen emerged—rouged and bow-tied, arm in arm—and teetered toward a table. They shared a cocktail (perfect Manhattans without ice) then launched into a plate of marrow bones, moved on to the sweetbreads with bacon, and blotted the grease from the corners of their mouths, and pushed off to the theater by 7:30 as they have done as a couple for over forty years. They have been an excitement and a fascination to me and my staff since we opened, and I love them inordinately. But they are not my neighbors.

Then we got reviewed. Cabs pulled up, and still clutching the review, these folks ordered only the dishes mentioned in the piece. They asked us to turn down the music. To get rid of our jelly jars and give them "real" wineglasses. With the third or fourth review, they got even more comfortable: They asked me to substitute the fish for the meat and the sauce for the vinaigrette and to hard-cook the egg and omit the garlic.

I was thrown. I thought that if you wanted world beat at a discreet level to accompany your tuna tartare and stale raisin-fennel semolina rolls, you would just go directly to the restaurant row on Park Avenue South. I thought that you would come to Prune precisely for the Johnny Cash on the stereo and the pasta kerchief with the warm oozy egg yolk in the center.

We started to scramble. Worried about their tips, the floor staff started filleting the fish tableside for customers who couldn't stand the sight of the head and bones. They "accidentally" broke all the jelly jars and replaced them with stemware. They begged me to substitute fruit for ice cream for the lactose-intolerant. I did it. I have come to understand the waiters' point of view. And to rely on it.

This funky bunch of people that work here—who leave their witch hazel pads and sparkle lip gloss and contact lens solution in the bathroom basket—cultivate a different kind of customer than I might. And I'm glad they do and are less strident than I am. I'm constantly having to snipe at them to do their chores, but they soften me and breathe a little expansiveness into my erstwhile way-too-principled and intellectualized restaurant. My actual neighbors walk by on their way to the falafel place around the corner. They spend their hard-earned money on things more utile than a good meal.

I hold the line now at things that really matter to me: no

well-done meat, no lite jazz, no diet soda. I decided that if we capitulated too much to the will of all the customers, we would lose what made us attractive in the first place, which, I believe, was our point of view. That we became attractive to a wholly different clientele than I had originally imagined is unimportant.

If I never imagined these customers as part of my neighborhood restaurant, I certainly never anticipated that they would become friends. Cherished friends. The Italian doctor who lives on the Upper East Side found us in the first few weeks after we opened. He was walking by and saw women in the kitchen. Missing his mother, he thought the food must be good and started coming in. On his second or third visit, he introduced himself and brought as a gift a loaf of olive bread he'd made at home. Hard as a rock. Tasteless. Heavy as a dinner plate and with as much life. A few weeks later—how could I not come to love this man?—he made a dry, metallic and insipid pork roast cooked in milk. I packed him off with a small container of braised rabbit's legs, redolent of stock and wine and mustard and thyme—it had started to snow—and gave him one of our tarnished silver soupspoons so he could eat it at the hospital. A doctor. An Upper East Sider. Everything my revolution would have taken out. Somebody's neighbor. But not mine.

What does it mean, then, to be a neighborhood restaurant, if you aren't feeding your neighbors? What do we call David and Gary, who live in Los Angeles and fly to New York just to eat here? And Mike in Texas, who plans his business trips to New York around his reservations at Prune? What about the lovely couple from Long Island who had never had a Meyer lemon before and whom I sent off at the end of their meal with a small sack of the perfumey things? These are my real neighbors.

The unemployed screenwriter who lives behind the restaurant, who sits around in his underwear all day—every clatter of our silverware and hiss of meat hitting a sauté pan a reminder of his lack of talent—is just not, in spite of his geographic proximity, my kind of guy. The pinched and brittle upstairs neighbor hurries disapprovingly past the luscious sight of a young couple in love at the window table, so caught up in the lustful project of mopping up anchovy butter with bread that their napkins have fallen unnoticed from their laps onto the floor. She must get home to spend the long evening contemplating her wheat allergy. If these are my neighbors, I'm not attached to ZIP codes anymore.

When I worked as a private chef and caterer, before opening Prune, I entered homes through the service elevator, the garage or the back door. No one that I'd fed had ever really wanted to talk to me, except for wanting to know where the ice was kept or how the vinaigrette was made. But now, here at the restaurant, these same people want to talk to me. To know me. Suddenly these people are looking me straight in the eye, talking to me, "the help," about books and wars and soup.

I can't overstate how much I have come to love these conversations. There is something unguarded and disarmed about a well-fed, well-taken-care-of person. An excellent sidecar and a perfect medium-rare rib eye and the ministrations of Dan, our floor manager, put people into a really lovely and genuine mind-set. They shed all of their importance and uptown bravado and just act normal. Approaching and approachable.

They tell me that the food at Prune reminds them of food they associate with their parents. "My dad and I ate canned sardines every Sunday doing the crossword puzzle." "My Jewish family ordered take-out Chinese every Sunday night, and I always ate the shrimp toasts." "We had butter-and-sugar sandwiches as an after-school snack every day in Italy when I was a boy." I hear these things all the time, and they lead to surprisingly open conversations. I, too, let my guard down. Lose the chip on my shoulder. Trade in the filterless cigarettes and *Communist Manifesto* of my twenties for something that is a little more nuanced and humane.

By the time people sit down to eat here now, it has become the little neighborhood restaurant in my vision, with our neighbors having dinner. They just don't live around here.

# Say Cheez

by Robb Walsh

from *Houston Press*

Walsh—who also this year published the authoritative *Legends of Texas Barbecue*—deftly navigates the Houston eating scene, armed with high standards but no haute pretensions. He has an uncanny gift for conveying the distinct essence of every place he reviews.

The Villanova, Temple and Penn State pennants on the wall give me a good feeling about Jake's Philly Steaks. Even more reassuring is the souvenir menu from Pat's King of Steaks, where the steak sandwich was invented. But when I reach the counter and spot a stainless-steel warming pot with a Cheez Whiz logo, I know I've come to the right place. I order a large Philly cheese steak.

The dining room is packed, so I stand by the counter surveying the scene and waiting for my order. I feel deep sympathy for the large man trying to remove a grease stain the size of a fried egg from his blue oxford dress shirt. He has a wadded paper napkin in his left hand and the bad-puppy cheese steak still cradled affectionately in his right.

A white-haired guy enters from the kitchen and stands behind the counter looking official. I ask him if he's Jake.

Turns out Jake was the previous owner. The current owner,

Robert Ginn, took over in 1993. The guy behind the counter is Robert's dad.

"So you like Pat's or Geno's?" I ask him, cutting to the chase. The two cheese steak joints are right across the street from each other in the City of Brotherly Love, and among Philadelphians each has ardent supporters. Robert Ginn and his dad took a trip to Philly and sampled both.

"Tell you the truth, I didn't see much difference," he says, with a Texas accent.

The Philly cheese steaks at Jake's will get even closer to the original next month, I'm told, when they start using rolls from Amoroso Bakery, the Philadelphia bread maker that sells the city's favorite hoagie roll. Amoroso ships partially baked and frozen rolls to sandwich shops across the country that are concerned with authenticity.

My cheese steak is delivered on a cafeteria tray. But something's missing.

"Hey, where's the Cheez Whiz?" I ask.

"I'll get you some," says Robert's dad, taking my tray over to the stainless-steel warmer. Careful reinspection of the menu above the counter reveals that Cheez Whiz is fifty cents extra.

Jake's No. 1, a regular Philly cheese steak, features lots of shaved rib-eye steak grilled with onions and then loaded onto a toasted baguette split lengthwise with provolone on each side. Cheez Whiz is indelicately drizzled all over the meat, but only if you request it. The Cheez Whiz has been relegated to optional status because so many diners find the stuff disgusting. But one glorious bite of crunchy bread, juice-squirting meat, slippery sweet onions and silky processed cheese goop reaffirms my faith in America. The viscous yellow liquid is the glue that holds the steak, onions and toasted bread together. Without it, a Philly cheese steak would be just another steak sandwich.

I look forward to sampling the Amoroso rolls as soon as they start coming off Jake's assembly line. I hope the thaw-and-bake variety is sufficiently crusty—there's nothing worse than a soggy cheese steak. That's why you shouldn't bother getting cheese steaks to go. I've developed an elaborate method for reheating these sandwiches that maintains some of the crunch (place a refrigerated cheese steak in a toaster oven on bake at 350 degrees for about ten minutes), but the best plan is to just sit down and eat your cheese steak on the spot.

I discovered Jake's Philly Steaks at bestcheesesteaks.com, a Web site where former Philadelphians swap info about sandwiches around the country. The Houston correspondent, Joe Ciliberto, had spent the first forty-one years of his life in Philly before being transferred to Space City. "For the first year I was going through serious cheese steak withdrawal," he wrote. "But about six months ago I found Jake's Philly Steaks on Chimney Rock between Richmond and Westheimer. That's about a forty-five-minute drive from my house, but I make the trip several times a month." I admire that kind of dedication.

Jake's makes a hell of a cheese steak, but it isn't far from my house. So just to make sure I don't favor it out of laziness, I also stopped by Texadelphia (2420 Rice Boulevard), a Texas-Philadelphia fusion restaurant where the house special is a cheese steak with picante sauce. Continuing the Texas theme, tortilla chips and salsa come with every sandwich. The meat here is a flavorful shaved Black Angus sirloin, served with grilled onions and your choice of several sauces, including ranch dressing. But the cheese is mozzarella, a dramatic departure from cheese steak orthodoxy. There are lots of extras, including mushrooms, jalapeños, and lettuce and tomatoes. They don't have Cheez Whiz—even as an option.

I also tried Joey's Philly Cheese Steaks (5177 FM 1960), where the No. 1 Philly cheese steak comes with onions, green peppers and provolone. There was a lot of meat on the sandwich, and I really liked the addition of grilled peppers. But Joey's didn't have any Cheez Whiz either.

Gooey, ripe French Livarot on walnut bread, smelly Swiss raclette melted over potatoes and pickles on a heated pewter plate, a fondue of fromage d'alpage, a Gruyère made in Alpine mountain meadows—these are a few of my favorite cheeses. But there are the times when only Cheese Whiz will do.

What is Cheez Whiz, exactly? Kraft called it a "pasteurized process cheese sauce" when the company introduced it in 1953 as a shortcut for busy homemakers. In an article in *Chemical and Engineering News* ("What's That Stuff?" February 7, 2000), a Cheez Whiz lover named Steve Ritter explores Title 21, Part 133 of the U.S. Code of Federal Regulations, a.k.a. the cheese rules.

Pasteurized process cheese, reports Ritter, can come molded in a loaf or a plastic-coated single. But Cheez Whiz uses a slightly different formula so that the product remains in a liquid state to be sold in a jar. But whatever its form, process cheese is essentially a combination of cheeses (like cheddar and colby) with extra milkfat added. It's heated, along with an emulsifier, then watered down—so it melts more easily. Of course, since it's watered down, salt, artificial colors and flavorings have to be added.

I have agonized over such pasteurized processed American cheeses in this space before; they are the secret to old-fashioned Tex-Mex cheese enchiladas. (See "There's Something About Larry's," May 23, 2002.) But just as enchiladas have been "improved" over the years with better cheeses, so has the Philly cheese steak been yuppified by earnest culinary reformers. I understand the impulse. My brother Dave, a cheese steak lover for many years, insists provolone is a better idea. He speaks for the majority when he says, "Cheez Whiz is disgusting. Nobody in their right mind eats that stuff."

But I referred my brother to www.patskingofsteaks.com, the Web site of the revered Pat's King of Steaks. The site explains how Pat Olivieri, bored of eating wieners every day, invented the prototype of the steak sandwich at his hot dog stand in South Philadelphia in 1930. It also gives the restaurant's Philly cheese steak recipe. While the substitution of provolone is allowed, Pat's King of Steaks recommends Cheez Whiz.

Maybe you're deck enough to insist on a Philly cheese steak made with authentic Cheez Whiz, and maybe you aren't. But either way you've got to applaud Jake's Philly Steaks for preserving the sandwich's proud, processed cheese traditions.

# An Ode to Sloppy Joe, a Delicious Mess

by Andrea Strong

from the *New York Times*

> Childhood taste memories can be curiously persistent, as Strong attests in this recipe article about an old school lunchroom standard. A tony chef may put a gourmet spin on it, but you cannot overwrite the complicated associations.

Some foods are memory triggers, meals that send you back to long-forgotten moments in your life. The sloppy Joe sandwich is one such time machine. Finding it on the menu at Drew Nieporent's sunny version of the neighborhood deli, TriBakery, took me back to the lunchroom of my elementary school in Queens.

It was a puberty-driven war zone, where hair-netted lunch ladies ladled heavy spoonfuls of chopped meat and tomato sauce onto puffy, perfectly round hamburger buns, the sort of rolls that were often turned into ammunition when pulled apart, rolled into tiny pellets and used in battles waged against the boys seated across the lunchroom.

The sandwich was just this side of awful. The entire messy mass, oozing a greasy, beef-scented tomato sauce, left my fingers and lips stained deep orange for hours. Nonetheless, some twenty years later, standing in line at TriBakery, surrounded by tall men in suits, I had to have one, if only to feel twelve again.

Surely, those elementary school cooks in Queens tried hard, but they have nothing on TriBakery's consulting chef, Chris Gesualdi, formerly of Montrachet. His sloppy Joe sandwich ($6.75), a tribute to the one his mother, Rose, used to make for him as a child, is perfect: a sweet and spicy hill of thick sautéed ground beef spilling out of a toasted homemade kaiser roll. Topped with melted Cheddar, it is a terrific antidote to adulthood.

Mr. Gesualdi is not the only chef experimenting with this stain-inducing sandwich. Tim Kelley, the new chef at Zoë, the American bistro in SoHo, makes Asian sloppy Joes in honor of his own somewhat traumatic experience with school lunch.

"I grew up on a farm in Oregon, and my mom used to make me these crazy vegetarian lunches," he said. "When you are a fourteen-year-old kid and you show up with these hippie sandwiches, well, I used to get hit. I mean there were sprouts everywhere."

Mr. Kelley stashed the hippie sandwiches in his locker and began eating in the lunchroom, where sloppy Joes became his favorite meal. "It was the total opposite of my mom's cooking," he said. "It's a very fond memory for me."

For his Asian-tinged sloppy Joe ($14.50), Mr. Kelley simmers pulled pork in a fiery tomato-based sauce, brightened with ginger, garlic and Vietnamese chili paste, then piles the saucy meat on a buttery house-made scallion bun and tops it off with a handful of fresh mint and cilantro leaves, a soothing balm to the pork's chili-driven heat.

While Mr. Kelley's Joe is far from traditional, it is delicious. It is the sort of sandwich that makes you want to be twelve again, if only to lick your fingers boldly at the table and adamantly refuse to share.

A Cuban version of the sloppy Joe is on the menu at Isla, a sexy Havana-inspired restaurant in the West Village. It is essentially a ropa vieja sandwich, a meaty tangle of marinated pulled skirt steak stewed in an aromatic tomato sauce with garlic, cumin, tomatoes, peppers and chilies, loaded into the center of a pillowy Cuban steam-oven bun ($9).

The owner, Diane Ghioto, says it is a tribute to a sloppy Joe sandwich that originated in Havana.

Cuba? The sloppy Joe smacks of American inventiveness: it's a classic example of the Depression-era trick of stretching hamburger meat. But Ms. Ghioto insisted that the sandwich originated in Havana.

"Sloppy Joe's was a bar in Havana in the 30's owned by a guy named José García," she said. "The bar got its name because his place was always a mess and the ropa vieja sandwich served there came to be known as a sloppy Joe. As far as I can tell, the American version is a bastardization of that sandwich."

Andrew Smith, editor in chief of the *Oxford Encyclopedia of Food and Drink*, said that he had heard a dozen different stories about the first sloppy Joe sandwich. "As far as I know, there is no definitive answer to the question of the origin of the sandwich," he said.

He did not completely discredit the Havana connection, pointing to the fact that the first print use of the term "sloppy Joe" was probably in reference to a bar called Sloppy Joe's in Key West, Florida.

One of its regulars was Ernest Hemingway, who also spent a good deal of time in Cuba. Indeed, according to the bar's site, Hemingway had suggested the name in tribute to Mr. García's Rio Havana club, which sold liquor and iced seafood. Because the floor was always wet with melted ice, his patrons "taunted this Spanish Joe with running a sloppy place . . . and the name stuck."

Jean Anderson, author of *The American Century Cookbook* (Clarkson Potter, 1997), who was unfamiliar with the Havana theory, said that her research pointed to a cafe in Sioux City, Iowa, where a cook named Joe made loose meat sandwiches—a Midwestern term for seasoned ground meat cooked loosely in a skillet—that eventually came to be known as sloppy Joes.

Support for Ms. Ghioto's Cuban theory came from Leonard Zwilling, general editor of the *Dictionary of American Regional English*. He confirmed that a sandwich was indeed served at the Sloppy Joe's bar in Havana and that a version of it wound up on the menu at the Town Hall Deli in South Orange, New Jersey, in 1936, when it was (and still is) not a messy chopped meat sandwich but a triple-decker deli sandwich. Jack Burdorf, an owner of the Town Hall Deli, knew the sandwich's history. His father had worked at the deli and then bought it with a partner.

"Around 1934 or '35," Mr. Burdorf said, "the Mayor of Maplewood, Robert Sweeney, used to vacation in Havana and hang out at an old saloon called Sloppy Joe's. When Sweeney returned to New Jersey, he described the sandwich he used to eat there to my dad, and asked him to recreate it."

The result, Mr. Burdorf said, was a sandwich that to this day is called the original sloppy Joe: layers of ham, tongue and Swiss cheese topped with coleslaw and Russian dressing, served on long, thin slices of soft buttered rye bread and sliced into four squares ($16.45).

If the original sloppy Joe was a giant club sandwich, what of the messy manwich of a meal so many Americans grew up eating?

The truth behind the humble beginning of the sloppy Joe may never be known, whether it was a triple-decker created from the memory of a mayor who visited Havana or a loose meat sandwich born in a cafe in Sioux City, Iowa.

What really matters is the place your mind goes when you pick one up, take that first bite and feel the slow trickle of greasy sauce down your chin. Because in the end, memories are more potent than any definitive version of history. One woman's Havana is another woman's Queens.

## Sloppy Joes
(Adapted from TriBakery)

*Yield: 12 servings.*

*Time: 1 hour 20 minutes*

2 tablespoons olive oil
1 cup finely diced onion

1 teaspoon minced garlic
2 pounds lean ground beef
1 cup tomato paste
2¾ cups tomato purée
½ teaspoon chili powder
½ teaspoon Tabasco sauce
1 teaspoon puréed canned chipotle in adobo
1 bay leaf
12 kaiser rolls or hamburger buns
12 slices Cheddar cheese

1. In a large skillet over medium heat, warm oil, and sauté onions until translucent, 5 to 6 minutes. Add garlic, and sauté for 30 seconds. Add ground beef, and sauté until well browned, 15 to 20 minutes.

2. Add tomato paste, tomato purée, chili powder, Tabasco, chipotle and bay leaf. Stir until blended. Raise heat to bring to a boil, then reduce heat to low. Simmer mixture, stirring occasionally, until thick enough to spread on a sandwich, about 45 minutes.

3. To serve, heat a broiler. Slice the rolls open and place them under the broiler until lightly toasted, turning as necessary. Ladle about ½ cup onto the bottom of each roll, and top with Cheddar cheese to taste. Return bottom halves to the broiler until cheese just melts. Top with the remaining halves, and serve immediately.

# Bread Winner

by Susan Choi
from *Food & Wine*

> Even the humble sandwich can be elevated
> to a work of art by the right hands. Choi's
> profile of an unsung artist makes us rethink
> how much we take our most casual food
> for granted—until it's not there.

When I was growing up in Northern Indiana, my father and I would buy a loaf of rye bread, grab the mustard jar out of the fridge and cross the state line to the Michigan town of Three Oaks. In a shop there, beneath the wicked gleam cast by a portrait of JR from *Dallas* (Larry Hagman was a mail-order customer), a man named Drier made magnificent sausages. We'd slice one of them with a pocket knife onto the mustarded rye and eat reverently.

That was a rare island in an otherwise battering sea of not-good, or plain bad, sandwiches. I happened across another one this past fall: A new sandwich guy at one of my neighborhood delis in Brooklyn sometimes made suggestions when I couldn't decide what I wanted. The more often I took his suggestions, the better the sandwiches got. When I finally noticed, I think *he* noticed: He unleashed an astonishing sandwich, of small veal meatballs, sautéed mushrooms and gravy on toasted ciabatta, as if he'd been waiting for my full attention.

It may sound grandiose, but when you eat a sandwich almost

every day, as your sole break from work, that sandwich is important. In the days that followed that meatball sandwich, I ate only great sandwiches. Some were inventions, like the sandwich of grilled chicken sausage with a tangy carrot slaw. Others were classics, like roast beef, but impeccably done, with deft touches of coarse salt and horseradish. Most of the time, the guy made what customers asked for—although you'd catch him tinkering, covertly adding butter or salt or substituting a real farmstead cheese for slices from the brick of Boar's Head. But it was when you let the guy "just make you something" that he shined brightest. One day, a few weeks into what I had privately dubbed the Golden Age of the Sandwich, the guy said, "I'm so glad you came in! I want to make you my favorite sandwich." It was a fresh execution of a classic: home-baked ham, Pavé d'Affinois cheese, slivered red onion, tomato, intimations of mustard and salt on buttered ciabatta. And it was fantastic, of course—but it would mark his last day on the job.

As they used to say at the end of old Westerns, "Who was that sandwich guy?" I needed to know who he was, if only to tell him how much I'd enjoyed that last sandwich. I finally went to the deli and asked for the guy's name and number. He turned out to be Dan Segall, age twenty-seven, originally from Sharon, Massachusetts. An aspiring playwright and director, he had more than one day job. In baseball season, he shot T-shirts out of an air cannon into the stands at Mets home games. "Who were you?" he asked on the phone when I called him. I'd barely started to explain when he said, with nostalgia, "The meat girl. You liked to eat meat."

Going to meet him, I panicked: What if Dan Segall was some kind of sandwich idiot savant? A misplaced concern, it turned out. "My philosophy of the sandwich?" he mused as we sat at a cafe in Brooklyn. "More like my manifesto. My rules of engagement." A man of many plans, Segall meant to present his manifesto in a convenient trifold format to his customers, but he never had time— he was too busy putting principles into action. To explain, he quoted no less a luminary than chef Thomas Keller of Napa Valley's French Laundry on the law of diminishing returns: "The

initial bite is fabulous. The second bite is great. But by the third
bite . . . the diner loses interest." Keller serves many small courses
to patrons at his restaurant, but what to do within the confines of
a sandwich? Every bite of a sandwich is the same, so each bite must
*contain* differences—vivid contrasts, like sweet mozzarella and salty
prosciutto. Segall's ideal sandwich, he explained, possesses the unity
and complexity of any great dish.

Of course ingredients have to be excellent. They must also be,
if not easily bitable, cut down to size: "You don't want to fight with
your sandwich," Segall said. Bread shouldn't be "inappropriate,"
too sharp-edged or chewy or thick. Adjacency should be considered: Raw onion should be next to cheese. Layering ought to
be logical. For example, Segall never puts lettuce on top, because
the bread slides right off. And butter is his first fundamental,
because it's not just delicious but also keeps bread from getting
soggy. "It's like a little raincoat for your sandwich," he marveled.
"Why do so many people avoid it?"

But these are like the rules of fine carpentry, invisible if practiced correctly. Eventually the rules give way to what Segall lov-
ingly called the "shared pursuit" of sandwiches. I learned that I'd
been just one of his sandwich compatriots. There was the customer who longed for the world's spiciest sandwich, driving Segall
to perfect his own hot-pepper oil. He had customers whose
requests he refused, like the man who wanted prosciutto with
Cheddar (he talked him into a happier pairing). What we all had
in common was the sense of partnership, a rule proved by exceptions, like the man who ate turkey on rye with ketchup. "I gave it
to him without comment," Segall admitted. "With that, there was
no arguable point."

It's hard enough to find someone who understands that making
sandwiches requires artistry. It's even harder to find someone
devoted to the *craft* of the thing. Even the completing gesture, of
wrapping the sandwich in paper, was so satisfying to Segall that he
went through a period of being disturbed by the imbalance of

handing over something he had made and receiving mere cash in return. "I'd think, make me a card or something. Give me your T-shirt!" This phase passed, luckily, but the desire to "put everything in *right*" remained. And this was why he left the deli, and also set the theater aside, to attend cooking school. He was only sorry he'd never realized his plan to write one-page playlets about sandwiches to slip into customers' bags.

After we parted, it occurred to me that among the myriad ways to offer a sandwich to the world, Dan Segall's way was improvisational. The deli was not his, and the raw materials were not of his choosing. For every customer like me, who would try anything, he had many more with rigid and habitual demands. Yet this was what made his art great: his capacity to find endless possibility in a realm over which he could never have total control. It was all starting to remind me of my own kitchen, where I often find myself confronting an array of foodstuffs that seem to have been forced upon me from on high. Meeting Dan Segall reminded me that when the daily question "What shall I eat?" yields as its answer the humble sandwich, that's a chance for élan and excitement. I think it no detraction from Segall's talents when I say that since I met him, my homemade sandwiches have vastly improved.

# Salumi

by Min Liao

from *The Stranger*

Can a restaurant reviewer ever be totally objective—and, more to the point, would you trust such a critic's opinions? Liao, who covers Seattle's dining scene for an alternative weekly, fesses up to her lack of detachment, which makes the ensuing "non-review" all the more reliable.

For those of us who love meat, going to Salumi is like going to church.

Here, at Armandino Batali's busy, narrow storefront/counter/tiny restaurant in Pioneer Square (just look for the little orange flag with a pig on it), you can find house-cured Italian meats—a.k.a. "salumi," premium-quality artisanal cold cuts, if you will, all made by Batali and his talented staff—along with hot and cold sandwiches ($6.25-$8) and platters that feature cooked meats (sausages, meatballs, and, my favorite, ox tails; $8.50) as well as cured meats (various salamis, coppa, pancetta, prosciuttos, tongue, and cured lamb; with bread for $9). Very little is more satisfying than walking up to a counter and saying, *Yeah, I'll take the "Hot Meat Plate," thanks.*

There are also good cheeses and olives and red table wine, and takeout items, which include homemade sauces and gnocchi, and, of course, meat by the pound. Daily lunch specials depend on season/whim: Last week, I had a delicious lasagna with lots of cheese and porchetta ($7), which is "Salumi's tribute to the pig"— roasted pork, stuffed with sausage meat and spices. I tried a bowl of "white gazpacho" with cucumbers and roasted grapes, and loved rolling all those flavors around in my mouth. I eyed a watermelon salad with fresh mint and onion, but who orders a salad in Meat Church? And lately, for summertime, they've been offering a nice prosciutto sandwich with fig confit and Coach Farm goat cheese. A lomo sandwich (cured pork loin, beautifully pink and peppery, $8) stacked with fresh mozzarella, onions, and peppers also made me blissfully happy. And I'm still thinking about those stuffed ribs.

Okay, confession: I've been trying to write about Salumi for the longest time. Since, like, February. But each time I start to do it, I just . . . can't. I've been putting this off since forever. I'm still not convinced I can do it now. I'm terrified of sounding like a wannabe epicurean jackass, of messing up the details, of sounding like a dumb gushing kid. Of just doing it WRONG.

The problem is that I've got a clumsy, unrequited crush on the place—I go in there and suddenly I'm Molly Ringwald in *Sixteen Candles*. I can't speak. I just end up feeling awkward and in the way, gazing at the menu board and other people's food. I get shy, lose my ability to make a decision and communicate it. Batali smiles at me; I blush.

I sit at Salumi's single communal table, where everyone eats with elbows tucked in, the tabletop cluttered with bread baskets, a wine bottle or two, containers of silverware, little plates with pools of olive oil. Batali clears dishes, checks on people, chats with regulars, asks how my lunch is. My mouth goes dry, and I can barely answer him. I just grin and chew, nodding like an idiot.

Apparently, I'm not the only one. The Man Who Cures the Meat has charmed the pants off local chefs, foodies, and food writers since he first opened up shop in the late '90s, after an East Coast apprenticeship and an educational trip to Italy, where Batali learned the art and craft of making salumi from skilled, authentic Italian *norcini* (a *norcino* is an Italian pig butcher and salumi expert). The Batali-Salumi story has taken on folklore status: You can't read an article about Salumi without it inevitably turning into a loving profile of Batali and his Meat Journey—his thirty-one years working for Boeing, his post-retirement passion, the Italy trip, the success of his second career, and the success of his son Mario, a New York City restaurateur/best-selling cookbook author/Food Network personality/celebrity chef. (Those Batali boys know what to do with a piece of veal, know what I'm saying?) Even the esteemed Jeffrey Steingarten, one of my favorite snooty food writers, admiringly mentions Salumi in his column this month in *Vogue* ("Cuts Above," September 2002), with an accompanying Irving Penn photo of various salumi that's like the *Playboy* centerfold of cold cuts.

I think this is why I'm such a neurotic mess about Salumi. It's so tempting to fall into the trap of fetishizing the older Italian gentleman who tends to his little shop, an irresistibly cozy human-interest story. It's so easy to read articles like Steingarten's and start to geek out about curing techniques and pig parts and spices and regional methods and the difference between Tuscan and Calabrian soppressata.

"[Salumi] is fermented food!" Steingarten writes. "It is the cheese of meat, the wine of pork, and sourdough of flesh! It is alive!" And the trivia *is* fascinating—from organic pig to preparation to a temperature-and-humidity-controlled cellar to a curing environment that involves high acidity, nitrates, and a benign lactobacillus colony. (Relax. It's all perfectly safe because the curing environment is, according to Steingarten, "completely inhospitable to harmful bacteria," and trichinosis has been eradicated for decades.) But despite the potential graduate thesis or *Saturday Evening Post* essay that could result from being a Salumi faithful, I STILL CAN'T FIGURE OUT HOW TO EXPLAIN THE PLACE.

Looking back at notes I've taken over the year, they read like a moony diary: *"today was depressing and I snuck down to Salumi for lunch soup, tomato-based broth but clear, square hunks of zucchini, some corn, too. . . ."* Or *". . . galette, mashed-potato-pie thingy, with melted cheese and vegetables, the perfect food, windy day, cold hands. some awesome oregano salami. Brought home a tub of meatballs in marinara."* Or *"Braised pork cheeks today. leeks and other stuff . . . amazing fennel sausage* [pork, cracked fennel, garlic] *and lamb sausage* [orange and cumin], *Emily had a grilled lamb sandwich—excellent."* Show up often enough and you'll realize that the allure of the place is not about its hype or exclusive products or the owner's son or prestigious clientele; it's about the cream-colored room itself, warm and crowded and filled with good smells. It's about the Tuscan finnochiona salami ($13.50/lb), studded with fennel seeds, and the best spicy soppressata ($13.50/lb) I have ever tasted—complex, slightly smoky, and a vivid red (perhaps from smeared red peppers. . . ?). Hold up a piece of any one of Batali's salamis and you'll see a carnal kaleidoscope, with bits of rosy hues and solid or clear whites, a slice of careful handiwork.

Show up during an intense lunch rush, and get in that long line, with the sweetest guys busting their asses behind that counter, and you'll witness the beauty that is the relationship between Man and Meat Slicer. Show up after 2:30 P.M. when things slow down, and feel as if you're part of the neighborhood: I've indulged in some catty gossip at that table; I've also read three chapters while inhaling some pasta. One afternoon a friend of Armandino's suddenly stood up and burst into Italian opera while Armandino ran around pouring wine into everybody's glasses. Another afternoon I wanted to strangle the schmuck sitting next to me, bleating on his cell phone while eating. And on one particularly dark day, I bought an entire pound of that heavenly soppressata, took it home, and ate nearly a half-pound in the bathtub, right out of the bag.

# I See London, I See France

by Jonathan Gold
from *Gourmet*

Normally pounding the Manhattan restaurant beat for *Gourmet*, Gold took a busman's holiday, eating his way through London's gastronomic hotspots. He deftly sketches some dozen-and-a-half restaurants, but more to the point is his shrewd analysis of the scene as a whole.

Some people travel to London for neckties, and some to take a peek at the Turner watercolors in the Tate. Virgin jumbos bulge with Americans eager to transform themselves into finely tuned machines dedicated to the consumption of theater, catching a bit of the Ye Olde, or dancing until dawn. Then there are those poor deluded fools like me. I went to London looking for an epiphany of cuisine.

More specifically, I was hoping to be thrown out of Gordon Ramsay's restaurant on Royal Hospital Road, which, with three *Michelin* stars, is officially the best restaurant in Britain. Getting thrown out of Ramsay's is what one does in London, apparently, as one might attempt a bit of heli-skiing in British Columbia or an audience with the king when in Tonga. Some of Britain's finest restaurant critics have been tossed out of Ramsay's for disparaging the soup or slighting the chef's term as a teenage footballer with Glasgow Rangers, and the sweep of his famous temper was prominently displayed on *Boiling Point,* a six-part kitchen documentary that aired on Channel 4. Any twit with a functioning American Express card can arrange to be fawned over—I wanted the full treatment, the sort of personal service that London chefs such as Ramsay, Marco Pierre White, and Nico Ladenis are uniquely situated to provide.

I had done my homework, of course. For years, Americans have been hearing about the London restaurant scene, reputed at one point to be the most robust in the world, and though I had never tasted a speck of food prepared by Marco, Nico, or Gordo, I seemed to know everything about them from British journals like *The Times, The Observer,* and a short-lived foodie lad mag called *Eat Soup:* their cars, their kids, their politics, their favorite football teams, their sexual proclivities, and in whose restaurant's back room Posh and Becks held their engagement party.

When artists were hip, Marco did a brasserie with Damien Hirst, then re-replaced all the art with his own glittering masterpieces when the two had their inevitable row. When the '90s financial boom made mere kitchen work seem like a mug's game, Marco and Nico gave back their hard-won *Michelin* stars and concentrated on building their respective empires rather than cooking for the Man. Gordo, in the meantime, muscled in on the ultra-luxury hotel-restaurant game with the vigor of an East Jersey don.

White, the most famous French chef in the country, bragged at one point that he had never been to France. In the introduction to his first cookbook, Ladenis asserted that the customer is not always right. My shelves groaned under the weight of volumes from Ramsay, White, Rogers and Gray, David Thompson, Pierre Koffmann, Gary Rhodes, the Roux brothers, and a place called The Ivy, where reservations were said to be fantastically difficult although the recipes seemed to be of the sort common on first-class airline menus.

Half the movies coming out of London seemed to feature mad chefs, from the cannibalistic *cuisinière* in Peter Greenaway's *The*

*Cook, the Thief, His Wife, and Her Lover* to the lunatic creations (Clams and Ham, Liver in Lager) in Mike Leigh's *Life Is Sweet,* where restaurant excess stood in neatly as a metaphor for pure, unchecked Thatcherism.

It must be said, the news trickling from London didn't exactly make me want to catch the next flight out—when the food press finally got around to describing the actual dishes, they sounded incredibly overwrought, the three-ingredients-too-many school of British cooking that Calvin Trillin once characterized as "Stuff-Stuff with Heavy," only laced with black pudding instead of *sauce mousseline.*

On my last trip to London, in 1988, during the Acid House season that the music magazines were calling the Summer of Love, I managed to hit some of the high points of London cuisine without really trying. My wife and I went to Sally Clarke's, where I remember being knocked silly by a piece of farmhouse Cheddar, and we had a *bollito misto* at the River Cafe that was almost as good as the ones you get in Modena. We had the haddock and chips at the renowned Sea Shell, near the Marylebone tube station, oysters and Champagne at Bibendum, and a nouvelle pheasant banger at Alastair Little, on Frith Street—it made us laugh out loud to see the tiny sausage, no bigger than a child's curled pinky, marooned on an acre of naked crockery. We had a vaguely Asian-influenced meal in a restaurant in Hampstead that had been extravagantly praised by the *Evening Standard,* although it would barely have passed muster back in California. I would like to say that we made a pilgrimage to Harvey's restaurant, in suburban Wandsworth, where Marco Pierre White was already beginning to make an impression as a gastroterrorist, but the night we planned to visit, we somehow ended up eating doner kebabs on the street outside an all-night rave in Brixton. Once, I arranged for a meal to be delivered to our room from Bombay Brasserie, which happened both to be close to the hotel and London's swankest Indian restaurant at the time, and my wife, still convinced that I had chosen it randomly from the telephone directory, continues to think of it as the best Indian meal she's ever eaten.

Still, for one reason or another, we never got back to London.

Now that I'm back, it is less the bizarreness than the Frenchness of London restaurants that is most puzzling: In dining rooms of a certain class, it is French commands you hear barked by headwaiters; French that you hear muttered in appreciation when a particularly lovely woman walks across the room. English farmhouse cheeses may be among the most exciting in the world at the moment, but you are far more likely to find a St.-Marcellin than a cheese from Wensleydale. There is something deeply ironic about stopping into a restaurant around the corner from Trafalgar Square, where you can't see the pavement for the pigeons, and dining on squab imported from Bresse.

Where the chef happens to be British, the trappings are still likely to be French. At the Lindsay House, where Richard Corrigan is revered as one of the new stars of British cooking, you may recognize the maitre d', Walter Lecocq, from his years with Alain Ducasse in Monte Carlo and New York. At The Square, where Philip Howard runs the kitchen, your wine will be chosen by a young man who, like many of his wines, hails from France. The menu basically shared by Ladenis's restaurants Deca and Incognico reads and tastes as if it were lifted from an ambitious train-station bistro in the Loire. At Le Gavroche, where the Roux family has been serving Mayfair for thirty-five years, English is spoken with less enthusiasm than it is in most of the great restaurants of Paris.

Even at the extremely English fish and game restaurant Wiltons, where the St. James's set has been drowsing off over the trifle since gout stools were all the rage and the smartly aproned waitresses seem to have been chosen for their resemblance to somebody's beloved nanny, the kitchen has been taken over by refugees from the long, Escoffier-style regime of Michel Bourdin at The Connaught (which has been transformed into, of all things, an Italian restaurant by the inevitable Ramsay), and although the primary effect of this so far seems to have been a slight improvement in the potted shrimp and sole meunière, it may be, perhaps, further evidence of the gallification of English taste. What the French couldn't win at Waterloo, they may be gradually conquering through their mastery of the English palate.

The phenomenon could plausibly be stretched to include the meal I had at Nahm, a dreary hotel restaurant in Belgravia where Australia's David Thompson just happens to spin phantasmagorical riffs on nineteenth-century Thai cuisine at stunning expense—fantastically complicated spicy crab relishes and lobster salads and southern-Thai venison curries all meant to be enjoyed with fine French wines. Even Charles Fontaine's deft menu at The Quality Chop House, a worn, crumbling restaurant in the ancient printing district, a roster of East End standards like jellied eels and steak and kidney pie—no doubt served a century ago, when the dining room was new—is leavened with things like lobster salad and lemon sole with olives.

It also probably encompasses Mju—where the much-esteemed Japanese-Australian chef Tetsuya Wakuda apparently consulted just long enough to institute a stale brand of French-fried Japanese fusion cooking that wouldn't pass the smell test at a Holiday Inn restaurant in Toledo, Ohio—and the lived-in cheer of J. Sheekey, a venerable West End fish restaurant whose timeless menu of prawn cocktails and salmon fish cakes extends these days to roasted bream with olive oil and herbs, a delicious *cassolette* of monkfish and sweetbreads, as well as happy nursery sweets. If you have ever had the urge to sample spotted dick, a steamed suet pudding dotted with currants, this might be the best possible place to do so.

I suppose Wapping Food came closest to reproducing what I thought the new London restaurant thing might be, a looming former hydroelectric plant with a few dozen tables tucked in among bits of the old machinery, and an utterly simple menu—I had a few grilled sardines, half a roasted guinea fowl with green beans, and a bowl of poached cherries garnished with a scoop of clotted cream the size of a cricket ball. The chairs were midcentury modern, and were for sale. The wine list was all-Australian. (Is this where to mention that an alarming percentage of the creative culinary minds in London—including David Thompson, Will Ricker of the pan-Asian bistro e&o, and Peter Gordon of the wonderful Asian fusion restaurant Providores, among others—come from the antipodes?) Though the food clearly exists in support of the Wapping Project's art performances and lecture series, the beautiful exhibition space, and the clanking electronic music on the loudspeakers, this is the London I used to dream of as a teenager: the rotting Victorian ruins, the bleakly gorgeous industrial landscape commemorated by Throbbing Gristle and Cabaret Voltaire, which has mostly been replaced by glistening office parks. I loved Wapping Food; I don't expect you to.

We can all agree, though, on St. John, Fergus Henderson's unapologetically British palace of meat: heaps of sizzling marrowbones, great slabs of pork from the rare Middlewhite breed roasted with potatoes, skewered eel broiled with Old Spots bacon, gooseberry fool—plain, deeply flavored food that may now be the most thrilling in London. "I have been to St. John," confessed a young French waiter at a Soho bistro, "and I had a beautiful piece of beef that had been . . . only put in the oven. The food is tasty, yes, but it is the farthest thing from French."

Precisely so.

To understand the new London restaurant, it may be necessary to begin with the classic English breakfast, known as a fry-up, at a classic London caff—perhaps the well-known Borough Cafe, a couple of steps from the Borough Market, near London Bridge. A proper fry-up is an intimidating sight to a novice, a big plate sluiced with tinned baked beans, surmounted by a couple of fried eggs, a fried tomato, a fried slab of black pudding (which is to say blood sausage), a slice of fried bread, fried mushrooms, two or three rashers of streaky bacon, and a terrifying hillock of bubble and squeak—potatoes fried hard with cabbage—which all leaks a sort of pale, orange grease that puddles across the plate in rude abundance. You may be tempted to flee to the nearest Starbucks, but it's gruesomely fascinating to see small-boned Englishwomen tearing through these absolutely enormous plates of food.

Modern British cooking can be defined thusly: anything but that.

So the morning after England eked its way into the second round of the World Cup by tying Nigeria—an event celebrated by lager louts across the land—I was not wholly surprised to walk into Gordon Ramsay's restaurant on Royal Hospital Road, a long, flag-draped walk from Sloane Square past an immense veterans' hospital, and find . . . a restaurant that might have been twelve paces from the Arc de Triomphe, with a French sommelier, a French maître d', and a cheese cart, bereft of even a single English specimen, that ranged from Epoisses to Cabécou.

I was seated at first in a sort of foyer, where I was furnished with salted nuts, a copy of *The Daily Telegraph,* and a flute of Dom Perignon for which I was destined to pay about thirty-five dollars. A waiter brought out some breadsticks and a little dish of cream cheese heavily scented with truffle oil. I rattled the sports page—if nuclear war had broken out that week, it would have been pushed to page fourteen behind news of David Beckham's injured toe. A headwaiter looked alarmed and substituted a menu for the newspaper before I could get to the summary of the England-Nigeria game. If I guess correctly, he whisked the paper off to be ironed.

Then Ramsay walked by (he has other restaurants, but this is the place where he seems to be) and I leapt at the chance to chat him up. He gently changed the subject from the inadequacies of the England eleven to the succulence of the new season's lamb before I had so much as a chance to blurt out a single "Oi! Gordo!"

I gestured toward the crystal panels and the blond wood and

smirked. "Very Arpège," I said, referring to the Paris restaurant that Ramsay's interior is probably meant to recall.

Ramsay just smiled.

I waved toward the canapé, telling him that I had always considered truffle oil to be the Heinz ketchup of the overbred, and a corner of his mouth twitched at my rudeness, but the head-waiter came by just then to lead me to a proper table. Ramsay shrugged and wandered back into the kitchen.

I would evidently not be thrown out of Gordon Ramsay's restaurant today. (Nor would I be when I visited his gorgeous new restaurant at Claridge's a few days later, where the menu was strikingly similar.) I would, on the other hand, consume a thoroughly conventional luxury-French meal, starting with a consommé spiked with tiny favas, chervil, and more truffle oil, continuing with a foie gras terrine overpowered by its larding of smoked goose, a single ravioli stuffed with a rubbery, overemulsified bolus of lobster, and a pretty, if overcooked, bit of John Dory moistened with browned butter and garnished with delicious little cubes of spiced celery root. A lamb loin, very rare, with a salt-marsh funkiness, was served on a bed of melted cabbage.

Ramsay was right: The new season's lamb was pretty spectacular.

Still, with all the brashness, all the hype, I had been expecting at least a cuisine of big flavors from London, something with a punch, but what I had been experiencing was as mild as lemonade. When I finally took a trip to Marcoland, or to one outpost of his kingdom anyway, a wonderworld in Mayfair called Mirabelle, I found a fantasy of '50s posh, with neither wild attitude nor blood sausage in sight. The menus are as tall as *The Sunday Times,* and the wine list— actually, I just saw the training-wheels version, magnificent in itself—is one of the deepest in London. The truffled stuffed pig's trotter, a borrowing from La Tante Claire's chef Pierre Koffmann that was always part of the Marco legend, was almost refined, at least as refined as it is possible for a huge, naked pig's foot to be.

These days, when you go to a restaurant run by Marco Pierre White, you're buying a branded product. You can't be accused of lacking class for going to an MPW restaurant, where you can be pretty sure you'll go the route of sole meunière, haddock-stuffed "omelets Arnold Bennett," and reliably good steak frites. The old MPW delighted in sea-pirate prices and cowering customers; the new one just wants to sell you dinner. Mirabelle was all right in its way, but I felt like a rock 'n' roller who never got around to seeing the Beatles on stage and is now making do with Wings.

# The Myth of Caviar

by Inga Saffron

from *Caviar*

Philadelphia-based journalist Saffron approaches the history of this Russian delicacy as a case study of international relations, world economics, and environmental concerns. But she keeps us aware of why caviar matters: its sumptuous taste, the epitome of high-class luxury.

Myths are one of the key ingredients in caviar. Stripped of its shroud of legend and tradition, caviar would just be fish eggs. Most caviar dealers are loath to admit it, but when caviar is properly made and eaten fresh, the different brands are as much alike as two kinds of baking soda. Yet, I can hardly remember a time when I did not associate the name Petrossian with caviar. The sound of the word itself, with its double *s* hissing like a Caucasian wind, calls up an image of a village in those high, jagged mountains, a place where meals are served on velvet-soft carpets, with warm flatbread, scented tea, and a cool bowl of fresh caviar.

The person who knows the story of the illustrious caviar house best is Armen Petrossian, one of Mouchegh's sons. He had taken over the family business in the late 1980s from his older sister, Tamara Kotcharian, who had followed her father and Uncle Melkoum into the caviar trade. (There was also another brother, Christian, who ran the American operation for a while.) Tamara,

Christian, and Armen have a double pedigree in caviar; sixteen years after their father opened his Paris shop, he married a Mailoff girl. The Mailoffs were also refugees from the revolution, but before fleeing to Paris, they had operated an armada of sturgeon boats in Baku. The children of this merger grew up across the street from the family store on Latour-Marbourg, all of them eating caviar from the time they were babies. I was eager to meet Armen and have him show me where the Petrossian caviar house originated. After several rounds of faxes, he invited me to have dinner with him at the restaurant he had recently opened over the family shop.

There was no mistaking Armen Petrossian as I approached a small group of people standing at the restaurant's bar. He might have been transported directly from nineteenth-century Astrakhan. His mustache was waxed and curled to sharp points, and he wore a jaunty bowtie. Despite his ample girth, he managed to convey a silver-haired elegance. If Petrossian was a throwback to another era, the restaurant designed by his brother Karen represented up-to-the-minute minimalism. The walls and carpets were a pale gray—sturgeon gray—while the chairs and trim were all lacquered a gleaming black—caviar black. The Paris restaurant was a sign of Petrossian's resurgence as a force in the caviar business after a long, hard decade of being shunted to the sidelines.

Before I left for Paris, I had gone to see Petrossian's American director Eve Vega at the firm's New York restaurant, which had occupied the ground floor of the elegant Alwyn building near Central Park South since the mid-1980s. Vega was as unfussily down-to-earth as Petrossian was swank, and spoke with a familiar New York accent. While we sat around scooping dollops of fresh beluga, osetra, and sevruga onto warm toast, she confided to me that the firm had nearly gone under with the Soviet Union, when a flood of cheap caviar was unleashed on the market. "A Wild West mentality prevailed," Vega said. "All this cheap stuff was coming in, in suitcases, avoiding customs. They sold it cheaper than we did. I had chefs telling me to lower our prices. I lost a lot of accounts." Pausing for a moment, she suggested that I forgo the warm toast that the waiter had left by my elbow. "Use the back of your hand," she instructed, licking a clump of eggs from the top of her fist.

When the Soviet Union was around to set prices, caviar was exempt from the gravitational pull of supply and demand. But once the Communists were out of the picture, the roe became just another furiously traded commodity. The early 1990s were a time when anyone with enough cash, daring, and a willingness to deal with the Caspian buccaneers could start a caviar house. Prices tumbled as Russian emigrés, fish dealers, and gourmet food companies shuttled in more and more caviar. In Europe, the official statistics show imports declining slightly during the same period. But that is because suitcase smugglers were bringing in so much caviar that many retailers and restaurants didn't even bother buying the legal stuff. Between 1991 and 1997, the official amount of caviar imported into the United States tripled from thirty-two to ninety-five tons annually, although the real increase was probably far greater.

It is safe to say that during the 1990s the United States became the single largest consumer of caviar outside of Russia, surpassing the Germans, the French, and the Japanese. Caviar had always been available in America, usually in specialty shops and fancy restaurants, but around late 1994 it suddenly burst into view in the most quotidian places—in department stores, train stations, airports, suburban supermarkets, on the Internet. It was the Internet, more than the other venues, which made caviar accessible to anyone, anywhere. To buy caviar on a whim, you no longer had to live in a place that was big and sophisticated enough to have a gourmet food store. With a click of the mouse, you could call up the Web page of one of the new caviar distributors, order as much as you wanted, and have it overnighted on a pack of dry ice to your front door.

When caviar became mainstream, it also became cheap. By 1995, Macy's was selling a kilogram of osetra for $310, even while

Petrossian was still bent on getting more than $1,000. Americans could well afford to indulge. At the exact moment when caviar prices were tumbling to record lows, Americans were making record salaries. By the mid-1990s, the booming stock market had plumped up portfolios of many middle-class investors. Caviar trickled down from Wall Street brokers and dotcom millionaires to the ranks of college professors and company managers. Not only did middle-class people have money to splurge on the luxury of sturgeon eggs, their palates had been primed for its sensuous, salty-sweet flavor. Having become more adventuresome in their tastes, people all over America were buying extra virgin olive oil in supermarkets and drinking espresso at highway rest stops. Caviar was a logical frontier for the food conscious masses. Affluence had the same effect on Americans as it did on the newly wealthy industrialists in nineteenth-century Germany: it made them crave the exotic.

The democratization of caviar took Armen Petrossian by surprise, he told me as we sat down at one of the pale gray tables in his restaurant. In the beginning, he had hoped to ride out the market turbulence by doing what Petrossian had always done, which was to sell its caviar in an atmosphere of exclusivity and luxury. The strategy failed, and by the mid-1990s he was forced to lower prices to stay competitive. He promoted a new label, Dom Petroff, as a way of selling second-grade caviar without compromising the Petrossian name. "It was a very difficult time," he recalled. "A lot of people were saying, 'Why are you charging so much? Why don't you buy the poached caviar?' . . . The new market was driving me crazy." What Petrossian didn't say, but was becoming clear to me, was that people were buying the cheap caviar because, to them, it tasted pretty much like the expensive stuff.

Armen Petrossian could see that caviar was becoming a mass-market food. The challenge was to find a way to make the Petrossian experience unique. It was no longer enough merely to sell caviar. Petrossian was at heart a shopkeeper, who still lived next to the store, and yet he knew that Petrossian's strength lay in the power of its name to evoke a special kind of opulence—an opulence with a pedigree. Rather than retrench, Petrossian decided to expand. The office over his father's shop would become a restaurant and would use the Petrossian name. But unlike in the family's New York restaurant, sturgeon roe would not be the main focus. Just as his father and uncle had built their business by redefining a well-known luxury, so would he. In 1999, he hired one of France's top chefs, Philippe Conticini, and together they began working on the menu for the new restaurant.

Petrossian was now perusing Conticini's menu and trying to decide what I should eat. Conticini had been famous for his desserts before he took charge at Petrossian—the French press describes him a "virtuoso of sugar"—and Petrossian boasted of the sweets that lay in store for us. But first we were obliged to have dinner, he reminded me. Petrossian explained that the menu was designed so that "you can have caviar or no caviar." I would start with "no caviar," he said. "No caviar?" I asked. "You will have the swordfish," Petrossian announced.

Our plates arrived papered with transparent leaves of smoked swordfish, so delicate and buttery that they nearly evaporated the moment they touched my tongue. Petrossian had the waiter bring us a very good red wine and an elegant, giraffe-necked bottle of water, then began to tell me the history of Petrossian. The French, he began, had known nothing about caviar before his father and uncle arrived in Paris. Petrossian was repeating the same claim I had seen on the Petrossian Web page. "French people didn't like caviar at first," he continued. "They were suspicious of eating something from the inside of a fish . . . But after eighty years, because of Petrossian, caviar has become a French tradition. That is an extraordinary thing."

Petrossian leaned back for a moment, taking pleasure in his family's accomplishment. Around him, the restaurant was populated by the kind of very thin, very tan women of a certain age who are found in great numbers in Paris, each one with a Hermès famous Kelly bag at her feet. I knew Petrossian's claims were greatly exaggerated and wanted to challenge them, but in a way that wouldn't sound too aggressive, especially since there were three more courses to go.

"What about Rabelais? He mentions caviar," I ventured. "And wasn't caviar the rage in France during the Belle Epoque?"

"Maybe French fishermen ate it," was all Petrossian would concede.

I could see that I had already put him on the defensive. "Petrossian not only brought the idea of caviar as a delicacy to France, but as a luxury," he added vigorously. "That's why we are so well known. We are the only caviar that has a trademarked name. We are recognized as synonymous with caviar . . . The shop is an institution. People come to visit it like a museum."

As if to punctuate his words, Petrossian announced that we would now eat caviar with blini. In my mind, I saw half-moons of thin, folded pancakes, and inside, a dollop of black eggs forming a bullseye against the white of the crème fresh. But when the waiter appeared, he was carrying a plate, with a large brown oblong form perched in the middle. It turned out to be a soft-boiled egg that had been entombed in a shell of deep-fried blini. Miniature crab cakes stood at its feet like sentries. The top of the oblong ball was crowned with a ring of tiny black grains that turned out to be osetra. I was eager to taste the caviar. But the moment I grazed the caviar with my fork, the blini broke and a lava of runny yolk sent them sliding onto the plate. I picked up a few individual eggs between the tines of the fork. The blini, if it could be called that, was as rich and delicious as the swordfish. Conticini enjoyed merging ingredients, textures, and tastes in unexpected ways. The next course was even more elaborately composed, a wedge of fried rouget balanced precariously atop a stewed tomato, which itself sat in perfect equilibrium atop an egg roll, but it was clear now that caviar would have only a minor role in the meal.

I tried to steer the conversation back to caviar, particularly the anarchy that was threatening the Caspian sturgeon. "There are no rules anymore, except who is stronger," Petrossian told me. He missed the Soviet days, when everything was more orderly. But he was no longer worried about the sturgeon's survival. The international community, he believed, was now acting to protect the stocks. Petrossian, meanwhile, was preserving the tradition of making caviar, he said, with a secret recipe. "The fish is not the most important thing," he explained, "the maturation is." I had never heard any caviar dealers speak of maturation before. I had eaten caviar out of an ikryanchik's bowl and it had tasted heavenly. It is true that as the salt penetrates the casings of the eggs, the taste deepens, but by two months the caviar has usually reached its peak. After a year, it is on the decline.

Petrossian persisted. "You must let caviar mature, two months to one year. The merchandise should be aged, controlled like salmon or vodka. The maturation is what makes Petrossian caviar unique." I mentioned that Dieckmann & Hansen didn't keep their caviar so long. "The Germans," he sniffed, "think of caviar as an industry. The French think of it as a delicacy."

Later, after I said good-bye to Petrossian, I stopped in front of the Petrossian shop, which was closed, to look in the windows. The streetlights cast a glow over the tins inside. The front window was decorated with a variety of Russian folk art—painted wood eggs and samovars. Petrossian was right. The shop was just like a museum. And then, epiphany struck. I had just spent three hours with Petrossian in the elegant restaurant that bore his family's great name, eating a sumptuous four-course meal and dining on ethereal desserts, yet I had consumed barely a dozen grains of caviar.

In the same instant, I realized that this was the future. Petrossian may not have introduced caviar to the French, as they liked to claim, but the firm had certainly helped shape the way we thought about caviar. The Petrossian name evoked a more luminous time when Diaghilev's Ballets Russes and the Lost Generation of expatriates were all living it up in Paris, nursing their exile with caviar and cocktails. Petrossian was so effectively associated with the mystique of caviar that the actual substance was less crucial to the experience. It was like Magritte's painting of a tobacco pipe that proclaimed it wasn't a pipe. The Petrossian name represented the idea of caviar, just as the painting represented the idea of a pipe. This was a very useful quality at a moment when fewer and fewer sturgeon were coursing up the Volga to deposit their eggs. Of course, you could still order a plateful of caviar at Petrossian's restaurant, but the dish was no longer the main attraction. You didn't have to eat any caviar at the Petrossian restaurant to feel you were participating in an aristocratic indulgence. Somehow, Petrossian had managed to pry the essence of luxury from the atom of caviar, serving everything associated with the delicacy except the delicacy itself. That was a lot more amazing than selling cheap caviar.

The Petrossians weren't the only ones to perpetuate the aura of caviar. Throughout the twentieth century, writers, artists, and restaurateurs larded the delicacy with myth, turning it into a touchstone of culinary nirvana.

Ludwig Bemelmans, the creator of the Madeline books, devoted an entire chapter of his memoirs to his caviar experiences. Though Bemelmans is primarily known for his whimsical drawings, rhyming couplets, and spunky Parisian schoolgirl, he once dreamed of a more pragmatic career in the hotel business. As a young man, he spent long days serving an apprenticeship as a busboy in the kitchen of the Ritz Hotel in New York. It was there that he developed the habit of helping himself to a few generous spoonfuls of caviar, which he would devour after hours with his fellow busboys in a dark corner of the empty ballroom. "Those were the best caviar days I can remember," he wrote. From then on, caviar would always be a guilty pleasure for Bemelmans.

M.F.K. Fisher, who turned her epicurean memoirs into a literary form, was similarly transformed by her youthful encounter with caviar. It happened when she was just twenty-three and traveling around Europe with her parents. After a hard day of sightseeing in Paris, the three decided to treat themselves to an indulgent lunch at the Café de la Paix. Fisher ordered a portion of caviar. They liked it so much, they ordered another, and then another, until the waiter simply bestowed the entire tin on their table. "That was a fine introduction," she concluded, "to what I hope is a reasonably long life of such occasional bliss."

Henri Soulé, proprietor of Le Pavillion restaurant, one of the few impeccable French restaurants operating in New York, in the 1950s, played an important role in preserving caviar's high reputation in the dark days of the Cold War. Whenever anyone ordered caviar, he insisted that it should be served with the maximum of theatricality. The caviar was wheeled out on a silver cart, flanked by an honor guard of waiters, who presented the dish as if it were a holy sacrament. One waiter would place a crystal bowl heaped with eggs on the table with a small bow, while the others discreetly introduced a retinue of warm toast, chilled Latvian vodka, and shredded egg whites. The restaurant's reputation for good caviar got around, and its devotees flocked to Soulé's tables. He personally selected the caviar served in his restaurant and made a point of opening a fresh tin for such favored guests as the Duke of Windsor.

Though the duke's fellow Englishmen were late in embracing caviar, once they did, it became an obsession. When Winston Churchill dispatched Lord Beaverbrook to discuss the war with Stalin in 1941, he instructed him to return with an agreement and twenty-five pounds of good caviar. In the pages of *Brideshead Revisited,* Evelyn Waugh's bittersweet look back at the England that existed before World War I, there are many descriptions of food, but few so sensuous as his account of a meal of caviar and blini, when "the cream and hot butter mingled and overflowed separating each glaucose bead of caviar from its fellows, capping it in white and gold."

Everyone had his own opinion about the best way of eating

caviar. Aristotle Onassis demanded pressed caviar when he took his meals at the Hotel de Paris in Monte Carlo. Christian Dior liked to drape a lightly fried egg over his sturgeon roe. On a visit to San Francisco in the 1930s, Somerset Maugham took his caviar with a two-fisted ensemble of champagne and martinis spiked with absinthe. Pablo Picasso loomed large in the art world, but was convinced that the tiny pinprick sevruga eggs ruled the caviar world. Ian Fleming preferred the nuttier osetra and so, we may assume, did James Bond. Edward Ruscha, an American pop artist, liked to make a subliminal connection between his family name and Russia's most famous export by slathering caviar on his canvases. Too bad he never charmed the Russians the way Charlie Chaplin did with his little tramp character. Although the Soviets did not believe in paying for copyright permission, they made an exception for the beloved film star when they printed a thousand-word excerpt from his autobiography in *Izvestia*. Chaplin's royalty payment was nine pounds of caviar, roughly a teaspoon per word.

# Untangling My Chopsticks

## by Victoria Abbott Riccardi

from *Untangling My Chopsticks*

Often it is the outsider who can really discern what a culture is all about. Riccardi's detailed account of her year in Japan learning the art of *kaiseki*—the elaborate food accompaniment to formal tea ceremonies—picks up every nuance of how food expresses the Japanese mindset.

It was to be a fifteenth-century-style Zen Tea kaiseki, considered the precursor of Rikyu's modest style, which meant the meal would be composed of one soup and two side dishes.

Stephen was already working in the kitchen when I called from the outside gate. A woman named Joyce, who was studying tea, came out to let me in.

Stephen still appeared pale and his face looked drawn. His arm quivered and the limp made it difficult to get around the kitchen. Yet, despite his limitations, he had managed to pick up all the ingredients for the chaji, as well as buy lunch for everyone.

For the next several hours, Joyce and I slivered vegetables and helped Stephen prepare the sweets. We pulled out all the tea kaiseki serving dishes and utensils and arranged them on the tatami in the order we planned to use them.

Choosing appropriate wares for a tea kaiseki requires knowing about their various characteristics and paying attention to the season at hand. Evoking a sense of warmth in winter months and coolness in the summer months is essential. So at a July tea kaiseki, for example, raw fish often arrives on a bed of cracked ice in a glass or chilled metal dish. In January it would likely show up in a stoneware vessel glazed in dark earthy tones.

But variety is also important, which is why wood, lacquer, porcelain, glass, metal, and stoneware are used throughout the meal. Not only do they add visual appeal but a tactile one as well, since soup is drunk directly from lacquer bowls, rice bowls are cradled in the palm, and serving receptacles and utensils are picked up, passed, and admired.

The Japanese also know that unrelieved simplicity or ornamentation becomes tedious. That is why, for example, after a succession of black lacquer and plain stoneware, a striking red sake bottle embellished with flowers will arrive. It provides a refreshing contrast and, because it is unexpected, makes a lasting impression.

"I'm going to get lunch," announced Stephen, hobbling outside to retrieve three cardboard bento boxes of sushi he'd left chilling on the back doorstep. I jumped up to help, but he waved me away. "It's part of my therapy." He returned balancing the sushi boxes in the crook of his good arm. I filled three water glasses and carried them over to where Stephen and Joyce were sitting on the tatami counter area inside the kitchen.

"You guys know what *sushi* means, don't you?" asked Stephen, lifting off the lid of his bento box. I looked at Joyce.

"Sure," she said, putting down her water glass. "Fish on vinegared rice."

"Wrong," said Stephen, popping a shrimp in his mouth. "*Sushi* means 'vinegared rice.' *Nigiri zushi* is the correct term because the verb *nigiru* means 'to grasp, or hold tight,' as in a rice ball, and the Japanese spell and pronounce sushi with a *z*. So nigiri zushi means 'stuff over vinegared rice that you can grasp.' Seafood is the most popular topping, although there are others, like omelet and *natto*."

I loved natto. Most foreigners despise the slippery brown

fermented soybeans, saying they smell like stale sweat socks. But when you mix the beans with raw egg and scallions and spoon them over hot sticky rice, they taste like a combination of syrupy espresso and a ripe runny cheese.

"The second style is maki zushi," said Stephen, dipping his tuna into soy. "*Maki* means 'to roll' and this style of finger-food is made by spreading vinegared rice over nori, filling it with stuff, and then rolling it up and cutting it into rolls. If you ask for a hand roll, then you get a cone of nori packed with all kinds of good stuff." His eyes sparkled with excitement.

"And you both know the pickled ginger is to cleanse your palate between different bites of fish, right?" We both nodded.

"And you know never to add wasabi to soy when eating sushi?"

"What do you mean?" I asked, quickly swallowing a huge slab of yellowtail.

"You only add wasabi to soy when you're eating sashimi," said Stephen, "because the chef has already smeared wasabi over the rice for nigiri zushi or maki rolls."

"Then why does the chef give you a cone of wasabi when you order sushi?" asked Joyce.

"It's like putting salt and pepper shakers on the table at a fancy dinner party," answered Stephen. "It's a formality."

"And if you do add wasabi to your soy when eating sushi—" I started to ask.

"The chef thinks you're shit," butted in Stephen, chuckling. "That's because he's seasoned your food perfectly, and you're telling him otherwise."

I cringed, thinking of all the sushi chefs I had insulted over the years.

"And," said Stephen, "when you go to a zushi bar, if you're going to drink sake, order it before dinner. Because sake is based on rice and the Japanese consider drinking it with sushi to be redundant." He wiped a dribble of water from his chin with his shirtsleeve.

"Kind of like ordering a side of bread to go with your sandwich?" asked Joyce.

"Uh-huh," said Stephen, eating a pinch of pickled ginger.

After lunch we went out for coffee at a nearby café, since David was running errands and would not return for several more hours. Then the three of us trooped back to Stephen's house to rest.

Around 5:30, Stephen and I went into the kitchen to prepare the final sauces and garnishes, while Joyce changed into a majestic ice-blue kimono embellished with snow-white pine swags. Since it had begun to turn dark, David, now back, placed candlelit lanterns along the stone path.

The particular type of tea ceremony that Stephen and David were hosting goes by the name Yobanashi, or "evening talk." It is usually held in winter. To warm up the guests and stimulate conversation, Stephen filled four small mugs with hot *amazake,* a thick fermented rice drink made with the fermenting agent koji. For a nip of heat, he grated fresh ginger into each cup.

"Here," said Stephen, passing me an extra mug. I had first tasted amazake at a teahouse in Nara with Tomiko and her mother the day after New Years. It was creamy and sweet and tinged with the flavor of sake. Stephen's version was like sipping a warm ginger frappé.

We prepared the first tray, beginning with the miso soup. When properly made, miso soup for a tea kaiseki can be likened to a fine wine. The first taste strikes the palate with a burst of flavor, followed by deeper savory notes. It is the "finish" that matters. The chef wants the flavor reverberations to be so hauntingly delicious, the guests will yearn for more. Seconds are almost always served.

The secret to creating such a tantalizing flavor lies in blending together different kinds of miso. In winter, for example, a small amount of savory red miso combines with the rich white variety. As the days become warmer, more and more red miso is incorporated to balance the heavy sweetness of the white. At the height of summer, only salty varieties are used to create the lightest possible lingering sensation.

To give his soup depth, Stephen stirred red and white miso together before smearing it over the flattened underside of a wooden pot lid. He held the cap of miso over a gas flame, moving the lid in circles, until the soybean paste bubbled and charred all over. He kept scraping and turning the blistered paste with a knife until it became thick and concentrated, then whisked it into a pot of heated dashi. To achieve a satiny consistency, he poured the soup through a small woven bamboo sieve several times before ladling it into the bowls.

Miso soup served at a tea kaiseki fills roughly one third of the bowl, not two thirds, as in restaurants. The amount is supposed to equal three sips, which are supposed to be interspersed with bites of rice. Proper form in the tearoom calls for guests to take one bite of rice, a sip of soup, more rice, then more soup, until the soup is gone (but never the rice, to avoid having the host feel obliged to serve more). If guests request a second bowl of miso soup, they receive double the amount of the first serving, approximately six sips.

Unlike the miso soup served in restaurants, however, which contains lots of little goodies, like seaweed and diced tofu, the miso soup served at a tea kaiseki usually features one central ingredient that breaks the soup's surface. Depending upon the season, you might encounter a square of bean curd, a ball of wheat gluten, or a wheel of daikon radish simmered in dashi until butterscotch sweet. These central ingredients are usually cooked separately before being placed in the soup bowl and crowned with a seasonal garnish, such as fall chestnut, peppery spring shoot, or fragrant summer herb.

Stephen chose spinach-like greens as his focal point, which he blanched in water, squeezed dry, and mounded into the center of each bowl. He carefully ladled the miso soup around the greens and garnished them with a blob of mustard that he pushed off the tip of a butter knife with his finger. When the guests opened the lid of the soup, they would stir the fiery condiment into the broth to add a charge of heat.

Although Japanese cooking aims to spotlight the natural flavors of ingredients, zesty accents often appear to provide contrast. A blast of pungent wasabi counterposes the oily richness of raw fish. A shake of spicy herbal sansho cuts through the fatty succulence of grilled eel. And a dab of stinging yellow mustard offsets the mild sweetness of boiled greens.

Joyce and I placed the matching black lacquer covers over the bowls and set them in the bottom right-hand corner of each tray. Black lacquer is favored in tea kaiseki for its ability to trap heat, as well as its elegant luster. The exception is when cinnabar lacquerware is used to serve vegetarian tea kaiseki, a carryover from the olden days when tea kaiseki featured vegetarian temple food in August to avoid the risk of meat and fish spoiling in the heat. The cinnabar wares were chosen to mimic the everyday red lacquerware the monks use for their vegetarian temple food.

Stephen scooped the rice into the shape of the figure and placed it in the black bowl. He chose the linear shape because at David's tea school it represents *ichi,* meaning "one," and refers to the number one place of honor rice holds in Japan. Aside from being a staple food, rice symbolizes life and all beginnings. Each tea school shapes its rice differently, however, in order to set itself apart. At Mushanokoji our tea kaiseki teacher, Sen Sumiko, told us to form the rice into a small ball, since the round shape represents a vestige of the *mosso,* the rounded implement used in Zen monasteries to measure out cooked rice.

Joyce and I placed the lacquer lids snugly over the rice bowls. One of the pleasures of removing the lid is to see the pearls of condensation that have gathered underneath; it evokes the purity of early morning dew.

At the top of each tray, Stephen placed the mukozuke, a small dish of sea bream sashimi tossed with light Kyoto-style soy sauce, a bit of dashi, and zesty yuzu juice. Unlike restaurant sashimi, which arrives with a separate saucer for wasabi and soy sauce, raw fish at a tea kaiseki comes seasoned in advance with a delicate dressing that harmonizes with the rest of the meal's subtle flavors. A bit of dashi or sake usually lightens the soy sauce, while a squirt of citrus adds brightness.

In keeping with the tea kaiseki philosophy of serving hot foods in heated dishes and cold fare in chilled ones, we had soaked the stoneware in cold water (and likewise had warmed the miso soup bowls in hot water). The wet ceramic would provide natural refreshment, like a rock at the beach dampened by waves.

In the center of each tray, we placed a small welcome dish. It was a sort of pâté of abalone liver lightened with dashi. Rare and unusual foods seldom appear at a tea kaiseki because they belie the meal's "simple" nature and might unnerve the guests if they had never eaten them before. Nevertheless, each person received a tea-spoon of the pâté, which I placed on a spicy, mint-like *shiso* leaf and garnished with nori filaments.

After wiping dry the Rikyu-bashi chopsticks, I laid them along the bottom edge of each tray. Stephen then signaled to Joyce that we were ready.

In traditional Japanese fashion, Joyce knelt with the first tray in front of her knees before partially sliding open the fusuma, which separated the tearoom from the kitchen. Joyce wasn't positioned to face the guests, but instead knelt with her right shoulder to the panel, so close to me I could touch her. After she pulled open the sliding door, she rose, stepped inside, and then sank down again onto her knees, whereupon she reached over to her left for the tray, slid it in front of her knees, then pushed the panel shut. Although I couldn't see what happened next, I knew from talking with Stephen and David that Joyce would stand up with the tray in one swift movement and carry it to David. He, in turn, would crumple to bent knees and slowly hand the tray to the principal guest, who would inch toward David to receive it with both hands.

When all the trays had been delivered in this manner, Stephen and I readied the wanmori, or climactic dish. In a large black lacquer bowl decorated with graceful gold brushwork I placed a dragon ball, a deep-fried round of juicy tofu stuffed with crunchy chopped carrots and lotus root. Stephen had purchased the golden balls at Nishiki market; we had simply placed them in his steamer to reheat them for the wanmori. He twirled hot-cooked soba around chopsticks to create a right coil, then tucked the nutty noodle nests next to each dragon ball. I ladled a small amount of dashi over the noodles, after which Stephen grated a juicy white daikon radish over each bowl to resemble winter slush.

One of the many delights of an "evening talk" tea is the tease of hot and cold dishes, both visually and in terms of temperature. This interplay symbolizes the frigid weather outside in contrast to the cozy warmth of the tearoom.

Therefore, having just served a hot dish, Stephen and I prepared an "extra" offering that was light and cold. It was a refreshing snarl of slivered red carrot and chopped daikon tossed with vinegar, soy sauce, and water. When the guests had finished that, for contrast we grilled unctuous teriyaki-marinated butter-fish for the yakimono and sprinkled it with tongue-numbing sansho. "Put five small pieces on the dish," instructed Stephen, as I divided up the fillet.

Food arrangement in Japan involves a multiplicity of factors beyond mere composition, including the auspiciousness of certain numbers. For some Japanese, serving one slice of any food is bad luck because *hitokire* (one piece) can also mean "kill someone." Four pieces are also avoided because *shi* (four) can also mean "death."

On the other hand, even numbers are yin, or dark and negative, while odd numbers are yang, or light and positive. As a result, most people tend to serve foods in clusters of odd numbers, such as three, five, or seven.

So based on Stephen's recommendation, I placed five pieces of the grilled butterfish on a single dish. But I didn't just spread them out on the plate. I overlapped them in the "piled-up" style, so that the burnished morsels would retain their heat and, when one piece was removed, the whole stack would not collapse.

Joyce delivered the fish along with a container of rice for extra helpings. Rice appears several times during a tea kaiseki. And each time it does the texture changes slightly. When it initially appears on the first tray, the grains are wet and soft because they have been skimmed off the top of the pot. The second time rice shows up it tastes more firm. By the third serving, after the grilled dish, the texture has become quite sticky. The final offering is the crusty shards stuck to the bottom of the pot that are served in warm salted water.

At this particular tea kaiseki, however, the grilled fish was the last course. The guests received no chopstick wash, no tray with tidbits from the mountains and ocean, no extra dish to go with more sake, no additional offering to use up leftover ingredients, no pickles, and no crusty brown rice bits mixed with salted warm water. The tea kaiseki was over.

David, who was now outside the tearoom, hovered by the sliding panel with one ear tipped toward his guests. Approximately five minutes later all chatter ceased. Suddenly, there was a *clack!*

In traditional tea kaiseki fashion, the guests had dropped their chopsticks on their lacquer trays in one synchronized movement to signal they were done. It was a subtle moment unbroken by the coarse call of human voices.

David gently slid open the panel to tell his guests he hoped they had enjoyed the modest meal. They responded with a soft chorus of "*Gochiso sama desbita* (Thank you for your hospitality)."

While Joyce cleared the trays, David set the charcoal in the brazier. All the guests spoke English, because I overheard them asking David all kinds of questions, such as: Where did the teakettle come from? Who made the incense container? Those were the kinds of set questions guests are supposed to ask the tea master at that point in a chaji. Sometimes I wondered if people ever strayed from their script. ("Say, David, how was your trip to Tokyo?" "Oh, fine, thanks for asking.")

I suspect the reason for limiting conversational topics in the tearoom is to set the tone for the ceremonial tea to come. After all, when you're headed on the path to nirvana, why take a detour to Tokyo or elsewhere?

Back in the kitchen, Stephen, Joyce, and I began to arrange the sweets on small plates. In keeping with the traditional kinds of confections fabricated in the fifteenth century, each guest received a whole dried persimmon, a chestnut, and a shiny shiitake mushroom cap that had been "candied" in a braising mixture of soy, mirin, and sake. None of these treats contained refined sugar because it wasn't widely used in tea sweets until after the first Portuguese trading ships came to Japan in 1543.

After the guests had quietly eaten their sweets, David invited them outside for some brisk air and a stretch. This interlude would give David time to ready the tearoom before making the ceremonial bowls of tea. He would roll up the scroll and replace it with an arrangement of flowers in order to honor the Shinto belief that all living things manifest a divine spirit. He would also light incense to evoke the fragrance of Buddha's paradise. Time out of the tearoom would additionally allow the guests to reconnect with nature, thus further purging themselves of any material concerns.

The guests spoke in hushed tones in the garden, since listening is a delight and necessity in tea. Hearing the rustle of the wind through the trees is a highly pleasurable experience; so is the soft scratching of the tea master's broom as he sweeps clean the tatami. These sounds elicit a flow of emotions that go beyond the actual sound itself. To hear the leaves flutter suggests an awareness of the breeze. Where has it come from? Where will it go? Whose cheek has it brushed? Is it the same wind Sen no Rikyu heard?

The sweeping of the broom conveys a sense of purity. This religious symbolism would be repeated during the tea ceremony when David purified the tea bowl and wiped the tea utensils with a special cloth.

When David was ready to receive his guests, he gently tapped a bell, just the way a Zen master does to call the monks to meditation. The idea of not speaking is important in tea. Often, the guests and host use little signs and noises to express themselves. The gentle ring told the guests it was time to leave the chill of winter behind and return to the cozy warmth of the tearoom. In a way, the tea master is a kind of Zen priest facilitating his guests' journey to enlightenment. Had it been sunny out, David would have hit a gong, since its low yin tone complements the bright yang of day.

While David made thick tea and then thin tea for his guests, we cleaned up, whispering and washing as quietly as possible to avoid being heard through the panel.

Around 9:30, the swish of fabric and scuff of tabi on the tatami indicated that the guests were getting up. I could hear them softly thanking David for the incredible evening in genuine tones of appreciation. Thinking about it, the gathering must have been sublime. How could it not have been? Imagine tiptoeing off into the woods to gather in a small beautiful room with an intimate group of friends, then sharing an exquisite meal and a bowl of tea that holds the promise of transcendence.

Since it was late, I said my good-byes and pedaled home. Around 10:30, I pulled into Tomiko and Yasu's driveway, my legs still vibrating from the ride. The light in their family room shone out through the metal blinds, so I knew they were up.

Still chilled, I kept on my fleece jacket and sat with them in the family room eating a cold rice ball that I had picked up from a nearby 7-Eleven store. It was a triangle of sushi stuffed with sweet pickled gourd and wrapped in nori. I had grabbed it unknowingly from the store's many offerings, since I still couldn't read much kanji. Tomiko made coarse green tea to warm everyone up and pulled out a box of pine nut cookies from her snack cupboard. As we sipped, and nibbled, and talked about everyone's day, we had our own tea ceremony of sorts, which became the crowning touch to an extraordinary birthday.

# Local Bounty

by Calvin Trillin

from the *New Yorker*

> An undertow of hilarity gives punch to Trillin's immensely satisfying food writing. As a confirmed New Yorker, dedicated eater, and avowed non-cook, he is perhaps the perfect writer to sing the joys of that rarely acknowledged ritual: dialing for take-out.

Although a grandparent who arrives on the scene after the birth of a child is traditionally pictured cooking dinner for sleep-deprived parents or stuffing the freezer with casseroles, I can tell you that these days it's mostly takeout. That is not simply the narrow view of a male grandparent who, admittedly, would have little to offer by way of home-cooked meals once he'd served the second dinner of meat loaf, accompanied by a salad of pre-washed mesclun and a reminder of his mother's belief that meat loaf is one of the many dishes that always taste better the next day. As I was about to leave for San Francisco last spring to inspect my daughter Abigail's first baby, my son-in-law's mother had just completed a similar visit, and Abigail reported to me, "We had some good sushi while Brian's mom was here." Brian's mother is not Japanese. Abigail was referring to takeout sushi—or carryout, as they say in San Francisco, since, she warned me in advance, San Francisco is a place where restaurants are, in general, happy to prepare food to go but not happy to deliver it. In carryout, the accepted role of a visiting grandparent is to duck into the restaurant for the pickup while one parent waits behind the wheel of the double-parked car and the second parent remains at home, holding the baby with one hand and setting the table with the other.

The one exception, Abigail said, seems to be Chinese food, which does come directly to the door. In Manhattan, the victuals customarily referred to as Takeout Chinese—essentially, a separate cuisine, if that's the word, from the food available in Chinatown— tend to make the trip from restaurants to apartment houses dangling in plastic bags from the handlebars of rickety bicycles. (The proprietors of Chinese restaurants apparently feel about baskets the way proprietors of National Hockey League teams used to feel about helmets—sissy stuff. The restaurant proprietors still feel that way about helmets.) Manhattan is essentially flat—I've been riding a bicycle around the city for at least thirty years, and I have yet to shift gears—but San Francisco is, famously, not. When my mind wandered during the flight from New York, I could picture one of those impassive delivery boys from a Manhattan Chinese restaurant trying to make it up a nearly perpendicular San Francisco hill, his determination unaffected by breathlessness or leg cramps or the fact that the weird angle has already caused a container of hot-and-sour soup to burst open on his trousers.

When my mind wasn't wandering, I was thinking about whether to present the home-delivery issue to Abigail as one more reason why it made sense to live in New York rather than San Francisco. I could imagine myself delivering the pitch: "Are you saying that you're willing to raise this child—this innocent child— in a city that has virtually no delivery, depriving her of the attention of whichever parent has to make the pickup or interrupting her schedule for a totally unnecessary car journey or, God forbid, cooking?" I could also imagine Abigail, who works as a legal-services lawyer for children, replying that, according to the laws and precedents she's familiar with, the sort of behavior I'd just described would not, strictly speaking, constitute child neglect. San Francisco's lack of takeout delivery wouldn't have been completely out of place among the arguments I have used to bolster my case for living back East. After I'd arrived for my baby inspection, one of the first items that caught my eye on the bulletin board in Abigail's kitchen was a *Times* clipping I had sent her and Brian, who also practices law of the humanity-helping rather than the disgustingly lucrative sort, about young professionals who had left the Bay Area in the wake of the dot-com collapse. The subhead of the piece read "Dot-Commers Who Once Flocked to San Francisco Are Turning Elsewhere." I had pasted on an additional subhead of my own composition: "Many Lawyers, Complaining of Inferior Bagels, Are Also Leaving."

I suppose there are studies that connect the ubiquitousness of takeout in Manhattan with the increase in two-job families or the supposed hatred of cooking by yuppies, some of whom are said to live in expensive apartments that have no kitchens. I have never actually run across an independently confirmed case of yuppies living in an expensive apartment with no kitchen, although a friend from that generation told me that he once sought to use the oven belonging to someone with whom he'd become romantically involved and found that she was using it to store fashion magazines. It is also possible that the Manhattan restaurant industry simply came to realize that a city so compact that even prosperous families often do not own an automobile is an ideal place for developing a delivery business; literally thousands of customers live within a quick walk or a basketless bicycle ride from any restaurant. However it came about, it came gradually. When Abigail was born, in the late sixties, and her parents were thus sentenced for a while to a wearing but oddly pleasurable form of house arrest, the closest we got to takeout was for me to go to an accommodating Italian restaurant across the street and have them pack food in plastic containers that looked as if they were designed for some other purpose.

Sooner or later, though, the distribution of takeout menus became so relentless that a lot of New Yorkers began to see it as a form of commercially viable littering. I would guess, from my own experience, that most residential buildings in Manhattan receive menus from at least one restaurant every day. For a while, in fact, it was common in my neighborhood, Greenwich Village, to see signs on doors saying "No Menus"—sometimes in both English and Chinese. I never thought of posting such a sign myself. Yes, I occasionally get irritated when the steps in front of my house are littered with paper menus from two or three Chinese restaurants of the sort that seem to acquire their food from one gigantic kitchen, presided over in a dictatorial but not terribly inventive way by General Tso. But my attitude toward takeout menus is reflected in that brilliant slogan the New York State Lottery uses in its advertising: "Hey, you never know." It was a takeout menu, slipped through the mail slot of my door, that alerted me to a splendid little sushi restaurant on West Fourth Street called Aki, whose chef's experience working for the Japanese Ambassador to Jamaica had inspired him to put on the menu a roll that includes both jerk chicken and hearts of palm.

Delivery by a restaurant of Aki's quality reflects a second stage of development in the New York takeout scene. When delivery of Chinese food consisted strictly of Takeout Chinese, for instance, I did not think of it as an acceptable alternative even to scratching around in the refrigerator for some leftovers that were way beyond what my mother would have considered their second-day peak. When we had some reason to eat our Chinese food at home rather than at a restaurant, I drove to Chinatown with my daughters and two or three of the dinner guests, everyone having been assigned to pick up a certain dish at a certain restaurant according to a split-second schedule—a food-gathering exercise we referred to as an Entebbe Raid.

Then, several years ago, Joe's Shanghai, a Queens restaurant that was noted for its soup dumplings, opened a Manhattan Chinatown branch that became a huge hit with the pasty-faced citizens the Chinese in America sometimes refer to, when in a benign mood, as "foreign devils." Soup dumplings, which are often called steamed buns on menus, get their name from the fact that the dumpling skin holds not only a core that is often made of pork and crab—Jewish connoisseurs sometimes refer to soup dumplings as "double-trayf specials"—but also a liquid so tasty that diners tend to be sanguine about the clothing stains they acquire while trying to get to it. Not long after Joe's Shanghai appeared on Pell Street, Goody's, a rival soup-dumpling destination in Queens, established a Manhattan beachhead a few blocks away. Soon, a similar Queens restaurant called Shanghai Tang opened close enough to the Village to put my house comfortably within the delivery area.

Shanghai Tang—which, in the Chinese-restaurant name-changing custom that turned, say, New York Noodletown into Great N.Y. Noodletown and Chao Chow into New Chao Chow, soon became Shanghai Tide and then Shanghai Tide in SoHo—listed on its menu, in addition to soup dumplings, dishes like Dry Fish Tripe with Pork Sinew. (Until some tweaking was done in the translation department a few years after the restaurant opened, that dish was actually on the menu as Dry Fish Stomach with Pork Sinus.) I don't often find myself yearning for Dry Fish Tripe with Pork Sinew, but I'm comforted by the notion that I live in a city where someone will bring Dry Fish Tripe with Pork Sinew to my door.

I wouldn't claim that Abigail's neighborhood was completely without eating possibilities. Several years ago, for instance, Yuet Lee, a restaurant on the edge of San Francisco's Chinatown, put a branch about three blocks from Abigail's house. Yuet Lee is a Hong Kong–style restaurant that turns out a spectacular version of fried squid—a dish I otherwise think of as routine bar food, often consumed by the sort of people who use their ovens to store fashion magazines. On a late afternoon of 1987, I was walking from an appointment near San Francisco's financial district when I discovered, by coming across little clots of people gathered in the streets, that the stock market had just had its largest single-day drop in history—what became known as Black Monday. Yuet Lee happened to be only two or three blocks away, and I went straight there. Within a few minutes, I was downing an order of fried squid that I had just watched emerge from the wok. It occurred to me that I might be the only thoroughly content person within several square miles. A branch near Abigail's house obviously enhanced my visits to San Francisco, but within a couple of years it closed. I managed to restrain myself from saying to Abigail, "I can't imagine what would keep you here now."

Why did I restrain myself? Because I'd like to think I'm above that sort of parental nagging. Also, I couldn't deny that Abigail's house remained within walking distance of the Mission—a neighborhood that is world headquarters for the San Francisco burrito. In San Francisco the burrito has been refined and embellished in much the same way that the pizza has been refined and embellished in Chicago. The San Francisco burrito, which is customarily wrapped in aluminum foil even if you have no intention of leaving the premises, is distinguished partly by the amount of rice and other side dishes included in the package and partly by sheer size. ("Out to Eat," the Lonely Planet guide to San Francisco restaurants, describes the Mission burrito as "a perfect rolled-up meal," and I would differ only in describing it as "two or three perfect rolled-up meals.") It is also so good that at times I've been tempted to put it on my list of favorite dishes that rarely seem to be served outside their place of origin.

Serious eaters in San Francisco tend to be loyal to their own burrito purveyor. Abigail, for instance, is a Taquería La Cumbre person. In the spirit in which a rabid baseball fan from St. Louis might hand out Cardinals caps, she once presented me with a T-shirt whose front is almost totally taken up by La Cumbre's logo—a heroic painting of a sort of Latinized Ava Gardner wearing crossed bandoliers and carrying both a bugle and an unfurled Mexican flag. My childhood friend Growler Ed Williams, who teaches Spanish literature at San Francisco State, is a Taquería Pancho Villa person. I know perfectly respectable people whose loyalty is to Taquería Cancún, which is only a few blocks from Abigail's house. I have had terrific burritos at all three. I can understand a reluctance to leave a place within easy shooting distance of the Mission.

After a couple of days in San Francisco, in fact, I had to admit to Abigail that the Mission was a pleasant spot for a grandfatherly stroll even aside from the availability of burritos: people raised in the Mexican culture know how to express their appreciation of a particularly stunning baby. As it turned out, a lot of the restaurants we used for carryout were in the Mission. Some of them were outposts of gentrification, described by Abigail as "in the Mission but not of the Mission." So we might be picking up tamales one night, followed the next night by "seared dayboat scallops with organic spinach and black-bean sauce." I wouldn't want to leave the impression that I thought eating carryout in San Francisco was a hardship. In fact, I tried to arrive at a fair appraisal to give Abigail as I left to catch my plane to New York. I finally came up with "It was O.K. for out of town."

Here's what I did when I got back to New York: I sorted my takeout menus. When I got through, I thought it was a pretty impressive collection. I had a wad of Indian and a wad of Mexican and a wad of Chinese (not just Takeout Chinese, either) and a wad of Japanese and a wad of pan-Asian and a wad of Italian and a wad of Middle Eastern and a lot of menus I found unsortable. I had about seventy-five menus. I could picture Abigail on her next visit, looking on with interest as I placed the various types of menus in neat piles on the dining-room table, like the organizer of a bank heist divvying up the loot. The Chinese pile, I notice, is about an inch thick. "What's your pleasure?" I say to Abigail.

"Chinese? Thai? Indian? Middle Eastern? Venezuelan? Malaysian? Italian? How about some octopus salad and artichoke ravioli from Da Andrea? How about risotto? There's now a place on Bleecker Street called Risotteria that offers about forty kinds of risotto, delivered to your door."

Abigail shrugs. "I guess Italian would be O.K.," she says, still noncommittal.

"Or we could do what we call a walkaway," I say. "Limiting ourselves to restaurants within a few hundred yards. It's a nice evening—we almost never get fog here—so maybe we could just stroll over and pick up, say, French fries at Petite Abeille or some zatter bread and marinated-chicken pitza at Moustache and bring them back here. If we feel up to walking an extra couple of hundred yards, of course, we could bring back lobster rolls from Pearl."

Abigail is beginning to look impressed. Maybe she had forgotten about Pearl's lobster rolls.

Then I'm offering all sorts of delivery possibilities—English fish-and-chips, Indian chaats, Japanese ramen, Singaporean fried rice. Menus are being flashed in front of her. I mention roasted chicken, the simple tuna-fish sandwich, soup dumplings. Yes, soup dumplings! I tell her that if she'd like to finish off by having Cones, just around the corner on Bleecker Street, bring over a pint of hazelnut gelato, that, too, can be arranged. "I think it's fair to say, Abigail," I tell her as I continue to flip through the menus, "that there's practically no type of food that can't be found within a few blocks."

Abigail shoots a meaningful look at my T-shirt. By chance, I'm wearing the La Cumbre shirt she gave me. At least she thinks it's by chance. Suddenly, like Ricky Jay producing a ten of clubs out of thin air, I open a menu that has appeared in my hand. "Speaking of which, here's a place that might interest you," I say. "It's called Kitchen/Market, in Chelsea. You'll notice it says 'Delivery.' " I show Abigail the menu. Near the center is a group of ten items. The heading above them reads "San Francisco Burritos." Abigail looks very impressed.

# Someone's in the Kitchen

# The Cooking Game

by Adam Gopnik
from the *New Yorker*

In a special August 2002 *New Yorker* issue devoted to food, the magazine's highly versatile staff writer shadowed five talented young kitchen Turks flexing their culinary muscles in a special cooking challenge. Gopnik's affection for cooks and their art is persuasive.

I enjoy the company of cooks. I admire them because they are hard workers, and because they make delicious things. But, more than that, I like to contemplate the way they have to think in order to make the things they make. They are the last artists among us who still live in the daily presence of patronage. In the two centuries since the Romantic revolution, the arts have, one by one, been Byronized, set free from the necessity of pleasing an audience—a process that began with the poets and painters and took in the architects and novelists and has swept up, most recently, the rock musicians and shoe designers. All have taught themselves that they are there to instruct and puzzle an audience, not to please it.

But although cooks are a source of romance, they are not themselves Romantic. They practice their art the way all art was practiced until the nineteenth century, as a job done to order for rich people who treat you as something between the court jester and the butler. Cooks can be temperamental—cooks are *supposed* to be temperamental—but temperament is the Byronism of the dependent; children, courtesans, and cooks all have it. What cooks have in place of freedom is what all artists had back before they were released from the condition of flunkydom: a weary, careful dignity, a secretive sense of craft, and the comforting knowledge of belonging to a guild.

I also enjoy the company of cooks because I have always wanted to be one. A surprising number of writers I know, apart from the bitter ones who dream about being publishers, share this fantasy. Words and food are bound together in some inexplicable way, a peculiar communion that lends grace and mystery to what otherwise would seem to be a simple exchange of gluttony for publicity.

Overt collaborations between writers and cooks, however, are rare, and I was therefore happy and surprised last March when two cooks whose company I enjoy a lot asked if I would, so to speak, write them a meal. The two cooks were Dan Barber, of Blue Hill, in Greenwich Village, and Peter Hoffman, of Savoy, in SoHo. It was Peter who called me first, and asked if I would be interested in organizing a *jeu de cuisine,* a cooking game. The game, he said, had been invented by Robert Courtine, who, under the name of La Reynière, was the gastronomic columnist of *Le Monde* for many years. (He had been a full-fledged collaborator with Vichy during the war; afterward, he became a reactionary of the table, and flourished.) In the early seventies, when nouvelle cuisine was just appearing, Courtine chose a list of ingredients from the Paris markets, and then had five cooks prepare a menu from them. Peter told me that five young New York chefs had agreed to cook for a week from a list of ingredients of my choosing from the farmers' market in Union Square. The cooks would use the foods I chose in whatever way they wanted, with whatever else they wanted to add. (It wouldn't be a competition, he said, in the tone in which extremely competitive people say those words.) I agreed, of course, although I later explained to him and Dan Barber that they would have to be responsible for my education: I had to confess that I had never visited the green market. They seemed unsurprised by this information; whatever they were coming to me for, it wasn't expertise.

I have known Peter since 1990, when he opened Savoy, a lovely, neighborly restaurant, with a golden-lit Arts and Crafts-style room, all blond wood and copper mesh and candlelight and welcome, eclectic food. Dan Barber was a more recent friend. A year ago, I wandered into Blue Hill, which he oversees with his fellow-chef Mike Anthony, expecting the kind of well-meaning meal you get from a young guy who has cooked for a couple of years in France, and instead ate as good a meal as any I have had outside the three-star places in Paris. Describing food is difficult, not because we can't capture in words things that are sensual—we do fine with painting and pubic hair—but because memorable description depends on startling metaphors, and startling metaphors depend on a willingness to be startled. Nobody did much with landscape, either, until it suddenly became respectable to compare a Swiss mountain to the whole of human destiny. We don't allow that freedom when it comes to what's on our plates. If someone wrote, for instance, that Dan Barber's foie gras with ground coffee beans is at once as inevitable as a tide and as astonishing as a wave, the reader's first response would be to think, quite rightly, that it is not, at all. (And yet it is.) People used to feel this way about metaphors for sex—the English still do. They have just got over Evelyn Waugh writing "I was made free of her narrow loins." But we all still resist "I was made free of his thick loin chops."

Dan is not merely an aspirant to intellect but a real live émigré from academe. In 1991, he had been waiting to go to China on a Fulbright in political science when his grant program was cancelled, and he set off instead to a job at a bakery. "Dan has this whole right-brain, left-brain thing going, which is rare for one of us," another cook said. There was something almost Salingeresque about him. He grew up on the Upper East Side—a Dalton lifer, kindergarten through high school; he cooked for his father after his mother died—and the way he generally looks and talks (acerbic, observant, self-critical), added to the natural diffidence of chefs, puts one in mind of the way Zooey Glass would have, had he chosen cooking over acting.

The three other chefs were to be Philippe Bertineau, of Payard Pâtisserie & Bistro, on the Upper East Side; Sara Jenkins, of Patio Dining, in the East Village; and Romy Dorotan, of Cendrillon, in SoHo—one French cook, three Americans, and a Filipino. All of them did most of the shopping for their kitchens at the farmers' market in Union Square, and all of them were, directly or indirectly, sons and daughters of Alice Waters, the Jeanne d'Arc of Chez Panisse, in Berkeley, who brought to America the Doctrine of the seasonal, the organic, and the sincere. The doctrine includes the belief that all shopping, if humanly possible, should be done at a farmers' market, that small producers are better than large, and that the cook should decide only after seeing what's in the market what he or she wants to cook that night.

When I got home and told my family that I had been specially selected as the point man for a demonstration of the virtues of the seasonal and the natural, of farmers' goods and nature's bounty, they were unimpressed.

"Will it be like Iron Chef?" my son, Luke, asked. He has become a great fan of the bizarre Japanese cooking competition that is broadcast on the Food Network every Friday night. On this program, two grim-faced chefs have an hour in which to cook a four-, five-, or even six-course meal, built around a single ingredient chosen by the host—a strange, melodramatic figure in black, who spits out Japanese. The special ingredient rises from beneath the floor, like the Phantom of the Opera's organ, in dark expressionist lighting.

"You'll be the guy in the black leather pants," he said, and barked "Tuna!" in a mock Japanese accent.

"No, I won't," I said. "This is not going to be a competition. Just an exhibition. Like the Dodo's race in *Alice's Adventures in Wonderland*. All must have prizes."

• • •

After years of Paris markets, with their abundance and bad faith—
the Marché Biologique, the organic market on the Boulevard Ras-
pail, sells a lot of terrific produce, but I have always doubted that
pineapples are actually being grown organically on the Île-de-
France—I confess that I found the pickings at the Union Square
green market on a spring morning a little scrappy. The rules of the
market insist that only a narrow band of local farmers can participate, and this limits your choices, especially between seasons.

"There's a lot of ramps and some good rhubarb" was the kind
of cheering but not exactly inspiring summation you would hear
on an April morning. "And some nice storage potatoes and some,
uh, storage apples." (I didn't even know what ramps were, though
I quickly learned: they are small wild leeks, which have suddenly
become fashionable. Why this should be is hard to say, the appeal
of a wild leek not being so great that it makes you regret that leeks
were ever tamed.) In truth, the chefs, too, found the market disappointing on most mornings, and that, I realized, was exactly what
appealed to them. Instead of ranging through the market like
cooks in a television commercial—squeezing an apple, smelling a
ramp, feeling up a chicken—they tended to go where they knew
they wanted to go, seeing at a glance if what they were looking for
was there, and then quietly taking as much of it as they could get.
They didn't taste much, because experience with the vender and
the look of the article told them what it would taste like. Expertise, I was reminded, isn't seeing all there is. Expertise is knowing
what you're looking for.

And knowing what you're looking at. Peter could station himself in front of a fruit and give you twenty minutes on its pedigree
and possibilities, like an Icelander telling you her family history.
Once, we stopped in front of a crate of strawberries at the stall of
Franca Tantillo, one of the more vivid farmers at the market.
"These are the only good strawberries," he said. "Franca and the
people at Fantasy Fruit are the only two people who are growing
those strawberries right now. They're day-neutral, which means
they completely ignore the usual Circadian cycle. They continue

to flower even though the day is getting shorter." I tasted a couple. They were nothing like the familiar American Driscoll's strawberries—bright-red outsides and hard white mealy insides. Instead, they were sublime tiny berries with the fragrance of a *Fraise des bois,* perfumed and intensely sweet.

On another visit, we stopped at a table of desultory-looking green leaves—the kind of things you cut off the ends of leeks before you put them in a soup. It was a cold and rainy morning, and there didn't look like much that was worth taking the subway for.

"These are scapes," Peter said. "And to understand what they are, you gotta understand the truth about garlic. There are two major groupings of garlic: hard neck and soft neck." We were examining the hard neck. It looked like garlic with a leek stalk. "Hard-neck garlic grows a flower stalk that pulls energy away from the bulb. So you have to cut the flower off each plant, which takes forever, and only a handful of farmers are willing to do it—they cut off the flower stalks and we call them garlic scapes. Real hard-neck garlic came from Central Asia, and it requires a cold winter to get that juicy, full, pungent garlickness. We have a very Central Asian-, Afghanistan-garlic-type winter here." I tasted a scape. It had a sharp and intense garlic flavor, and a green, leafy undertone.

"You know, we have to put up with certain frustrations," Peter went on, as we tramped through the market. "But that's part of the whole expression. What produces great taste? One thing. *Stress.* French winemakers are always pushing the limit of viability. You can't really grow grapes in Champagne because it's too damn cold; and you can't really grow grapes in Châteauneuf-du-Pape because there's no soil there—but you force the vines to adapt to the environment and search for nutrients, and where the season is short enough and you have to crop close enough you get terrific flavor. What drives great taste in the field is stress."

"Thanks, Peter," Dan said dryly. "I'm going to tell that to everybody in the kitchen tonight."

One morning, as Dan and Peter and I walked around the market, I complained about how little meat was on offer. "Well, for the best veal you have to meet Amy, this woman upstate," Dan said. "You know, most veal is white, and it's sort of awful and immoral how they raise it, because they want white meat. But she has a dairy farm, and instead of getting rid of the male calves she just, well, she brings them up like her own children." Dan's eyes glowed. "They're grass-fed and she lets them run as free as you or I. It's a hard sell for a restaurant, because it's a reddish meat and customers expect white, but it's absolutely delicious and she's a completely admirable person. I mean, she's amazing, the way she treats them. She really brings them up like her own children."

"She brings them up like her own children until they're nine months old and she slaughters them," Peter said equably.

I soon became a convert to the limited palette and small victories of the green market. I started coming home with a satchel filled with New York City produce: scrappy, hard-necked, stressed-out.

"We're going to have greens with scapes and ramps," I announced.

"Can't we just have chicken fingers?" Luke asked.

"Scapes and greens and ramps: it sounds like a Ted Hughes poem," my wife said dubiously.

Over a few dinners and many post-market breakfasts, I came to know the chefs involved in the game, and thought that I had begun to glimpse something about their curious mix of entrepreneurial savvy, high principle, sensual engineering, and mordant despair. There was, for instance, a story Dan Barber loved to tell about the moment he thought he had identified the *Times* food critic William Grimes incognito in his restaurant.

"So by this point, I know, I mean I *know*, that this is Grimes. I mean, it's obvious, he's coming in night after night, he's trying different bits of the menu, very professional—it's obvious that the guy is a food critic, and I see him and I sort of recognize him." A visit from Grimes determines a restaurant's mood, because a Grimes review will determine its future. Dan Barber paused, and there was a quick, is-this-O.K.-in-front-of-a-civilian? glance between him and the other chefs before he went on. "We even put it out over the credit-card line. That's this informal system a couple of chefs have where they fax the fake credit-card names of the *Times* critic to all the other restaurants." He shrugged. "So the very next day, Grimes actually calls from the *Times* and asks for a wine list. Now, this guy, let's call him Mr. Hudsucker, had taken a menu with him—but not a wine list! So, I mean, now we're getting obvious." He went on, "That Friday, a 'Diner's Journal' article comes out that lists all the dishes Mr. Hudsucker ate at the bar! So, O.K., the next week H. M. Hudsucker makes another reservation, and we flip over backward for him, creating all these tasting menus, and the servers going through hula hoops. You have to be careful about that stuff, of course, because it's like the Enigma secret—you want to use it, but you don't want it to be obvious you've broken the code. Anyway, finally someone comes into the kitchen and I say, 'That's Grimes!' and he says, 'No, it isn't. I know Grimes, and that's not Grimes.' And I say, 'That's not Grimes? Then who the hell is that?' Later, a waiter went over without my knowing it and said, 'You seem so, uh, *passionate* about food, Mr. Hudsucker, are you in the business?' And he said, 'What business?' And the server said the food business. And Mr. Hudsucker said, 'The food business? I'm in the insurance business. I just like it here.'

"And the really terrible part of the story is that he came back and we didn't do anything for him—not because we're malicious. It's just, just that at this point we're sort of disillusioned with H. M. Hudsucker, no fault of his own. And he walked out upset. It's ironic because . . . *he was the ideal diner!* He ate like a food critic without being one! The ideal guest."

Cooks, I learned, indulge the gaping outsider—I want to run away with the circus!—without even trying to explain to him what they know too well, that the tricks are easy; the hard part is preventing the clowns from committing suicide and the lion trainer from getting in bed with the ringmaster's wife. They're glad that people like the circus, but they understand that the circus is not the show; the circus is the ring around the show.

Though cooks worry about food and carp about critics, they obsess about their staffs. (I once saw Dan Barber struck dumb—speechless and incapable of movement—by the news, conveyed to him at the morning market by one of uptown's snazzier French chefs, that he had just hired away Dan's first-rate general manager.) This is partly because they have to, or there will be no one there to serve, but also because, just as good baseball managers know that an awful lot of what looks like pitching is really fielding, restaurant owners know that a lot of what tastes like good food is really good service. "The thing is, what's a good taste is a feeling, not just a sensation," Peter Hoffman said once. "So if you're feeling welcomed and warm, right then the food tastes better—the whole feeling is better, and you're not going to start prying apart your sensations, unless you're a writer. You just know you're having a good time, and you tell the next person, 'The food's wonderful there.' Once, we had a girl seating people and some friend of the house came in and she said, 'Just a minute, please.' *Just a minute, please.* Not rude or anything—but, for that person, everything we've been working to build up about Savoy is *gone* in that moment."

The craft secret, I realized, was that the craft was not the secret. There are lots of good cooks. The quality of the cooking in a good restaurant really depends on the daily preparation of a context, a hundred small sensations that precede any one bite and transcend it. The understanding that the food was not the thing from which all else came but the thing to which all else led was shared by all the harried and overworked cooks in the *jeu.* (The chefs who owned restaurants felt it most keenly, of course, but even those who worked for other people knew that the quality of the cooking depended on choices that were made before the cooking even started. No cook will ever talk about "a great recipe.") Philippe Bertineau is the perfect Frenchman—he was the original sous-chef at Daniel—and the American cooks looked on him as their Horowitz, their technical genius. He has the worried, harassed, ironic eyebrows that French cooks always seem to have. He grew up on a farm in the Poitou-Charentes region, and was perplexed by the American cooks' belief that their doctrine was a doctrine, rather than a revealed truth. "On the farm where I grew up, everything came from the farm," he told me. "Where else could it come from? I can't *believe* how impatient Americans are. They want to start"—he shrugged and made a mournful O with his mouth—"oh, mixing trout and cumin seed after they've worked in the kitchen for a day, before they know how to fillet a turbot."

Sara Jenkins, it turned out, was the daughter of an American foreign correspondent, and grew up in Spain and Lebanon and on a farm in Tuscany, and she practiced Tuscan farm cooking with an exceptional sincerity and purity of spirit. She believed in the doctrine with the conviction of someone who has given up "sophistication" in order to believe. She was a true Daughter of Alice, with the wide-eyed, militant innocence of the Salvation Army girl in "Guys and Dolls." "I think *anything* can be delicious, if it's really fresh and seasonal," she told me once over coffee. "I've always had problems with frog, for instance, until I went to Cambodia one summer. And, I mean, you may *think* you don't like frog, but what you don't like is frozen frog. These Cambodian frogs had been caught and skinned only minutes before, and it was . . . once you've had fresh frog, you have a completely different feeling about what frog can be."

Romy Dorotan, the Filipino cook of Cendrillon, had been working part time at a restaurant in Philadelphia while he got a degree in economics at Temple in the seventies. One day, the cook quit, and he had to take over. He managed, he explained, because he had read a lot of books by the gloomy British sensualist Elizabeth David. "She really showed me the way," he said. "I would read a bit of Elizabeth David every day, and her writing gave me the courage to cook." It turned out that it was Romy who had been the Courtine reader.

I was drawn to Dan Barber, though, because, alone among the cooks, he had what every doctrine ought to inspire, and that is doubts, and not just doubts but Doubts. At the time we were going to the market together, *Food & Wine* named him and Mike Anthony two of the best new chefs in America, and they posed on the cover in their whites. But he still wasn't sure he wanted to spend the rest of his life cooking. He is in the position of a trombone virtuoso who never exactly intended to be a trombone player. "I mean, do I really want to spend my life doing this?" he said one morning. "It's incredibly hard to have a happy family life if you're a cook. I've heard about people who have, but I've never met any. And the money—I mean, we make money, but you could make more money by investing it in a C.D." Chefs, like writers, are wrung out by the work. "It's insane, insane, insane, *insane,*" one said cheerfully. "All cooking is monotonous," another said. "No matter how varied you think your technique is, you always end up taking something flabby and making it crunchy on the outside, tender on the inside. Food is always crispy out and tender in, over and over and over again."

Dan even had doubts about the doctrine. One spring morning as we were walking through the market, we saw some hydroponic tomatoes. The other cooks walked right past them. "Now, this is a problem for me," he said, stopping in front of the red pile. "You see, I mean, here it is a nice day, it's a hot day, and someone is going to come in and ask for a tomato salad, and a steak, and I'm going to have to be the virtuous guy who tells him, 'No, you can't have it.' I mean, is that a slightly weird role for me to be playing? The tomatoes are good, this local guy is growing them, and I have to be too goddam virtuous to serve them because they aren't dirt-grown in August? It worries me a lot, so I'm always trying to make compromises. I mean—Alice, forgive me, but I don't know if I always want to be that pure. Tonight, we'll do a cold tomato soup with coriander—and we'll press that on the tomato-hungry public."

Peter walked over to the tomato stand. "The way I see it," he said, "it's part of the pleasure of the seasons—waiting. I want to be satiated with tomatoes when tomato time comes. I want to wait."

"Yeah, but the stockbroker or whatever doesn't want to wait."

The conversation turned to a new restaurant that had just opened, three stories high and full of restaurant theatre (specially designed uniforms, that kind of thing).

"I love that stuff," Dan said brightly.

Peter stopped. "You're . . . kidding, right?"

"No, I'm not. I love that stuff." He shrugged. "I guess I'm not reverent enough."

It would be easy to be irreverent about what might be called the snob appeal behind the doctrine. All status, including the status of what we eat, depends on invidious comparison. At the turn of the last century, when only the wealthy could obtain out-of-season ingredients—strawberries in December, oranges in August—hothouse fruit had the prestige that organic fruit has now. When anyone at any time can go to the Food Emporium and shop for cherries and raspberries, glory attaches to someone who has the leisure to go to a market and shop for ramps and rhubarb.

But then all values in real life get expressed as manners; the mistake is to think that values are *only* manners. Everything is a show; what matters, as the bishop said to the mermaid, is what you're showing. "Seasonality," whatever snobbishness it may express, also expresses a desire to connect, to a region, a place, a locality. (The larger, ecological point of the doctrine, that agribusiness is bad for civilization, is, of course, independent of the aesthetics of taste, but that point, in turn, could be met by the counterpoint that agribusiness of one kind or another is, on a desperately overpopulated planet, necessary for the survival of civilization at all. And this conversation can turn round and round over a dinner table until you are hungry again.)

After a two-month marination in the farmers' market, I had come to my own conclusions about what in the market was affectation and what real gain. Some things that you could find outside the market—oranges and lemons and pineapples and onions, red and yellow, and eggplant, and the tougher cuts of beef and pork, even raspberries and cherries and fresh herbs—were perfectly O.K. in their supermarket form. Other things, though—strawberries, potatoes, asparagus, fresh peas, green beans, poultry—had come to seem to me so inferior in their mass-produced versions that they ought to be made to do a perp walk from the produce bin to the compactor.

The list I finally decided on for the menus was composed of pale or delicate things: veal, trout, day-neutral strawberries, green garlic and its scapes, mustard greens, small sour cherries, snap peas shelled. The veal would be Amy's child-raised veal, and the trout from Max Creek farms at the market. (Of all the things I have loved to eat, trout seems to me the one that has almost disappeared from the world of tastes; farmed salmon is pleasant if uniform, but most farmed trout doesn't even taste like fish.) I threw in sorrel because I love it, and also because I have seldom seen it used except in a sauce for salmon. Since there was no starch, I allowed each cook to fill in as he wanted to.

The week after I chose the ingredients, we went from place to place, to see what each cook had made of the writer's list. As it turned out, each one created something far more individual than you could have imagined from the list of ingredients I'd e-mailed. At this point, of course, I should give out recipes, or at least pass around a platter of hors d'oeuvres. But I will do the best impression I can of Robert Courtines's sonorous style assessment and boldly unleash a raft of exotic metaphor. So let it be said that Philipe Bertineau's version of the menu was a visit to a region of France: the innards of veal, sweetbreads and kidneys, were crisped above the crunchy snapped peas; on one side, a little blush of color, the sour cherries were recused from dessert turned into chutney. Although Bertineau cooks high, his references are to regional cooking: all French food aspires to the condition of country cooking; all haute cuisine pines for the farm where it began. His trout was stuffed with the mustard greens, so that the sweetness of the trout was set off by the startling spice of the greens, and he snipped the sorrel with scissors and used it in a chiffonade, rather than the expected imitation of sorrel sauce.

Sara Jenkins turned the same list into a July day in Tuscany. Her veal got minced up, yet not dumbed down, into a ragù, and she mixed her mustard greens with fresh ricotta over rigatoni. A poached or sautéed trout was, I think, too finicky for her country heart, and so she served smoked trout as a starter, on bread. It was an American's Tuscany, perhaps, but all flax and terraced fields nonetheless. Romy Dorotan seemed to turn everything toward the East, with sudden juxtapositions of cool courtyards and hot sunlight (the farm-raised veal was curried; the sweet trout heated with cayenne; baby fennel chilled with watermelon ice) and yet the more time you spent with his menu, the more its European and Davidian origins emerged. Though the ambitious juxtapositions of flavor were Eastern, the idea of bringing those juxtapositions forward, instead of leaving them lurking in the shadows of tradition, was entirely French.

With the two chefs I knew best, not just their origins but their entire characters were evident. Peter Hoffman, whose commitment to the idea of the menu was most intense, made the most intensely committed menu. It was, if anything, too intense, too varied: he marinated the brook trout, for instance, so that it became a kind of superior, briny herring, and then married it with the mustard greens. We liked his dessert best of anything: a sour-cherry-and-day-neutral-strawberry compote, simple and sweet and acid, with buttermilk ice cream. Even Dan Barber's doctrinal doubts, I would insist, could be tasted in the menu he prepared, with Mike Anthony. They shelled the snap peas and turned them into a sublime sweet-pea purée, with yogurt and fresh herbs. It was a cultivated dish masquerading as a rustic one, from the market, certainly, but not entirely of the market. Their veal was slow-roasted in Parisian manner, with the mustard and garlic reduced to a single resonant tang.

Like I say, I should give out recipes. But, failing that, I can hand out an insight. It was not a game. The metaphor of the *jeu*, at least, was all wrong. Cooks have no time for games. They do what they have to do. I had not created a game for them to play. I had created one more stress in a life of stresses, and they had turned it into a taste.

• • •

When the week of the menu was done, I had the cooks over for Sunday brunch. They looked at one another's menus: part of the pathos of their work, I realized, was that they were too busy to eat out much. Dan couldn't make it. A Con Ed power failure had hit his restaurant on Saturday morning, and he and Mike had spent the whole day distributing their produce to other people's fridges, and then had to spend all Sunday collecting it.

The cooks asked how it had been for *me*, and the only metaphor I could come up with was a homely one. I said that it had been like listening to each of them talk, and then, as they ate and argued, something else became clear to me. Searching for an occult connection between cooking and writing, I had missed the most obvious one. They are both dependencies of conversation. What unites cooks and writers is that their work flows from the river of human talk around a table. People cook to bring something to the table; people write to keep something that was said there. I enjoy the company of cooks, I realized, because I love the occasions they create for conversation.

Everyone agreed to try the game again in the fall, and, over bagels and lox, Peter said that he and his wife, Susan, had decided to remodel Savoy—to take out the beautiful candle-lit room and put in a bar and new décor, with framed black-and-white photographs, to make it more accessible to the Armani-shoppers who now fill SoHo. Their idea had always been to make a first-class neighborhood restaurant; now that the neighborhood had changed, they'd have to change, too. Cooks, it struck me, are even more immediately vulnerable to life's difficulties than writers are, and life, though it looks tender on the outside, is crunchy as can be on the inside, which may be why we prefer it with food.

# Where Recipes Come From

## by Benjamin Wallace
from *Philadelphia Magazine*

Every chef has his or her own story; Wallace's portrait of Nigerian chef Shola Olunloyo counts off all the ways in which he is unique, yet also reveals something about the creative process that burns inside every innovator at the stove.

On a January afternoon in West Philadelphia, Shola Olunloyo bounds around his third-floor walk-up in jeans and an untucked dress shirt. Chopin pours from an iMac, accompanied by a trippy, shape-shifting Screensaver. Olunloyo has given himself the day off, but just like every other day, he has been up since five thirty. He's plating lunch, and it ain't grilled cheese. We'll be eating a foie gras and unagi (eel) terrine, an Asian-inflected sea bass course, and an architectural dessert involving chocolate cake, pistachio sauce, and cow's-milk-cheese ice cream. "This is what excites me," he says. "I can't make an omelet."

A London-born Nigerian who studied finance at Drexel, Olunloyo toiled on the hot line at Le Bec-Fin for three years, then opened Blue Angel as co-head chef and Bleu as head chef before going into business for himself. Tall, lanky and photogenic, he has become more widely known in the past two years, a Rittenhouse Square fixture who's achieved a limited kind of one-name fame.

Thanks to his mouthful of a surname, just about everyone calls him simply Shola. He has accomplished this through his catering and through Studiokitchen, a prix-fixe dinner party of sorts that he hosts two nights a week, where he chooses the menu and gets to road-test new dishes for the restaurant he ultimately intends to open. Shola is the kind of guy who has a fridge plugged into the cigarette lighter in his SUV to keep food cold while he's driving around picking up ingredients. He fills sketchbooks with pen-and-pencil drawings of ideas for dishes he's contemplating. If a restaurant interests him, he'll methodically work his way through the menu, making a dinner of, say, four different desserts. Even before he started Studiokitchen and began catering in earnest, he'd rigged up his apartment as if it were a full-service haute French restaurant, with a wallful of copper saucepans, a freezerful of esoteric sauce bases (rabbit *jus*, mussel *jus*), a jury-rigged cold smoker, and a no-frills industrial oven with a makeshift exhaust vent sticking out the window. Now, he lives off Rittenhouse Square, and what used to be his apartment has become Studiokitchen. This is his laboratory, the place where he nurtures recipes to maturity.

Few of the powers ascribed to professional chefs have been so mythologized as the creation of a recipe. Nobu Matsuhisa, the celebrated Manhattan chef who gave Masaharu Morimoto his start, once credited a new dish to his morning golf game; bending to lift a ball from the rough, he spotted wild watercress, then proceeded to base a salad on it. Celebrity chefs routinely give interviews in which they evoke strolling through fragrant, bustling wholesale markets before dawn and being whimsically sparked—by crates of pristine, perfectly ripe quinces, or by a fresh haul of bay scallops still dripping seawater—to invent some audacious, paradigm-shifting flavor combo.

In truth, most busy chefs order their produce from trusted purveyors, sight unseen. And while chefs tend to come up with new recipes that make use of whatever's in season, as often as not they take their ideas from books, from eating at each others' restaurants, and from plain old experimentation in the kitchen. Most good recipes (i.e., not Pineapple-Asparagus Delight) are slight tweaks of tradition, or elevations of classic dishes. Witness, for instance, the mac-and-cheese at Jones, which spurs that comfort-food war-horse to higher ground with four different cheeses and a gratinéed sprinkling of bread crumbs. Thomas Keller, one of the greats in his own right, is upfront about cribbing his mascarpone sorbet directly from Alain Ducasse. "I admire that," Shola says. "I tell people to look up in the dictionary the words 'inspiration' and 'plagiarism.' "

Then there are the recipes, from the most creative chefs, that seem to spring from nothingness into being, the results of some culinary Big Bang—"Sudden odd things no one had thought of," in Shola's words. There's Jean-Georges Vongerichten and his famously unlikely yet delicious pairings: watermelon and tomato, caper and raisin. There's Thomas Keller and his oysters with tapioca. There's Gray Kunz and his barbecued sea trout with grapefruit-ginger-shallot sauce. These are the recipes that leave you asking: Where the hell did *that* come from?

On this day in January, Shola is working on a terrine inspired by a meal at Morimoto, which has an oyster-foie gras dish on its menu as well as broiled eel with avocado. As a veteran of the haute Le Bec kitchen, Shola enjoys making terrines, and he was intrigued by the irreverent idea of an Asian riff on France's culinary holy-of-holies. He searched the Web, his memory and his cookbooks for precedents, and found a few. With that starting point, he's ready to develop the idea. A well-constructed recipe is teleological. Every ingredient and every technique has a specific purpose, even when that purpose may elude the amateur cook. The bay leaf fleetingly used in the initial blanching of a vegetable may, in the final flavor, be undetectable yet have a subtle but crucial role. That garnish of minced chives may be there for color, or texture, or a little kick of flavor, or all of the above.

Today, as always, Shola's thinking about what else might go on the plate. "I'm moving away from ethnic assignment of dishes," he says. "I like affinity cooking, putting things together that go well together." Foie gras is often paired with fruit. Quinces are in season, and they're more interesting than the traditional pears. He'll poach them. He associates foie gras and aspic, the gelatin in which it is sometimes suspended, so he decides he'll also make quince jelly, reinforcing the quince flavor while providing an interesting "mouthfeel." For counterpoint, he'll throw in something bitter and crunchy, frisée lettuce; the vinegary tang of its dressing cuts the sweetness of the dish. He finishes with a sprinkling of chives, for color. So, taking a combination here, a variation there, a dash of personal idiosyncrasy, and then doing a little mix-and-match to achieve a harmonious balance of flavors and textures, Shola has his idea: a terrine of foie gras and broiled unagi, served with poached quince, a quince jelly, and a small salad of frisée.

That's the easy part. While the goal of a recipe may be to successfully combine a particular set of flavors, the recipe itself is essentially a sequence of solutions to anticipated problems in reaching that goal. Anticipated problem number one: If Shola layers the eel with the foie gras before cooking, he risks overpowering the velvety goose liver with the strong-flavored fish. Solution: He will cook them separately and only later combine them. Anticipated problem number two: The quince, with its floral, desserty quality, and the terrine, with its unctuous, meaty character, would ordinarily make for strange mouthfellows. Solution: Simmer the quince with bay leaf, an herb that works well with both sweet and savory and will therefore bridge them. Anticipated problem number three: The terrine has a fragility that will cause it to fall apart if cut with a regular knife. Solution: He will cut it with an electric knife. He ends with a flourish, scattering star-anise salt on the plate. One more texture, one last reinforcement of the Asian theme.

For an entrée, Shola has an idea to do something with a classic combination: celery-textured, licorice-flavored fennel and flaky white sea bass. He'll add some tomatoes, which he likes pairing with fennel. And it's a light dish, calling for a sauce of light broth, but he keys it to his Asian theme by steeping Asian ingredients like lemongrass, ginger, cilantro root, cinnamon and star anise in the broth. He also briefly infuses the broth with jasmine tea. Tea? "Random," Shola explains. "Sometimes you have to go in a different direction."

Again, a set of problems and solutions: Tomatoes are out of season, so he'll intensify the flavor of the current market's bland hydroponics by oven-drying them with herbs. Tea is astringent, so he counters it with sugar. He wants a clear broth, but the usual chicken parts and chopped vegetables would render it cloudy, so he bases the broth on a whole chicken and intact veggies. He doesn't want the broth to be too insubstantial, though, so he gives it a heftier mouthfeel by throwing some gelatinous chicken feet in with the other ingredients.

When it comes to cooking the fish, he does it two ways. He often makes simultaneous variations of the same thing, to figure out what works best. In this case, he pan-sears one filet, and prepares the other using a cutting-edge technique that he's trying for the first time: vacuum-sealing the fish in plastic using a special machine and then poaching it, like a Lean Cuisine pouch. The first method yields a nice brown crust and perfectly crisp skin, the second a super-moist filet whose essential taste comes through without distraction. Each is delicious in its own way.

Dessert is a riff on the mascarpone and lemon juice sorbet originally concocted by Alain Ducasse. Shola's version, an ice cream, substitutes a molten cow's-milk cheese called Chaource and creamy lemon curd. (Pure juice would separate the buttermilk required for ice cream.) As Shola well knows, all creation builds on what's already been done.

# The Culinary Underground

by John T. Edge

from the *Oxford American*

A peerless chronicler of Southern food-ways, Mississippi-based John T. Edge knows that it's not just about the cooking, but about the characters, too—and he's always turning up new ones. Only a Delta insider could get us into a place this odd and local.

"I met my idol on the first day of grade school," Norfleet Reichle tells me between pulls on a menthol-flavored Doral. "Willie D. Thompson was his name. I walked in the bathroom and there he was, standing on the toilet seat, taking a dump. Momma said I had wings 'til right about then."

It's five-thirty on a blustery Monday morning in January of this year. Norfleet, a solid fifty-two-year-old with a wide and welcoming face and a half-cocked smile, is holding court from a tattered recliner. Attired in khaki shorts and a v neck t-shirt, he wears neither socks nor shoes. Since about four-thirty, Norfleet has been peeling potatoes and shucking corn. I had planned to document his day from start to finish, but I couldn't wrench my bones from bed at four, when Norfleet usually rises. So I'm playing catch-up and gulping coffee in an attempt to clear my head. Norfleet, on the other hand, is at full cerebral gallop.

He heaves from his perch and heads for the narrow kitchen at the north end of his house, which he shares with his wife Sheila. "Did I tell you about how I jumped ninety-two feet into twenty-two feet of water?" he asks. He is way ahead of me. "Now, don't get me wrong," he says, pulling the top from a tub of marshmallow fluff and fixing me with a gaze devoid of even a trace of irony. "I like to take a drink of whiskey. But I wasn't drunk; I was just drinking."

Norfleet Reichle likes to drink. He also likes to cook. For the last two years, he has done more cooking than drinking. His wife is pleased. So are his regulars: the dirt farmers, fish farmers, doctors, and lawyers of Columbus, Mississippi, who stop by his house every weekday for lunch. Though his address is listed on state tax rolls as a bed and breakfast, and a cypress placard by the front door reads FLEET'S EATS, the ranch-style home in which Norfleet and Sheila live is best understood as a sort of liminal restaurant on the cusp of legitimacy, the kind of place where the laundry room serves as a staging area for iced-tea service and the carport does double-duty as a pantry.

The concept is not unique. Annie Keith's, a once beloved and now defunct meat-'n'-three in Atlanta, Georgia, began its path to legal status in the kitchen of a brick midtown bungalow. Good Ole Home Cookin' in McCormick, South Carolina, started serving midday meals to local laborers out of a doublewide garage. Customers at Colonel Hawk's in Bardstown, Kentucky, once announced their arrival by driving around back of the proprietor's home and clanging a bell. Without exception, these proto-restaurants are remembered fondly for their food, if not their stubborn homeliness and lack of pretense.

Perhaps it's the South's tradition of poverty-engendered enterprise—a similar legacy spurred the rise of Cuban home restaurants, known as *paladores*—but the informal economy of what are sometimes known as backdoor restaurants remains strong. Besides Fleet's Eats, I know of five other spots like it in Mississippi. Some, like Peggy's in Philadelphia, Mississippi—which still serves lunch from a makeshift plank buffet spanning the hallway of the Webb family home—have made the leap to legitimacy. Others, like a house restaurant in the capital of Jackson, operate thanks to a wink-and-nod arrangement that draws local glitterati to their stoop but, in the interest of keeping the health department functionaries at bay, forbids regulars from divulging the name and address of the kind lady who dishes up what may be the city's best fried chicken and sweet potato pie.

"If you're cooking two meats and five vegetables, sometimes you got to call the big dogs in," says Norfleet as he muscles tubs of vegetables from the refrigerator to the Radar Range to what passes for his steam trolley, a folding table topped with eight daisy-ringed Crock Pots and a ginger jar lamp. Purple hull peas go in one crock; fresh corn in another; mashed potatoes, cut with a block of preternaturally yellow oleo, in a third.

It's now about eight in the morning. Sheila (a doe-eyed paralegal from the Delta who fell hard for Norfleet's schoolboy-gone-to-seed charm) has been up since six-thirty, slicing bananas for pudding and mixing cornmeal batter for muffins. Between muffin batches, she works the phone, faxing menus to the likes of Highway 82 Pawn and First Baptist Church of Columbus, and taking calls from regulars. "Frank, you better come out here today," she chirps. "I got a butterflied pork chop with lots of fat on it, and it's got your name all over it."

When Norfleet takes another cigarette break, I turn my attention from scribbling notes to taking an inventory of my surroundings. What was once a sun porch is now overtaken by a ten-seat table and case after case of Fleet's homemade pepper vinegar, pea relish, and spicy vegetable juice. The dining room now boasts seating for ten. To accommodate four-seat and six-seat tables, the couch in the family room has been shoved against the back wall, between the recliner and the television.

Norfleet did not aim to be a restaurateur. Upon graduation from high school he pursued Jefferson's agrarian ideal by way of farming the rich prairie that stretches eastward from Columbus through the black belt of Alabama. Norfleet worked the land for more than twenty-five years, raising hogs and cattle, soybeans and winter wheat. At one point, he rented and cropped 1,300 acres. Two straight summers of too much rain, however, brought his farming career to a shuddering halt. In 1993, along with his first wife, Norfleet took over a plate-lunch joint on the outskirts of Columbus. "I didn't know a thing about running a restaurant," says Norfleet, "but I knew everything I needed to know about cooking." But when Norfleet lost his first wife, he lost his first restaurant. Another restaurant followed. It didn't take either. Fleet's Eats wasn't hatched as a third try. It evolved out of a catering and lunch delivery business that Norfleet and Sheila began nearly two years ago with the hope that they would pick up a few extra dollars until something better came along.

These days, although the personal lives of Norfleet and Sheila appear to be in retreat, the house is not wholly absent the trappings of a typical working-class home: Duck prints and cross-stitched homilies bedeck the formal living room; a bookshelf stacked with family portraits, volumes of the *World Book Encyclopedia,* and John Grisham novels stands tall alongside the fireplace; and pillows, appliquéd with doleful angels, dot a plaid couch in the family room.

Amazingly enough, the kitchen may well be the public room least affected by Norfleet and Sheila's stab at homegrown commerce. The Reichles use little specialized equipment. No Buffalo chopper, no Hobart mixer. In fact, if you arrive after Sheila has put away the two electric skillets in which she fries the chicken and pork chops, and you squint your eyes just right, you might believe that the oversized platter of deviled eggs on the counter is intended for a 100-year-flood family reunion instead of the midday crush of regulars at a renegade restaurant.

The midday meal comes early in Columbus. If, like many of the customers at Fleet's Eats, you begin your day at first light, then a ten-forty-five trencherman's lunch is the perfect answer to a five-thirty biscuit-and-coffee breakfast. As nine begets ten, prep work slows. By ten, Norfleet is standing ready. Ditto Sheila. All eight of the Crock Pots are full. The wall oven is stuffed with trays of fried pork chops. A napkin-wrapped basket of brown-and-serve rolls sits on the counter alongside a Tupperware tub of cucumber-and-onion salad. And row upon row of plastic-wrapped slices of apple pie—a result of Sheila's recent and intensive study of *Betty Crocker's Cookbook*—await the crowds to come.

Since sometime around daybreak, Norfleet has quit the recliner in favor of taking his cigarette breaks at the kitchen sink, flicking ashes down the drain. That's where he is when the first paying customer walks through the back door, tracing a path alongside the bright orange extension cord that snakes from a carport plug to the kitchen counter. Norfleet has yet to serve a meal, but, as he surveys what he has wrought, he pulls on a Doral with a sort of post-coital bliss, as if, seven hours into his workday, it's all gravy from here.

For the next couple of hours, Sheila pours tea and makes change from what was once the silverware drawer while Norfleet monitors Crock Pot levels. Though he does not shirk his duties, it's Sheila who shoulders the brunt of service. Norfleet is busy working the crowd, calling most everyone by name. Between tales of how he cooked a loggerhead turtle gumbo and what inspired him to strip the meat from catfish frames to make croquettes, dubbed "cat puppies," he steals glances at the Weather Channel, justifying interest in cable television by pronouncing, "Anybody with any damn sense is interested in the weather."

He rides the crest of the lunch rush for a good hour-and-a-half. But by one in the afternoon, he is out of red beans and rice, his back is cramping, and he is mortal once again. Before the day is over, he and Sheila will serve forty-five, maybe fifty lunches. If they're lucky—and if Norfleet doesn't lose a double-or-nothing wager to a table of farmers in the mood to gamble for a free lunch—the Reichles might net $150. It's barely a living wage, but that doesn't trouble Norfleet. "I'm not in it for the money," he tells me as he scrapes a plate. "I like people, I like cooking, and I gotta pay my bills, so I figured I might as well give this a try."

As he works his way through a stack of dirty dishes, the sink begins to empty, and, by my measure, Norfleet grows restless. Without the prospect of work to occupy his head and hands, his country-fried ebullience fades. I'm expecting a breakdown, some sort of epiphanic moment wherein Norfleet pledges to chuck it all for a job as an oil-rig cook.

But I've been reading his mood all wrong. When I slip on my coat and begin to say my goodbyes, he sidles up to me, intent on talking about his plans for the future, about how he's going to add seating for fifty patrons and convert the carport into a true restaurant kitchen. He proves to be a compelling door-talker. When I try again to take my leave, he asks, sotto voce, what I think about the prospect of making sardines by pickling catfish fingerlings. What I read as panic and pathos was actually the birth of a notion. "I'm thinking that I wouldn't have to skin the little fellas," he tells me, his face a mask of earnest intent, "but I would have to clip off the fins, and I *might* have to gut 'em."

# Life on the Line

by Jason Sheehan

from *Westword*

Words seem to pour effortlessly from Jason Sheehan; his pieces in Denver's weekly *Westword* are like funhouse rides, taking crazy loops off and around the subject of whatever restaurant he's reviewing—and yet somehow always landing with a meaningful conclusion.

S ean Kelly is no celebrity chef. His hands give him away. They're big, strong, the wrists thick from handling saute pans, fingertips mauled, palms rough as untreated leather.

Cooks know cooks from the feel of each others' hands, and they can gauge how long someone's been in the business from the thickness of calluses and slow accumulation of scar tissue. Blindfolded, I could recognize some of my own partners in crime with just a handshake. The kinked pinky from years of whisking the roux with the whisk held wrong, the fingertips beveled by slips of the knife, the occasional missing digit or truly noteworthy scar.

Not too long ago, I ran into a former boss who—like me—had hung up his knives for a kinder, gentler career path. He'd become a restaurant owner. After we exchanged the usual pleasantries, he asked, "So, how are your hands?" I told him that a few days earlier, my wife had handed me a cup of coffee straight from the French press and I'd had to set it down, fast, on the counter, because it was so hot. It was the first time in ten years I'd been able to feel heat on the palm of my hand. He nodded, commiserating.

We were both becoming sissies, useless in the real world of knives and fire and boiling duck fat. These days, the biggest threat of injury we faced was a really nasty paper cut. Our hands were getting soft.

But not Sean's. He's no overstuffed teddy-bear chef in spotless whites throwing out catchphrases to a rabid, captive audience. He's not a clipboard-checker, either, stabbing his gold-tipped digital thermometer into every entree coming off the hot line to make sure the entrecote for table twenty-two is going out well-done. Sean is a cook, and he has the hands to prove it.

He didn't have to stay in the kitchen. Things could have gone very differently after he closed The Biscuit and his much-loved Aubergine Cafe and walked away from the business in early 2001. In the wake of these much-publicized closures, investors were waiting in line to throw big, dirty bags of money at him. "I remember sitting down with these sixty-, seventy-year-old millionaires," Kelly says. "Guys who had all these ideas, who wanted to be restaurant owners and could toss around $40,000 like it was nothing. But that's not nothing. That's a year's work for someone like me. They were like, 'Oh, don't worry. We'll set you up with banks and loans and everything.' But you know what? Someday, someone's gotta pay all that money back, and I didn't want that kind of debt on me."

He could have done a deal with the devil and spent the rest of his days flitting around a swank dining room, taking all the credit for work being done by hordes of sweaty underlings soldiering away on the other side of the swinging doors. He could have become an institution. Restaurant Sean Kelly would have been wildly successful. An empire of Baby Aubergines and Kelly's-to-Go takeout oyster-and-bresaola franchises might have made him a very rich man.

But instead, he did exactly what no one expected. He became a cook again. After a year on the outside spent reading, cutting fish for a local supplier, doing some food writing and getting reacquainted with his family after years of fourteen-hour days, Sean Kelly's back in the kitchen, making your dinner at Clair de Lune. There's no sous chef, no line full of tattooed, felonious kitchen mercenaries brought in to communicate the "essence" of Sean Kelly to the masses—just Kelly himself, along with Terry White as garde manger, roundsman, prep and pantry cook, and Gustavo Murillo, who washes the dishes. They work together five nights a week in a tiny, bright, well-organized kitchen smaller than those in some starter apartments, and they do it because this—and not some Pandora's box of debt and celebrity and eighty-hour weeks—is what Kelly wanted. Something small, intimate and controllable. A place where nobody owned him, that was truly and totally his. And most important, a place where he could cook. "No investor would've gone in with me on a place like this," Kelly says, standing in the alley by Clair de Lune and describing the strange twists that led him to this cramped, pint-sized space on Sixth Avenue.

And he's right. I don't think there's a money man out there who would have risked his neck (or his credit rating) on the concept: eight tables in the dining room, most of them two-tops; five people on the staff most nights (including servers); one cook in the kitchen using local produce and meats—much of it organic, all of it expensive and some picked, grown, harvested or slaughtered just for him.

Reading Kelly's brief, compact French-Mediterranean menus is like looking at van Gogh's *Starry Night.* They're sketches, windows onto something larger, vignettes of perfect evenings done in food. Seared sea scallops with celery-root remoulade, scallions, capers and preserved lemon; simple straw-potato cakes; saffron couscous; walnut liqueur, creme anglaise, baked apples and cider reduction; salt-cured foie gras with earthy summer-truffle vinaigrette. Kelly's offerings change with the seasons, with his mood, with the chattering of a fax coming in from one of his local purveyors.

Whatever is good, whatever is fresh, whatever moves him, that's what he'll cook. "It's really pretty simple," he says. "One fish, one game, one meat, one vegetable. Then there's the antipasti, the fruits de mer, the cheese courses."

Yeah, simple but for the fact that most of the offerings change daily. The Reblochon for the cheese course was held up in customs, Kelly tells the staff at a pre-service meeting, so don't push it. The scallops looked good, so he'd gotten enough just for tonight. Tomorrow, it would be something different. "And you'll notice, again, that everything on the menu is pan-seared, pan-roasted, pan-broiled . . ." He flashes his copy of the night's menu across the bar, the margins filled with handwritten notes. The staff laughs. It's an inside joke. "Everything has to be done in the pan," Kelly explains. "I don't have room to do anything else."

In the kitchen, I watch as Kelly arranges a half-dozen sea scallops in a smoking-hot pan, laying them down in a perfectly spaced circle so that each one receives the same amount of heat, nudging one back into line with the knuckle of a thumb when it shifts just slightly. I watch as he stops in the middle of a heated discussion about Food Network chefs to lay out a leg and breast of Guinea fowl on a sizzle plate, leaving an unfinished sentence hanging in the air while he carefully pokes at each piece of meat, as if communicating with an old friend. Kelly follows his own rhythms at Clair de Lune, playing the restaurant game by a totally different set of rules— rules that he makes up and changes whenever it suits him.

You don't have to be in the kitchen with Kelly to appreciate what comes out of it. A few nights earlier, I'd sat in the tiny dining room, crowded with foodies in various stages of hoity-toity indulgence, surrounded by walls that were the color of an Impressionist sky. The plateau de fruits de mer, one of the few menu mainstays, was like a Long John Silver's sampler platter for grown-ups. Immaculately fresh Littleneck clams and Malpeque oysters—served on the half shell and carefully opened to preserve their liquor—lay like knobby gems on a bed of ice. I could smell their metallic perfume as they arrived at the table, the scent catching right at that juncture between throat and sinuses, like you're chewing a mouthful of pennies. The taste was briny, deep and green with no bottom. The texture like having suddenly grown a second, tiny tongue. When eating shellfish as fresh as these, you're immediately aware that this thing in your mouth was alive just an instant before it hit your plate, that it died for your pleasure. And as with the smell of truffles or the flavor of expensive port wine, the sense-memory connections they form in the brain are pure sex.

Also on the plateau were two spiced shrimp, huge and chilled, and half a lobster split straight down the spine as though following a diagram in an anatomy textbook, giving you the chance to taste the subtle differences between the meat of the tail, body, claw and head. There were dipping sauces as well: a shallot vinaigrette, a cocktail sauce jacked up with spices, and a tarragon tartar sauce, although the netted half-lemon provided was the only accessory this dish required. It says a lot that the lobster—usually queen of the fruits de mer—was the least interesting thing on the plate.

The plateau came with dipping sauces, as well: The antipasti misti, another regular menu item, was a wildflower drawn on the plate with sweet, bright-orange persimmon, powerful house-cured sardines, roasted red peppers, caper berries, black olives, little cubes of marinated chevre, homemade bresaola (a marinated tenderloin, air-cured, then sliced thin like an older, meaner, less cultured big brother to prosciutto), and crisp-fried baby artichokes drizzled with basil aioli. The baby artichokes are the only dish that Kelly resurrected from Aubergine. "I had to have them here," he says. "Or come up with some really good excuse why I didn't. There's people who would've never forgiven me otherwise."

On the menu that night was a vegetable tagine (a classic Moroccan preparation consisting of winter vegetables, preserved lemon and a tomato jus) served with solid, lemon-touched falafel and saffron couscous. There was also a wonderful, slow-roasted, aged Muscovy duck breast on an autumn sketch of braised apples, lemon, sweet potato, cippolini onions and a sweet cider reduction.

The duck was firm and musky, with crisp, fatty skin and meat that had been dried somewhat by the aging process but made all the more flavorful for the concentration. Generally, I like my duck rare, bloody and full of life; I like the classical preparations, the meat flame-kissed and pink. But that wasn't what Kelly was doing. Not this season. Youth and juiciness are spring sensations. This duck was hearty and ready for a long, cold snow.

By the time dinner was over, I'd accidentally gotten drunk as hell on Chimay Red, from the short, carefully considered wine list arranged by Karin Lawler. This wicked quasi-beer, made by monks, is highly carbonated and high in alcohol content (something that should probably be written in much bigger letters on the bottle, although having it come as a very blurry surprise is fun, too), with a flavor halfway between a very good beer and a very cheap champagne, which all conspires to make you drink a lot of it quickly and then inspires very un-monklike feelings in the casual imbiber. It's nice stuff. It was especially nice at Sean Kelly's place.

Clair de Lune is the restaurant that every burned-out, grill-scarred, sick-of-it-all veteran of the food industry dreams about when he collapses into a booth at the end of the night with his crew. I've been there, and I know the whole, tired spiel backwards and forwards: "Fuck it," he says. "Fuck it all. Fuck these hours; fuck this heat, these customers who don't know a gratin from a gaufrete. Fuck the fish guy and that stinking grandmother of a salmon he sent me. The investors crying over a slow Saturday. Fuck 250 covers at brunch. One of these days I'm gonna . . ." And it goes on from there. They all want a place to call their own, a place where they can work the rest of their days with the kind of simple happiness I saw on the face of Sean Kelly. A place like Clair de Lune.

It's small, yes—so small you will become intimately acquainted with everyone in the dining room, because you'll be able to hear every word of their conversations. But you'll get past that. Yes, the menu is in a state of constant (and welcome) flux. And no, your plastic is no good here: Kelly didn't feel right about giving thirty grand a year to credit-card companies for the dubious honor of using their machines when he could instead give that money to a dishwasher. You'll get past the cash-and-check-only policy, too.

Clair de Lune may be small, but the food served here is bigger than the walls, the block, the neighborhood. It's big enough to feed anyone who understands how rare it is for a cook with Kelly's resume and skills to be touching every plate that comes out of the kitchen. To be sure, it's too small for a celebrity, so it's a good thing there aren't any here. There's just a cook—a great cook, with the hands to prove it.

# Monsieur Feret Builds His Neighborhood Dream House

by Eric Levin
from *Food Arts*

> The perils of the restaurant business are well-known, but all too easy to forget when the food is delicious, service welcoming, atmosphere serene. This in-depth feature from a leading restaurant industry magazine reminds us of the tightrope every restaurant owner walks.

To open or not to open, that was the question Philippe Feret was wrestling with as the sun set on one of the bleakest days in American history. Feret was standing in the dining room of his restaurant, Brasserie Julien, on Manhattan's residential Upper East Side. About eight miles south, on the opposite side of town, the World Trade Center lay in ruins, black smoke rising higher in the sky than the towers had stood only hours before.

A few of his employees had called and said they wouldn't be coming in. None of the day's deliveries had arrived, so the kitchen would have to make do with what was on hand. "Was it even appropriate to open?" Feret, a chef by training, and his wife, Cecilia, an MBA and marketing veteran who manages the business, asked each other. "If we do, will anyone show up?"

They looked up and down Third Avenue and saw that some of the other neighborhood restaurants were opening. They decided they would, too.

Later that evening, Feret experienced a kind of epiphany. The place was packed. People were greeting each other with outstretched arms, filling the 2,500-square-foot restaurant with hugs, tears, and stories. "Quite a few people had been in the towers that morning," says Feret, a forty-two year old French émigré. "It was an amazing scene. That night I truly felt like the mask had come down, and people had nothing to hide behind. I felt I had to make the restaurant even warmer and more welcoming."

In the coming months, Brasserie Julien would make itself even more of a home-away-from-home for its patrons. In so doing, it would illustrate a key post-9/11 truth: that in shaky times, the neighborhood place is the bedrock restaurant business in a big city like New York.

On Friday morning, September 14, Feret rented a Ryder truck and jockeyed snarky traffic to the outlying borough of Queens and his favorite store, Home Depot. He returned with fifteen gallons of paint, plus brushes, rollers, and drop cloths. Around 11:30 P.M., after saying good-night to his last customers, he started painting. He painted all night, put in his usual sixteen hour day on Saturday (asking patrons to excuse the half-painted room), then pulled another all-nighter.

When Brasserie Julien opened on Sunday night, the walls had changed from austere off-white to mustard, the ceiling from white to burgundy. The forty-eight hour marathon would have done in most people. But it was business as usual for the small, wiry, limitlessly energetic Feret, a one-time competitive weightlifter, motorcyclist, and skin diver who seems to get happier the harder he works.

A literal mom-and-pop operation, Brasserie Julien is named for the Ferets' son, Julien, who had just turned one year old when the restaurant opened. Now that he's four, he loves to play mini majordomo, looking up at bemused patrons and announcing, "Hi! I'm Julien. This is my restaurant!" At least, that is, until he is trundled off to a rear table for a simple dinner with sister Elena, eight, and their parents, often functioning in tag team mode.

At a time when the American Dream is being sorely tested, Philippe and Cecilia, the daughter of Colombian immigrants, and their chef, Christophe Lachavanne, who was born in Montreuil, France, are working fourteen or more hours a day to bring their own American Dream to life. In an era of big-budget restaurants, Brasserie Julien is a do-it-yourself phenomenon—an unlikely but winning mix of French tradition and Yankee ingenuity. Feret virtually built the place with his bare hands. While Feret hammers and Lachavanne chops, Cecilia works the phones and bangs out press releases as well as postcards and e-mails to customers for imaginative theme dinners and promotions. She also writes the folksy dish descriptions and designs and prints the menu on her desktop. Oh yes, and the Ferets run their high-end Allure Catering business out of the basement. "We don't have millions of dollars," says Lachavanne, "but we have millions of ideas."

The forty-eight hour paint job, in fact, was the least of the changes the team has made since the attacks. To hide the entrance to the kitchen, Feret designed and built a partition, a stunning wood-on-wood rendition of the art deco elevator doors of the Chrysler Building. On top of the partition sits a large ornamental clock—a French brasserie tradition. The clock doesn't draw a lot of double takes, but it should: it's set to Paris time. A Cecilia touch.

They also decided to soften and subdivide the dining room with semisheer burgundy curtains. Using flea market materials, Philippe soldered together pyramidal brass and stained-glass sconces for the walls. Not overlooking the utilitarian, the man whose friends call "the Home Depot chef" built a walk-in cooler in the basement, powered by a second-hand compressor. (Prior to 9/11, he had rebuilt the bar to make it more beckoning and installed three separate kitchens: for the restaurant, for pastry, and for catering.)

The best example of the Ferets' imagination and sweat equity are the two themed alcoves in the back of the restaurant, which have transformed former Siberias into hot spots. On the left, as you face the centered clock, is the mahogany paneled "Wine Cellar." It's really a wine wall—actually, three walls framing the back left corner of the room. On backlit bookcase shelves, rows of wine bottles stand side by side like toy soldiers. The presentation is as simple as it is alluring. Nestled in the space is a table seating up to eight, where winemaker dinners are served every Thursday night.

In the back right corner, Feret recently completed what he calls the "Chefs Family Table," under a dropped ceiling of illuminated stained-glass panels: In two seatings per night, Lachavanne presents a four course, prix-fixe family style menu averaging $45. "Sharing food helps bring people together," says Feret. "Brasseries were traditionally places where people went to entertain themselves when there weren't all the entertainment options you find today."

Surprisingly, Feret had little experience with power tools before 1995. The son of a pastry chef, he was born in Normandy, grew up in Paris, and arrived in this country fifteen years ago "with a hundred bucks in my pocket and a big dream." From his father he had learned baking and also the arcane art of sugar sculpture, which would become an attraction for Feret's catering clients. The dream was to own his own business rather than take over his father's bakery and restaurant.

In France he had earned his spurs cooking at the Michelin two-star restaurants Le Doyen and Maison Prunier and at the three-star Taillevent. At Prunier he had slaved over a hot stove—a giant charcoal-fired brute with a cooktop that would literally glow bright red. "It was like an old locomotive," Feret recalls. "It was impossible to regulate the heat. The quality of the charcoal, the weather—everything affected it. We moved the pots with long-handled forks; you couldn't get too close, it was so hot. There was no air conditioning, no exhaust system. It was a good experience."

In New York, Feret became banquet chef at Tavern on the Green and executive chef at the now-shuttered Maurice in the Hotel Parker Meridien. In 1994, he opened Cafe Centro for Restaurant Associates, and in 1996, under the late Joe Baum and

Michael Whiteman, reopened Windows on the World, which had been closed since the 1993 bombing of the World Trade Center.

His goal was to open his own place by the time he was forty. In 1995, to gain financial leverage, he and Cecilia bought a rundown seven room apartment on the Upper East Side. It cost $210,000, and he set about renovating it himself. "That was the only way I could afford to do it," he says.

It took him five years. He'd work late at night after fourteen hour days at Cafe Centro and later Windows. He became a shrewd scavenger, retrieving brass hardware and fixtures and hardwood doors from dumpsters outside big apartment buildings under renovation. In 1998, the apartment was valued at $640,000, and the Ferets refinanced, creating their restaurant nest egg.

The dream seemed to be on track, but it soon overheated like the stove at Prunier. In March 1997, when he was thirty-eight, Feret lost his job at Windows after the restaurant received a disappointing one-star review in the *New York Times*. At Windows, Feret had been a proponent of buffalo meat and, in various recipes, had made it a popular special. After leaving Windows, he teamed up with a man who had a buffalo marketing and distribution business. He thought they might open a restaurant together, but the relationship ended badly, with Feret claiming he was owed back commissions and expenses.

Despite a solid reputation, Feret found it difficult to attract investors. Landlords were equally hesitant. The reason? "I had never owned my own business before." The same boom market that made it possible to refinance his apartment for triple what he had paid put most desirable restaurant leases out of reach. In August 1998, the Ferets thought they had a deal to take over the lease of a struggling music-oriented night spot called La Folie, on Third Avenue between 79th and 80th Streets. But at the last minute, the lessee managed to come up with several months of overdue rent.

The search continued, and in September they leased a space on East 59th Street. It had been an Italian restaurant, but the Ferets decided to turn it into a brasserie and rename it Acacia. While the space was being gutted, they decided to run a lunchtime sandwich shop in the lobby of a residential building on East 57th Street. One month later, the landlord of the Third Avenue space called and told them things hadn't worked out with La Folie. "He said, 'The place is yours. Do you want it?' "

The Ferets agonized, then decided to try to run all three places. It was even crazier than that, because after the collapse of the buffalo venture, they started a game and fowl distributing business. This ended sourly, too, though they kept it going until spring 2002. They bowed out of Cafe Adriana, the sandwich shop, in March 1999.

Their adventure with La Folie began in late 1998, when they discovered that, apart from the live jazz, the place had nothing going for it—no dinner trade whatsoever. In his first fit of instant reinvention, Feret closed La Folie for two weeks, ridding it of its black ceiling and lugubrious drapery and painting the whole place shades of cream. In January 1999, the Ferets reopened it as Brasserie Julien.

Meanwhile, they were sinking piles of money into the transformation of Acacia, which finally opened in April. For the next two years, they desperately shuttled back and forth between the two restaurants. On the residential Upper East Side, lunch was a nonstarter, but Brasserie Julien quickly established a faithful dinner clientele. Acacia proved problematical from the start. Construction went $100,000 over budget, partly because the Ferets didn't realize how much work would be required to bring it up to New York City building codes. To bring in more cash, the Ferets started catering parties. By 2000, they were doing well enough with that to launch Allure Catering. Allure did Rupert Murdoch's seventieth birthday party as well as bashes for Mary Tyler Moore, the U.S. Navy, and the royal family of India.

But Acacia finally expired in spring 2001. "One thing they teach you in business school," Cecilia says, "is not to diversify too fast. We did. We wound up just skimming the surface of each business."

"It was like having a baby that's born sick and fighting seven days a week to keep it alive," says Feret, who estimates he and Cecilia lost $400,000 of their own money. "That's why at Brasserie Julien I'm doing everything myself. Last year we finally got to where we could put some money in the bank. That's when 9/11 happened."

Despite the stirring turnout on September 11, Brasserie Julien's receipts dropped 60 percent for the fourth quarter, compared to 2000. "Allure had thirty-six parties scheduled between September 11 and October 7," Feret says, "and not one of them happened. Another twenty parties were canceled between October 7 and December 31. In all, the cancellations cost us $500,000 in business."

Brasserie Julien is "a work in progress," Feret says. "As I go along, I decide what I want to do. Mostly my customers tell me." When some female patrons asked him if there was a way they could hang their purses while they sat at the bar, Feret put in small hooks underneath the bar lip. Lachavanne serves a mean three-cheese fondue Savoyarde, made with Chardonnay and kirsch. When the Ferets noticed a customer dipping grilled vegetables and charcuterie into the bubbly cheese, a light went on. Cecilia made it into a menu item.

The fondue is the perfect emblem of the Brasserie Julien style, which has reached a peak under Lachavanne, who has had extensive experience as a chef in France and in lower Manhattan. Lachavanne took over the kitchen three days after the attacks. Since then, his assured way with French comfort food has helped the Ferets make their brasserie even homier.

One of his best dishes is an appetizer of smoked Normandy herring. Forget your preconceptions about salty, vinegary herring. Lachavanne marinates the smoked fillets for at least ten days in canola oil, garlic, juniper berries, thyme, bay leaves, carrots, and onions. The dish is brought to the table in a large white oval tureen, along with crusty bread and a delicious creamy potato salad. At first, you wonder if there's been a mistake: there's enough for the whole table.

But it's no mistake—the sheer abundance is part of the power of the dish. The herring and vegetables, punctuated by the plump berries, lie submerged under the glistening surface of the clear canola oil. The flavors are so rich and the texture so silky that it's intoxicating—the essence of a traditional Norman dish.

Lavachanne first worked for Feret briefly at Allure in 1999. Before they met, they had each sworn they would never again work with anyone French. "Most French chefs have an ego bigger than the Eiffel Tower," says Feret. "They get upset first and think later." But they discovered they were two *pois* in a pod. After returning to France last spring to recuperate from a bicycle accident, Lachavanne took up the ladles at Brasserie Julien. Though they venerate tradition, both believe, as Feret says, in "cooking for the people who will eat the food." Feret had puzzled about American tastes for some time. "I wondered, 'Why is ketchup so popular in America?' It's because there's sugar in it. Americans have a sweet tooth."

Feret learned this lesson while developing recipes for Cafe Centro. He presented several salad dressings to the brass in blind tastings. The one with a hint of sugar got the nod. At Brasserie Julien, Lachavanne adds about a teaspoon per quart to his mustard/ lemon vinaigrette. Lamb shanks also get a touch of sugar. Feret understands that a New Yorker is generally a larger, hungrier being than a Parisian. "In France, you would never put a twelve-ounce steak on the plate. It's too big. Here, not only would you serve it, you have to specify the size on the menu. In France you don't even mention it. It's the same with lobsters."

When Feret was a chef at Cafe Centro and Windows on the World, he used to pride himself on "running things as if it were my own business." Three and a half years of nurturing Brasserie Julien have taught him that "I was completely wrong about that. I was getting a paycheck, no matter what. When I was looking for investors, it used to frustrate me that people would say, 'But have you ever run your own business?' Now I understand where they were coming from. If you want to have your own business, first learn to be a handyman."

And learn to hold your breath. As a skin diver during his twenties, Feret used to train with the French Army scuba club, though he wasn't in the army. "We did twenty meter dives off the coast of Brittany, in cold water, in total darkness," he says. "You had to hold your breath for three minutes."

Good training for running a restaurant.

# My Education in Cooking

by Judy Rodgers
from *The Zuni Café Cookbook*

The chef at San Francisco's successful Zuni Café is known for many things—roast chicken, Caesar salad, pickles and polentas and buttermilk mashed potatoes—so the real surprise of this handsome cookbook is not the mouthwatering recipes but her elegant and expansive writing style.

My education in cooking began unassumingly in 1973 with a delicious ham sandwich on chewy, day-old *pain de compagne,* a spoonful of very spicy mustard, tarragon-laced cornichons, and a few sweet, tender crayfish as an hors d'œuvre. Jean Troisgros chose the menu for us and prepared our little meal with enthusiasm, surprising to me at four in the morning after a flight from New York and a high-speed seven-hour drive from Paris to Roanne. It was actually our second ham sandwich of the night; our first was a nondescript effort on stale baguette that we left half-eaten in an all-night autoroute *resto-stop.* But I am sure the redundancy was no coincidence; Jean had it in mind to demonstrate how good such a sandwich could be, and his dark brown eyes twinkled when I finished and then reached for another slice of ham. We ate standing in his kitchen, which was dark and quiet and gave no hint of its legendary status, except for the rich aroma of a veal stock slowly reducing to demi-glace. This was my first meal in the best restaurant in France. I had the singular good fortune to spend the year that followed under Jean's wing, and in the embrace of his brother, Pierre, and their extended family and staff at their restaurant, Les Frères Troisgros.

Chefs weren't stars in 1973; *nouvelle cuisine* had not been pronounced, and "California Cuisine" had just been seeded. As a sixteen-year-old from Saint Louis, I had never taken an interest in cooking, and nearly everything I ate in Roanne was as unfamiliar as it was delicious. Happily, I was prodded by the neighbor at home who had arranged for my stay with his French friends, the Troisgros, to document everything I ate there. As a result, and with the brothers' blessing, I recorded recipes for every dish on the menu, and then some. Their focus on raw ingredients was relentless, and the attention they lavished on each detail of every preparation was as routine for them as it was revelatory for me. Hearing about the traditions surrounding each dish made each one more memorable. What had begun as a high school exchange student sojourn veered swiftly away from academics and toward *la cuisine*. Although I had not landed at a restaurant, much less Les Frères Troisgros, by any design, observing this routine became all-consuming. As soon as I got home from school, I headed for the kitchen to watch, listen, and take notes. Jean relished calling me Mata Hari, and he punctuated the accusation with a thrust of his meat fork, which was his favorite all-purpose kitchen tool. Having made the joke, Jean would return to the *piano* (the edge of the stove), pause, and then dispense a bit of culinary wisdom as he checked the doneness of a *côte de bœuf.*

"Do you see how this pan is *à taille* (the right size)? This is the first and most important thing to know. Always choose a pan that is the right size. Too small, and you crowd the meat and steam it; too large, and you burn the fat you are cooking in, and it's not so good for the pan either. This is why we have the *batterie de cuisine.*"

He turned to the array of copper casseroles, six to eighteen inches wide, hanging behind him. Jean could always explain cooking techniques in a practical and logical way.

Following this unplanned curriculum, I learned many of the lessons I still apply daily, although I never really cooked at Les Frères Troisgros. Timidity and respect for their *métier* held me back. I occasionally summoned the confidence to help sort through spinach leaves with a *commis* (beginning cook), or gingerly pluck a thrush before dropping it whole into a Robot-Coupe for their famous *mousse de grives,* but mostly I watched, and wrote. But if my hesitation cost me hands-on experience, Jean, Pierre, and their cooks compensated; they made sure I tasted as many dishes, as frequently, and in as many stages of preparation, as possible.

"It tastes different today, the cream, *n'est-ce pas?* You see? It's more acidic and thicker. We'll use less lemon in the sauce."

Or, "Taste this. Do you like it? It's a truffle. First of the year. But they'll get better."

Jean had just popped a whole truffle steamed over Sauternes in my mouth.

I watched Pierre measure portions of aged Charollais beef by eye, carve them with nonchalant precision, and then taste a sliver of the raw meat that clung to his knife. Always checking. A lesson I have never forgotten.

A parade of Troisgros devotees from a dozen countries passed through the kitchen that year and most confided to me that this was not the usual three-star restaurant. It was not just the best food, it was also the simplest and purest, and the restaurant the most convivial. The seasonality and regional character of the food, coupled with lack of pretension, brought clients back over and over. The most frequent diners were business people, purveyors, neighbors, fellow restaurateurs, and the local taxman, all of whom stopped in the kitchen for a visit before Jean or Pierre prepared a simple lunch for them "off-menu." *Les amis* dined on a plain dish—an omelette, half a roast chicken left from the *repas du personnel* (staff meal), or the signature Troisgros escalope of salmon, but without their legendary sorrel sauce—just perfect local salmon, barely cooked, strewn with freshly chopped herbs, and moistened with olive oil and lemon juice. These clients ate very, very well.

And I learned from *le Patron*, Jean-Baptiste Troisgros, Jean and Pierre's father. I shared some of my most memorable meals with him. A proud Burgundian, Jean-Baptiste was the patriarch of the house, who held court at table and struck a mix of fear and adoration in all who attended to him. The *Patron,* feisty at eighty-six, wore wire-rimmed glasses with dark gray lenses that enhanced his mystique tremendously. Although he could have anything he wanted, on or off the menu, Jean-Baptiste favored simple food and became utterly euphoric when presented with a carefully fried egg deglazed with sherry vinegar, flanked by *pain grillé* (toast), and followed by a salad of *pissenlits au lard* (dandelion greens and bacon). Likewise, he was never more irritated than when he thought a dish was even slightly overwrought, not honest or *"généreux."* Le Patron admonished me never to be taken in by *"cinéma dans la cuisine"*— akin to saying "food for show." His culinary edicts were always passionate, and I wrote all of them down.

The Troisgros *sœur,* Madeleine Troisgros Serraille, also did her part. At least twice a week she'd fetch me from her brothers' restaurant and calmly produce a perfect family meal in her own modest kitchen—a *blanquette de veau, pot-au-feu,* or *gratin de nouilles* (macaroni and cheese, sort of). I loved her *miroton,* a homey beef and onion casserole, based on the leftover *pot-au-feu* she had deliberately made too much of. Madeleine was a champion of the salad course and was rigorous about its seasonality—she was visibly thrilled to dress the first mâche or tender dandelion of the season. She loved every leafy thing you could eat *en salade*—escarole, frisée, watercress, endive, *roquette* (arugula), Batavia or butter lettuce—and had a knack for choosing one or two nonleafy things—nuts, or croûtons, or hard-cooked egg—that made the salad more satisfying. Every leaf was in impeccable condition, and the ritual of dressing it at table was an important moment in every meal. There was never a leaf left over. Then, before clearing the salad plates,

Madeleine served the cheese. This course, never omitted, consisted of a few perfect cheeses, always in season, and just right for the dishes that had preceded—whether a local goat cheese, the regional Fourme d'Ambert, or a chunk of Beaufort she had brought back from the Alps. She never offered too many choices, lest they compete or clash or overwhelm. She tended to sample only one herself, knowing which was the best that day. Madeleine fashioned perfect meals; beyond being generous in flavor and tradition, there was a balance and focus to the menu: everything complemented everything else in an uncanny way. And there was always a simple dish with the *goût du revenez-y*—"the taste you return to" for another nibble that prolongs the meal. Her cooking never demanded your attention, it simply kindled conviviality.

Within a very few months, I had succumbed to the philosophy that guides Zuni cooking today. While growing international attention swirled around the more glamorous three-star restaurants, and parades of gastronomic pilgrims clamored after the fanciest, cleverest, and most exclusive truffle, lobster, and foie gras dishes incorporating exotic fruits and Japanese garnishes, I was taking thorough notes on how Michel made *hachis parmentier* (shepherd's pie *à la française)* for the staff meal. Or I was heading for the slightly drab but friendly café up the street with Jean on his night off for a hanger steak and perfect *pommes frites.* My mentor always congratulated the café owner on the delicious *bifteck* and insisted this was as good a meal as any, lest one think classical or *nouvelle cuisine* could challenge the virtues of simplicity. There was surely a place for creative new restaurant cooking, and even for classical cuisine, but it wasn't for every day. And Jean constantly reminded me that the food we eat every day ought to be taken just as seriously. It deserved to be just as well prepared, and just as celebrated.

# Le Plaza Athênée

by Jacques Pépin

from *The Apprentice*

For a man who didn't even learn English until his 20s, Pépin writes engagingly and well. He tells his story—how a provincial lad trained in traditional French kitchens became one of America's most popular TV cooking teachers—with a minimum of vanity and a great eye for detail.

I had come a long way. Or so I had thought until I presented myself to Lucien Diat, the executive chef at Le Plaza Athénée. Instantly, I reverted to that cringing boy who had come to Le Grand Hôtel de L'Europe in short pants.

"Presented myself" is not totally correct. No one presented himself to M. Diat. It would be more accurate to say that I was granted a brief audience before the Great Man (whose brother, incidentally, was Louis Diat, the famous chef at the Ritz-Carlton in New York). Enthroned in his glass-walled office above the kitchen, M. Diat—always Monsieur, never, ever Chef—received the documents I had been given at the Société in the dismissive manner of a king accepting the credentials of yet another ambassador from a small, inconsequential principality.

"You will be second *commis*," he proclaimed. "Get dressed and go to the *garde-manger*."

Once again, I found myself near the bottom of a kitchen hierarchy.

But this was a kitchen unlike any I'd worked in or ever would work in again. I felt like some kid from the minors finally striding out onto the turf of Yankee Stadium. No doubt about it, I was playing in the Big Leagues. Le Plaza Athénée had—and, now run by Alain Ducasse, still has—one of the very finest dining rooms in the world. To serve two hundred meals a day, the hotel employed forty-eight full-time chefs, four times the number of us who had served the same number of customers in Aix-les-Bains. M. Diat organized his kitchen in a rigidly structured brigade. Below M. Diat was the sous-chef, also called *l'aboyeur* (the barker), because his job was literally to bark out orders over the intercom system. Below that were ten *chefs de partie,* each in charge of a separate area such as sauces, the cold department, fish cooking, roast and grill, vegetables, and soup. There was a night chef, a turning chef to replace people who were off and another to fill in for any *chef de partie* on vacation, a *chef de partie* for the afternoon, and a chef in charge of the pastry department. Below each *chef de partie* was a first *commis;* below each first *commis* a second *commis,* and in some departments, third *commis* trainees.

At Le Plaza, the first *commis* were between twenty and thirty years old, and the *chefs de partie* between thirty and sixty years of age. Diat's machinelike brigade worked according to very strict and well-defined laws. The *chefs de partie* had their own dining room and locker room with showers. We *commis* had our own place to change, shower, and eat, and even there, the first *commis* dined on one side of the table, we second *commis* on the other.

Each of us stayed at one job until we had mastered it. Then, once we performed to M. Diat's satisfaction, which is to say flawlessly in even the most minute detail, we'd get moved to another department to start all over again. When a cook had made the rounds of all stations as a second *commis,* he would move through all the stations as a first *commis.* The result was a staff that had tremendous depth. A *commis* in the *garde-manger* knew exactly how to trim a veal chop because he had also spent months working at the elbow of a grill chef who would discard any cuts of meat less than perfectly trimmed. But bad cuts never reached the grill chef because the *commis* working the grill had also worked in the *garde-manger* and could whip out a knife and fix any problems on the spot.

During my stay at Le Meurice, none of the sixteen cooks had ever changed jobs. Unless someone had died or retired, I would have been the *commis* in Le Meurice's vegetable department forever. By contrast, M. Diat's style of management was more representative of the traditional French *brigade de cuisine,* and it was diametrically opposite to what often happens in kitchens now in restaurants in the United States, where the emphasis is on specialization. Today the idea is to take someone, often an immigrant from Latin America, and train him or her to do one specific task. And that's it. The person may know nothing else about cooking, but nobody will be able to touch him or her at that job, be it turning a carrot or grilling a hanger steak.

One thing that we were absolutely denied at Le Plaza was any room for what today would be called self-expression, though none of us would have thought of using that New Age term. All of our efforts were directed toward performing individual tasks in the precise manner of the house. There were no recipes or written procedures. Working beside M. Raimo, the *chef poissonnier* (fish cook), I watched his every move while making sure all the ingredients and utensils were at the ready a half-second before his hand shot out for them; I anticipated his moves with the foresight of an operating room nurse. After a time, the chef let me try my hand at a garnish. Finally, on a busy day, he had me cook. I imitated everything I'd ever seen him do, producing a fillet of sole that had the look, smell, and taste that only the sole at Le Plaza Athênée had. Not better than Maxim's or Le Meurice's, but as good as theirs and distinct from any other sole anywhere. Perfection was when a diner had no idea who was "cooking tonight" or had no occasion to ask such a question. Be it Jacques Pépin or any of twenty other *commis,* the sole would taste exactly the same every time. Ours was not the flash of star chefs. It was the toil of the many.

Every day as meal service began, M. Diat emerged from his office and descended upon the kitchen. Even if I was in the walk-in fridge, I would know the moment he entered because the noise level dropped by half. He crossed the room and stationed himself at the pass, the counter where chefs put plates for pickup by waiters. Not a single dish left the kitchen without passing through M. Diat's hands and receiving his blessing.

Lord help the poor cook whose work didn't meet M. Diat's standards—something that very rarely happened.

"What is this?" M. Diat would say, his voice never rising above conversational tones. "Put this back in the oven."

Or: "Present this platter again."

Then there was his *look,* a look that will recur in my nightmares as long as I live, not so much a look of anger as one of disdain, a gaze that lasted but a fraction of a second, yet made it clear that your pathetic little error was far beneath the level of his contempt. Quaver in the glare of those pale gray eyes, and you never made the same mistake again.

And if you did, there was The List. I first encountered The List one morning when I reported to work and came across a scrum of my fellow *commis* jostling for a glance at a piece of paper thumb-tacked to the wall. They were like schoolboys, and Teacher had obviously posted the results of final exams. Some of my coworkers left with their heads down, shrugging off their disappointment by saying, "It's okay. Maybe next time." Some strutted off with smiles. Most merely sighed with relief.

The List outlined our assignments for the next six months. Whether we had risen to a more prestigious station, fallen to one not so desirable, or stayed in place was the only way to tell if we were doing a good job. No one, certainly not M. Diat, would have dreamed of paying a direct compliment.

• • •

"Bone it out."

So much for the orientation session to my new post at Le Plaza Athénée's *garde-manger.*

The *chef de partie,* Chef Berutti, pointed to a leg of veal flopped over a butcher-block table. The appendage looked as if it had been hacked off the back end of a calf only moments before and hastily skinned for my benefit. Otherwise, it was still pretty much in working order.

My new boss's instructions, while explicit, were hardly detailed. I realized that the veal leg represented his version of a test. Pass, and he would know whether he could trust me. Flunk, and . . . well . . . Le Plaza did have those third *commis* positions.

It had been a long time since I had boned a leg of veal. Working from faded memories dating back to my apprentice-ship, I separated the leg into different muscles: top round, bottom round, top knuckle, top sirloin, and shank. I then trimmed each of these cuts. It was an exacting process. Affecting a false non-chalance that I was far from feeling, I concentrated on the job and finished it to his liking.

In the *garde-manger* at Le Plaza, I was exposed to esoteric, expensive, and often unusual foods: exotic fruits like papaya, mango, and cherimoya. But the strangest of all arrived one morning in a basket from Hédiard, a fancy specialty store. Chef Berutti placed the basket in the walk-in fridge and kept it under constant guard.

"What are those fruits Chef is so worked up about?" I asked another *commis.*

"*Des poires avocat,*" he replied. "Avocado pears."

I had a weak spot for pears. I adored all varieties: Comice pears, Anjou pears, Bartlett pears. To be watched over so carefully by Chef, a *poire avocat* must have been the ne plus ultra of peardom. I was dying to sink my teeth into one.

The opportunity presented itself the next time I found myself alone in the walk-in cooler. I glanced around for Chef. Not seeing him, I snatched the largest and juiciest-looking pear, polished it briefly on my jacket, and vigorously bit it. My teeth penetrated thick, leathery skin and stopped jarringly upon contact with something hard and slime-covered. I drew back, surprised and queasy. How could people eat these pears? Notwithstanding the skin and the pit, the flesh itself was oily, mushy, not at all sweet.

Avocado misadventures aside, I must have been performing satisfactorily because when M. Diat next posted The List he had promoted me to the rank of second *commis* at the grilling and roasting station, where I came under the tutelage of Chef Duclos, whose motto was a quotation from Jean-Anthelme Brillat-Savarin: "*On devient cuisinier mats on naît rotisseur*" (One can become a cook, but one has to be born a roast cook).

Chef Duclos was certainly born to his calling. Unlike most of the cooks in M. Diat's kitchen, who, contrary to stereotype, were trim and wiry, Chef Duclos was a short, almost perfectly round gent. He looked as if he had spent his life feasting on fat roasted capons and juicy racks of lamb. Despite his girth, Chef Duclos worked with the grace and artistry of a professional dancer. Dainty sliding steps, delicate twirls, deft arm motions—his every movement was orchestrated, economical, beautiful to the eye. He could put in an entire shift without moving his tiny feet outside the same two-foot circle. To accomplish this, his *mise-en-place* was arranged in a strict order with no variation whatsoever. If he had been suddenly struck blind, Chef Duclos would have been able to continue working by feel alone. The *beurre maître d'hôtel,* butter for use on steak, always rested just above his cutting board on the right corner, next to the watercress in ice water. His chopping knife lay on the right side of the board, with his spatula, fork, and paring knife on the other side. It was amazing to see him work; calm, deliberate, confident, precise, there was not one gesture lost, not one extra movement.

Chef Duclos prepared the best roast chicken I had ever tasted. He started with fine birds from my native Bresse region, chickens that had been allowed to run outside in the sunshine, flapping their wings, scratching for seeds and insects. Bresse chickens had firm-textured flesh with pronounced differences between dark and white meat and the slightly gamey taste that is true chicken flavor. The skin was crunchy, buttery, salty, and nutty. Chef let the best qualities of his chicken come through, seasoning it with nothing more than salt, pepper, and butter, cooking it to order in a very hot oven, basting every ten minutes or so. There was no magic in Chef Duclos's chicken. What made his chicken the best was the perfection of every small step. The best chicken and butter. A searingly hot oven. Just the right amount of carefully made stock. Removing the bird from the oven the second it was cooked.

To serve his chicken, Chef Duclos took the copper saucepan (there were only copper and cast-iron saucepans in Le Plaza's kitchen) from the oven, placed it on the edge of the stove, and transferred the chicken to a hot silver tray that he had grabbed from a shelf behind him, without looking. With one hand, he poured the fat out of the saucepan, added some white wine and brown chicken stock to the pan with the other hand, put it back on the stove for a few minutes to reduce the liquid, and then strained it into a sauceboat. He did this in one fluid motion in just a few seconds, without stepping to the left or right. Simultaneously, he closed the oven door with the toe of one shoe, blindly plucked a handful of watercress from behind him, and arranged it next to the chicken on the tray. Still without moving forward or backward, he took a tablespoon of butter and dropped it into a hot saucepan. When it had turned a hazelnut color, he poured it over the finished bird, then pivoted on his two feet. Holding his plated chicken in one hand, he grabbed the sauceboat in his other and placed them on the pass at the pickup station, where M. Diat awaited to render judgment.

Chef Duclos and I prepared a great deal of Dover sole and *loup de mer,* a type of striped bass, always over intense heat. We seasoned each piece with salt, pepper, and a dash of peanut oil, then marked it with an exact *quadrillage,* perfect cross-hatched grill lines. We removed the fish after a minute or two, brushed it with melted butter, and finished it in a hot oven. The result had a taste of charcoal yet was never dry or overcooked. In addition to the fish, we grilled lobster and langouste (spiny lobster) and flavored them with herb butter. However, it was the adjacent grill, where the meat was cooked, that was the busiest. *Entrecôte minute* (a thin slice of beef sirloin), filet mignon, *poussin* (a tiny, young chicken), and veal or lamb kidneys—each had to be grilled perfectly in its own time and with a specific intensity of heat.

The veal chops of Chef Duclos were nothing short of perfection. First he seared and marked them on both sides on the grill. Then he browned each one of the four edges, keeping the chop upright by leaning it against a chunk of raw potato, cut so its bottom could be wedged between the bars of the grill.

One of the most important things I learned from working with Chef Duclos was how to deal with the orders as they came in. There were no rules; each cook developed his or her own system. The orders arrived in groups, and as the sous-chef barked them out, the workers in each section had to register and remember their roles in the respective dishes. There could be no mistakes. When the waiter was ready to pick up a dish, it had to be ready or it would set back the table and, with a trickle-down effect, mess up the whole kitchen and dining room.

"Two trout, rack of lamb, chicken," the sous-chef announced. Immediately, two dozen cooks took note. In the vegetable department someone started the appropriate side dishes. A *commis* in the *garde-manger* cleaned the fish, trimmed the lamb, selected a chicken, and ran them to the appropriate stations, sliding for the last ten or fifteen feet across the sawdust-strewn floor. *Sauciers* corrected the individual sauces needed. It was organized chaos, but somehow synchronized. That table's orders, involving dozens of individual tasks, would arrive at the pass at the same instant, all perfectly prepared. I loved it. I felt invincible. Often, in the middle of lunch or dinner, the ordering, the cooking, and the plating of food became so rushed and so frantic that it gave me a high. Barked orders imprinted themselves in my brain automatically, even if I was simultaneously plating one dish while sautéing food for another. As the orders came in, I set out reminders for myself, an empty skillet on the stove, a clean plate in the middle of the cutting board, or a piece of parchment paper on the table, some memory jogger to tell me that I had a trout with almond to put in that skillet in a half hour, that a pilaf of rice and mussels was to go on that plate, and that the parchment paper was to become a papillote, or paper casing, for a veal chop that I'd have to start preparing ten minutes before the trout in order for the dishes to come out at precisely the same time.

Somehow, a year passed. The List appeared, and I found opposite my name the words "first *commis*." If a second *commis* is the buck private of a kitchen brigade, a first *commis* is more like a lieutenant, someone who has survived a few battles, who remains calm under fire, and who has earned a measure of trust. Before my second year was out, I had attained what was considered the ultimate first *commis* posting: the sauce. To be considered a great *saucier* was the highest accolade a cook could receive. The subtlety, intricacy, and lightness of a sauce could make a dish.

Stock is the basic ingredient of most sauces, and stock was critically important at Le Plaza's sauce station. Back in Bourg-en-Bresse, the only stocks Chef Jauget used were brown and white chicken stocks. For the brown stock, the chicken bones were roasted to a brown color in the oven before they were tossed into the stockpot, whereas for a white stock the roasting was omitted. In addition to these, we made white veal stock, white fish stock, and white beef stock for consommé at Le Plaza. Sometimes we reduced the white fish stock, usually made from sole, to a syrup to make an essence, or *glace,* to finish sauces for fish. We made brown lamb stock and brown veal stock that we reduced by half and lightly thickened for a *demi-glace*. The *demi-glace* had no salt and was basically fatless and fairly mild, so it was perfectly adaptable to various dishes. It took on the taste of a *bordelaise* with a reduction of red wine; of a *périgueux* with truffles and Madeira; or a *chasseur* with tomatoes, white wine, and tarragon.

A slight variation in seasoning, viscosity, reduction, or cooking time could make the difference between an average and a superlative sauce. Some sauces, such as veal and chicken velouté and béchamel, had to be cooked slowly for two to three hours to stabilize them so they would not break down when used to finish specific dishes. If a reduced veal stock had achieved the right taste and color but its consistency was still a shade thin, it was pulled off the fire and thickened with arrowroot so that it did not become too potent and had the proper consistency.

These stocks and sauces played an indispensable role in every dish, either as a thickener or as a flavoring agent. For example, creamed spinach, fresh spinach sautéed in butter and seasoned with nutmeg, salt, and pepper, with cream added, was brought to the right consistency with a tablespoon of precooked béchamel. A seemingly simple dish such as fillet of sole cooked with white wine and shallots might require three sauces: a fish velouté to give it the proper texture, a fish *glace,* a dash of hollandaise, and sometimes, a bit of whipped cream, if the fish was to be glazed under the broiler. There was a strict order to follow, but within that structure the talent of the chef could come through.

After we had boiled the beef and poultry bones long enough to be strained for stock—twelve hours—we would re-wet them, a technique called *remouillage*. We then simmered them again for another five to six hours. We strained the second liquid through the finest *chinois* (strainer), then reduced it to make a *glace de viande*. The *glace* was the color of caramel and had the consistency of heavy syrup when hot but was hard as a block of rubber when cold. Like the demi-glace, it had no salt and no fat, but it was very potent. It had transcended the level of a sauce and become a flavoring agent. The *glace* was the secret weapon of the cooks, an alchemist's gold that would transform an ordinary veal chop into three-star fare.

As first *commis* in the sauce department, I had the responsibility of producing the *glace de viande*. I inevitably made too much for the needs of the house, and I sold the extra to caterers in les Halles, sharing the profit with the *chef saucier*. This was an accepted part of kitchen tradition—a special bonus for the all-important *saucier* and his lieutenant.

# Boulangerie Poilâne

## by Dorie Greenspan
from *Paris Sweets*

In a culinary life split between Paris and
New York, writer Greenspan has collabo-
rated with such star chefs as Daniel Boulud
and Pierre Hermes. In this charming book
she shares recipes from top Parisian pastry
chefs, including this endearing sketch of a
master who died this year.

Walk anywhere in Paris, and you'll see small signs hung in
café windows that say, *"Ici, pain Poilâne."* "Here, we
serve Poilâne bread." It is a point of pride to serve large slices of
this traditional rustic bread hewn from distinctive grand rounds,
which are correctly named *miches* but have for decades gone by
the name *pain Poilâne,* to honor their maker. While you can find
*pain Poilâne* in Parisian cafés and supermarkets, it is always worth
the journey to go to the boulangerie on rue du Cherche-Midi.

The shop, established in 1932 by Pierre Poilâne, a first-generation
baker, and now—and for many years—under the dedicated propri-
etorship of his son, Lionel, is storybook perfect. The front room,
lined with wooden bread racks and filled with the alluring scent of
flour and yeast, is a study in browns, each shade a hue found in a loaf
of bread. The shop is so beautiful that you might not notice the
small back room, an office of sorts. Ask if you can peek, and you'll
find it is covered from floor to ceiling with paintings and drawings,

each in a different style, but all on the same subject: bread. The first canvas came from a customer, an artist, who paid off his bread bill with a painting. Soon others followed. It is an eclectic collection, topped off, literally, by a chandelier crafted in bread, made for the surrealist Salvador Dalí.

But the heart of the boulangerie is in the vaulted basement, where the breads are fashioned by hand, raised in linen-lined baskets, and baked in the wood-fired brick oven. There is something magical about the space, the heat from the oven, the aroma from the dough, the coolness from the stone walls, and the cloistering embrace of the low arched ceiling.

I remember, with great clarity, the first time, fifteen years ago, that I followed Lionel Poilâne down the worn stone steps to see this centuries-old bakery. That day, M. Poilâne, who is scholarly, encyclopedic, poetic, and passionate on the subject of bread, recounted his beginnings as a baker.

When he was fourteen years old, his father had brought him to the boulangerie and said, "Now you will begin your apprenticeship." The youngster, small and thin, artistic and creative, had known for years that this would be his life, but it was only when it became real that it became unimaginable. "I used to bury myself in the bags of flour in that corner," he said, pointing to where the flour is still kept today, "and cry, trying to keep my sobs from being heard. I did not want to be a baker. I did not want to live underground. I could not bear the thought that this would be my lot for years to come." Then, one day, the young Poilâne had an epiphany. He said, "I opened the oven door, looked into the red-hot hearth, and thought, 'This will either be the door to my prison or the door to the world.'" Anyone who knows that *pain Poilâne* is a household word throughout France and that Lionel Poilâne has established bakeries in Tokyo and London, as well as outlets in the United States, knows what that oven door became.

Considering how devoted Lionel Poilâne is to bread, it borders on surprising to find sweets for sale in his shop. What is not

surprising is that the sweets—there are only three: flan, apple
tartlets, and butter cookies called Punitions—are as exquisitely
made as his bread. But then, who would expect anything less from
a perfectionist?

## Punishments / Punitions
(Adapted from Boulangerie Poilâne)

*Makes about 50 cookies*

*Anyone who's ever been to world-renowned bread baker Lionel Poilâne's
boulangerie on rue du Cherche-Midi remembers the experience for many
reasons, not the least among them the sweet little butter cookies that are
there for the taking when you reach the counter. The cookies, piled in a
basket and replenished who knows how many times a day, are small and
round, with rickrack edges, a pale butter color, and a deep butter flavor. To
me, they have always been Proustian: I eat one and immediately remember
the butter cookies my maternal grandmother baked every Friday. Given the
memories these cookies conjured up for me, I should have guessed that they
are, in fact, grandmother cookies. As M. Poilâne explained to me, these
plain butter cookies had a special name among the grandmothers who made
them in Normandy, his birthplace. There, they were called* "punitions," *or
punishments, and, as Poilâne tells the story, Norman grannies would tuck
these sweet cookies behind their backs and, with a smile and a slight tease
in their voices, invite the little ones to come take their punishment. Need-
less to say, the lucky kids never had to be asked twice.*

*When Lionel Poilâne made these cookies for me in the basement of his
shop, he mixed the dough by hand in the time-honored way. He poured the
flour onto the marble counter and constructed a wall of flour encircling an
empty space, "the fountain," as bakers call it. The sugar went into the fountain, then a small circle of space was created in the center of the sugar, and
in went the egg. Using the tips of his fingers, and making sure to keep the
flour barrier intact, M. Poilâne worked the sugar and egg together until
they were light and smooth. Then he put the butter on the sugar and egg
and began working it, too, into the dough, squeezing it in his hand and*

*massaging it into the sweetened egg. Finally, working with the lightest touch, he began bringing the flour into the dough, taking a little of the flour from the inner edge of the fountain's walls and working his way out until all the flour was incorporated and the dough just this side of blended. Watching the dough come together was a lesson in deftness and an opportunity to see forty years of experience compressed into three minutes of work.*

*For sheer sensuality, nothing matches making dough by hand, but you can make a perfect dough for these cookies in a food processor. In fact, because the machine works so quickly, it is ideal—use the pulse mechanism and keep your eye on the dough's progress, and you'll achieve the quintessential sandy texture that is the hallmark of these plain cookies.*

1¼ sticks (5 ounces; 140 grams) unsalted butter, at room temperature
Slightly rounded ½ cup (125 grams) sugar
1 large egg, at room temperature
2 cups (280 grams) all-purpose flour

1. Put the butter in the work bowl of a food processor fitted with the metal blade and process, scraping down the sides of the bowl as needed, until the butter is smooth. Add the sugar and process and scrape until thoroughly blended into the butter. Add the egg and continue to process, scraping the bowl as needed, until the mixture is smooth and satiny. Add the flour all at once, then pulse 10 to 15 times, until the dough forms clumps and curds and looks like streusel.

2. Turn the dough out onto a work surface and gather it into a ball. Divide the ball in half, shape each half into a disk, and wrap the disks in plastic. If you have the time, chill the disks until they are firm, about 4 hours. If you're in a hurry, you can roll the dough out immediately; it will be a little stickier, but fine. *(The dough can be wrapped airtight and refrigerated for up to 4 days or frozen for up to 1 month.)*

3. Position the racks to divide the oven into thirds and preheat

the oven to 350°F (180°C). Line two baking sheets with parchment paper.

4. Working with one disk at a time, roll the dough out on a lightly floured surface until it is between ⅛ and ¼ inch (4 and 7 mm) thick. Using a 1½-inch (4-cm) round cookie cutter, cut out as many cookies as you can and place them on the lined sheets, leaving about 1 inch (2.5 cm) space between them. (You can gather the scraps into a disk and chill them, then roll, cut, and bake them later.)

5. Bake the cookies for 8 to 10 minutes, or until they are set but still pale. (If some of the cookies are thinner than others, the thin ones may brown around the edges. M. Poilâne would approve. He'd tell you the spots of color here and there show they are made by hand.) Transfer the cookies to cooling racks to cool to room temperature.

KEEPING: The cookies can be kept in a tin at room temperature for about 5 days or wrapped airtight and frozen for up to 1 month.

AN AMERICAN IN PARIS: To make these cookies even more like my grandmother's, I sometimes brush each cut-out cookie with a little egg wash (1 egg beaten with 1 teaspoon cold water), then sprinkle the tops with sugar, cinnamon sugar, or poppy seeds before baking.

# Personal Tastes

# Hamburger Rules

by Colman Andrews

from *Saveur*

As editor-in-chief of the glossy *Saveur,* Andrews has a highly refined palate, educated by decades of eating very well indeed. And yet, when it comes right down to it, he isn't afraid to declare himself a fan of one of America's simplest and most essential dishes.

I take a bite, and a world of flavors and textures reveals itself: the animal saltiness of well-seasoned, moist ground beef, its abundant juices soaking into the soft, sweet white flesh of the flour-dusted roll; the sourness of the vaguely chewy melted sharp cheddar; the crisp, saline, smoky authority of well-cooked bacon; the faint crunch of a cool iceberg lettuce leaf turned translucent by the warmth of the meat and cheese.

I am bewitched, seduced, transported. I am satisfied even before I have begun to digest. At times like this, I am quite prepared to propose the perfectly constructed bacon cheeseburger as proof of the existence of God.

I love hamburgers. When it comes to this variously enhanced, definitively American (but unquestionably universal) sandwich I am a true believer. I would rather eat a burger than a hot dog, a pizza, or a chunk of chocolate cake. I would rather eat a burger than a T-bone. If I were told that I had to give up either hamburgers or foie gras for the rest of my life, I'd swear off that fattened poultry liver so fast you wouldn't see my lips move. And if I were then told that I had to give up hamburgers anyway, I do believe I'd get old Doc Kevorkian on the line. They will pry this burger from my cold, dead fingers.

A culinary psychotherapist (and if there isn't such a beast, I'm sure one will pop up soon, probably on the Food Network—Frasier meets Emeril) would no doubt find evidence of arrested development, of *nostalgie de* baby-food, in my predilection for ground-up protein—which extends far beyond the hamburger and its cousin meat loaf, incidentally, to encompass sausages of every description, pâtés and rillettes, chicken croquettes, even fish cakes . . . Let them think what they want.

I mean, I've got perfectly good teeth and enjoy applying them to sirloin steaks and lamb chops and baby back ribs as much as the next carnivore. But there is something about meat or fowl or fish that has been ground or finely chopped or shredded, then properly seasoned and correctly cooked, that appeals to me immediately and viscerally, that gladdens my heart, that connects me with neither artifice nor irony to the sheer pleasure of eating.

A hamburger is literally a person or thing from the city of Hamburg, the great northern German port that was part of the Hanseatic League in medieval times. What this Teutonic municipality has to do with Big Macs and Whoppers is a subject of much speculation, some of it quite silly. The Hamburg New Media Association even devotes several pages of its website to the question. Like many other would-be authorities on the subject, the New Media folks trace the burger's beginnings back to the Tartar hordes who swept out of Central Asia about 750 years ago, supposedly riding across the steppes with slabs of raw animal flesh lodged between their saddles and their mounts. The meat was thus tenderized, it is said, and when the Tartars stopped for the night, they'd simply chop the meat up and dig in. (Think steak tartare.) How and why some saddle-softened Central Asian warriors' fodder became a "Russian delicacy" (as those New Media Hamburgers call it) in Hamburg and eventually found its way to America with a Hamburg provenance attached is not revealed.

"Hamburger steak" first appeared on an American menu as early as 1834, at Delmonico's in New York City—but the precise nature of the dish is unclear. The recipe for "beefsteak, Hamburg style" offered by Charles Ranhofer, former chef of Delmonico's, in his book *The Epicurean* (1893) is a mélange of chopped beef tenderloin and suet and chopped onions fried in butter, seasoned with salt, pepper, and nutmeg, shaped into four-ounce balls, flattened, rolled in bread crumbs, fried in butter, and served with "a good thickened gravy"—not exactly the burger as we know it today. Neither was Fannie Farmer's version. The recipe, generally credited as the first ever published, for "hamburg steaks" in her *Boston Cooking-School Cook Book* (1891) called for chopped lean beef, salt and pepper, and onion juice or chopped shallots, with a slightly beaten egg and "a few gratings of nutmeg" as optional additions.

Slightly earlier, circa 1888, James Henry Salisbury, a British physician, proposed simply seasoned ground beef, eaten three times a day, as a specific against anemia, colitis, tuberculosis, and other ailments. (Much later, *Salisbury steak* came to mean a fancified ground beef patty, often oval in shape, served without a bun but usually with a brown sauce or at least a sprinkling of parsley in upscale American or "Continental" restaurants.)

The good people of Seymour, Wisconsin, about twenty miles west of Green Bay, meanwhile, believe fervently that the hamburger was invented in 1885 by local son Charlie Nagreen, who is said to have improvised it at the Outagamie County Fair by flattening a meatball and sticking it between two slices of bread for his customers to eat while walking around the fairgrounds. Other claimants to the burger's paternity include Frank Menches of Akron, Ohio, (1892); Louis Lassen of Louis' Lunch in New Haven,

Connecticut, (1900); and Fletch "Old Dave" Davis of Athens, Texas, who took his burger to the 1904 Louisiana Purchase Exhibition in St. Louis, where it gained wide exposure.

No one can say for sure when or where the classic modern-style burger on a bun first appeared, with its traditional garnish of tomato slice, lettuce leaf, and sometimes onion, sometimes cheese. Its rise in popularity did seem to mirror that of the automobile, though, for it was the perfect "fast food"—quick to cook and easy to eat. You could even hold it to your mouth with one hand while keeping the other hand on the steering wheel. It is hardly accidental that many early burger joints were drive-ins.

The first nationwide burger chain was White Castle, which was founded in 1921 in Wichita, Kansas. Wimpy's (inspired by a burger-loving character in the "Popeye" cartoons), Bob's Big Boy, Steak n Shake, and A&W, among others, followed. Then one day in 1954, Ray Kroc, a Chicago-based milk-shake-machine salesman, visited a preternaturally bustling fast-food joint run by brothers Maurice and Richard McDonald in San Bernardino, California. The next thing anybody knew, he owned the name and the concept, and McDonald's had sold something like 90 gazillion burgers all over the world and changed forever our culture, our eating habits, and for that matter our burger.

I can't pretend to remember my first hamburger, but I almost certainly encountered it as a youngster at a drugstore lunch counter in Southern California, where it was almost certainly served on a sesame bun, in an oval wicker basket lined with waxed paper, nestled against a heap of french fries. I suspect that I was hooked immediately. Like so many children, though, I was a picky eater and wanted nothing but cheese on my patty—no lettuce or tomatoes, no pickles or onions, no mustard or ketchup or relish. I gradually came to appreciate lettuce, tomatoes, and onions (especially fried or grilled), but to this day I avoid pickles (their mocking pungent sweetness overpowers everything else), and I am alone among my friends and coworkers, I think, in eschewing all condiments. The purity of the undressed burger, with its elemental, guileless counterpoint of flavors and textures, is to me a thing of beauty.

Of course, just as everybody has a favorite burger joint—loyalty to such regional chains as Corpus Christi's Whataburger or Southern California's In-N-Out Burger, not to mention such local treasures as Hut's in Austin, Corner Bistro in Manhattan, Zip's in Cincinnati, Dick's Drive-In in Seattle, and suchlike, can be as passionate as football fandom—it's also true that just about everybody orders, or makes, burgers his or her own way.

The hamburger is very nearly a blank canvas—a lunch-tabula rasa. About the only absolute essential is a patty of cooked ground beef ("burgers" made of ground turkey or salmon or stuff like that are nothing but sorry imitations, imperfect metaphors, like "margaritas" made with wine or "pizza" topped with ersatz cheese), and even the patty admits some variation: things may be added to the meat—egg, bread crumbs, cheese, butter, parsley, onion, Tabasco, Worcestershire sauce, whatever; it may be seasoned with just salt and pepper or with soy sauce, lemon or lime juice, paprika, red pepper, and/or a number of other things; it may be small and thin in shape or broad and plump or anything in between; it may be fried, grilled, broiled, even boiled.

Then there's the question of the bun: slightly spongy, golden-brown-top classic (the prototype of which was supposedly invented in 1916), with or without sesame seeds? potato roll? kaiser roll? Portuguese roll? sourdough toast? rye toast (as in the great Southern California coffee-shop classic the patty melt)? english muffin (don't laugh; there are people who swear by it)? And the literally scores of possible garnishes—not just the traditional ones, but anything from bacon to arugula, sauerkraut to chili (as in another SoCal specialty, the open-face chili size)—and the countless jarred or bottled sauces or relishes. And the cheese, whether american, cheddar, swiss, jack, chévre, blue, or . . . Combine these variables in every possible way, and you've got probably thousands of potential personalized burgers, thousands of interpretations of this most emblematic of American culinary creations.

And emblematic the burger is—a triple-decker cultural affirmation for each of us who enjoys one, an edible symbol that announces three things: I eat meat. I am an American, perhaps in nationality but certainly in spirit. And I know what I like, which is simply this: my hamburger.

# Shark Bait

by Jesse Browner

from *Gastronomica*

Guys who cook often have a secret macho edge to their culinary ambitions. In this piece from *Gastronomica*—a fascinating culinary quarterly with an anthropological bent—novelist/magazine writer Browner owns up to the hidden agenda behind his "killer" sandwiches.

*The most common sign that an opponent is bluffing is if he'll look at you very briefly, offer a semi-smile and then glance away quickly. That's an attempt to look you in the eye and act unafraid. But the action is cut short because the player can't maintain the act under great pressure.*
—Mike Caro, *The Body Language of Poker*

Not long ago, I sat down to a game of poker with five old friends. About an hour into the game, long before the heavy betting began, Guy rose from the table to help himself to a sandwich from a tray I had set out earlier. He heaped some chips onto the side of his plate, grabbed a beer from the refrigerator, and returned to his place as a hand of stud was being dealt. From the corner of my eye, I watched as he retrieved his cards with his right hand and his sandwich with his left. He studied the cards as he brought the sandwich to his mouth and bit into it. An instant later, he glanced with apparent surprise at the sandwich, then, momentarily, at me. He blushed subtly and returned his gaze sheepishly to the cards without comment.

I smiled to myself. He had paid me a high, if silent, compliment, which was fair enough. More importantly, though, that evanescent embarrassment had told me everything I needed to know about the strength of his cards. Less than a minute later, with only a pair of fours in my hand, I bluffed him out of twenty-three dollars.

I have been playing in the same floating poker game—"neighborhood" poker, as opposed to professional—for about twelve years now. Most of us went to college together, but we do not have much in common other than our shared history and our love of poker. We were all single when the game began. Three of us are married now; some have children; some make more money than others. We often go months without seeing each other anywhere beyond the card table. The years have accentuated our differences; poker annihilates them. When I sit down on a Sunday night for six hours of card play with these men, I feel that I know them as well as I know anyone in the world, my wife and children included. That, of course, is an illusion, but, like so much else in poker, a useful one.

The sandwiches I had prepared were not ordinary sandwiches. They had been built of fresh rolls from a one-hundred-year-old Portuguese bakery in Connecticut; a brisket braised for over three hours; and a horseradish sauce prepared from a secret recipe. The dish was one in a repertoire of meals I've developed specifically for poker games over the past twelve years. Cooking for card players is governed by a slew of constraints—the food must be non-greasy, eatable with one hand, fit on a small plate, and so on—but you can still be creative and bring a delicate touch to it, if you're motivated to do so. The question is: what could possibly motivate you to do so? Why bother with such hyperactive hospitality, when far less would do? It's a question I've been asking myself for a number of years, but it was not until I saw Guy smile and blush that an answer began to coalesce for me around the nugget of a simple idea.

No one could argue against the basic premise that when you cook for someone you seek to please them. It would seem more or less self-evident that a guest's satisfaction must be the only response acceptable to an attentive host. "To entertain a guest is to make yourself responsible for his happiness so long as he is beneath your roof," says Brillat-Savarin in *The Physiology of Taste*. But of course, nothing—not even happiness—is ever as simple as it seems. We know, for instance, that there are two essential types of pleasure, as Epicurus teaches us: the "moving" pleasure of fulfilling a desire and the far superior "static" pleasure of being in a state of satiety. When you eat my good food, you are happy; but when you are full of my good food, you are in a state of *ataraxia*—tranquillity or serenity—that tends to overwhelm or dampen your other desires, including, perhaps, your desire to fleece or humiliate me at the poker table.

Here is Brillat-Savarin's description of the effect of a well-prepared Barbezieux cockerel on his guests: "I saw successively imprinted on every face the glow of desire, the ecstasy of enjoyment, and the perfect calm of utter bliss"—an extremely accurate demonstration of Epicurus's thesis. Now, it goes without saying that the perfect calm of utter bliss is not a condition in which you want to be risking the month's rent in a game of aggression, guile, and chance. So, I reasoned to myself, if my lamb-salad hero had even half the ataraxic effect of the Barbezieux cockerel, I would be unbeatable.

And so it has proven. Offered in apparent generosity and self-lessness—one old and trusted friend to another—my hospitality is in fact a Trojan horse, fatally compromising my rivals' defences from within. I watch my opponents eat; they smile, they stretch, they grow chatty and convivial. They let down their guard. I strike.

*[Gastronomy] examines the effect of food on man's character, his imagination, his wit, his judgement, his courage, and his perceptions, whether he be awake or asleep, active or at rest.*
                                        —Jean-Anthelme Brillat-Savarin

It strikes me that the central objects of poker—seduction and deceit—are also and ineluctably those of cooking. Each activity involves taking a finite set of elements, combining them in as resourceful a manner as possible in limiting circumstances, and passing them off as superlative. In both cases, what is ultimately at stake is neither money nor a decent meal, but the creator's ego. You cannot summon the will to bluff or to feed a tableful of guests successfully unless you are supremely confident that they will accept your offering and submit to it. This, of course, is a secret of life as well, but that is beyond the scope of my inquiry here. What I can say with some degree of certainty is that playing poker has made me a better chef, and that cooking has made me a better gambler, because each fosters the same understanding of underlying human motives and weaknesses.

A competent poker player, for instance, is only too happy—indeed, relieved—to throw down his hand when faced with what he is convinced is a better one. If he concedes, he knows that he will not be permitted to see his opponent's winning hand, nor does he wish to; he will always prefer to believe that he has lost to better cards—a circumstance beyond his control—than to superior psychology. Are you not in precisely the same position when you accept someone's hospitality? You willingly place yourself at that person's mercy and under his authority, assuming despite all your experience of human duplicity that they are a sort of divine mercy and benevolent authority, and that whatever may be served up is worth the price of submission. "Solitary eater and housebreaker!" accuses Athenaeus, and rightly so. If we choose to live fully and with pleasure, we must find ourselves again and again in the hands of someone who wants something from us in exchange for allowing access to the table—banquet or poker.

The exploitation of hospitality to impair a guest's judgement or to weaken his resolve has been an ongoing theme of Western lore, but it has generally been more subtle among the civilized tribes. The cautionary tale of Samson and Delilah is a case in point. Most people know how, for 1,100 pieces of silver, she lured him into revealing the secret of his strength and then betrayed him to the Philistines. What may be less familiar is the fact that she had to make four attempts before she was successful. It was only when she played the love card that he succumbed, and even then she had to exhaust him in bed before it was safe to shave his head. The seductions of Delilah's hospitality eventually proved too strong even for a man who could spend half the night with a prostitute in Gaza, then uproot the city gates and carry them all the way to Hebron.

Moralists as early as Plato, in his *Laws,* were cautioning men to gain firsthand experience of "the pleasurable attractions of the banquet" in order to be better capable of resisting them. Odysseus cautions Achilles never to send his men fasting into battle, and later takes his own advice by ensuring that he and Telemachus are well fueled and oiled before laying into Penelope's suitors. In Homer, as a rule, a war council never begins until the participants have had their fill of meat and wine. Philosophers followed the same rule: a symposium was the drinking *(potos)* that followed supper *(deipnon).* Even the muse needed to be seduced.

Or just consider this: When Beowulf arrives in Denmark, he finds Hrothgar and the Danes greatly demoralized by Grendel's gruesome predations. Night after night, the monster raids Heorot and carries off up to thirty hapless warriors to his lair; and yet, night after night, the king feasts his company, slips away with his queen to a secluded sector of the royal compound, and leaves his men to settle in for the night. This is genuinely strange. Has no one ever asked why these valiant defenders of the realm sleep night after night in the one place in all Scandinavia where they know their invincible foe—a "God-cursed brute," a "shadow-stalker," a "captain of evil"— will seek them out in their most vulnerable condition? Even if we take it for granted that there were few rocket scientists among these sixth-century pagan barbarians, how are we to understand the Danes' obdurate self-destructive compulsion?

In a word, the Danes have been seduced by their leader and his hospitality. "Time and again, when the goblets passed/and seasoned fighters got flushed with beer/they would pledge themselves to protect Heorot/and wait for Grendel with whetted swords." But they never did wait, did they? They fell asleep every time, and "When dawn broke and day crept in/over each empty, blood-spattered bench,/the floor of the mead-hall where they had feasted/would be slick with slaughter." Hrothgar is described as humiliated, bewildered, and numb with grief, and yet the poet explicitly describes the haven to which the king and queen retire every night as being protected by God against Grendel. In other words, every night, this brave king fills the bellies of these simple boys—under the circumstances, "simple" must be taken as a charitable characterization—with free beer and roast game and their ears with cheap flattery, then creeps off to his divine sanctuary, but not before ensuring that they have pledged their lives to defeating a creature they will be too drunk to rise and challenge.

From Calypso to Tom Jones, the seductions of hospitality are innumerably documented, its goals being anything and everything from sex to murder. In the ninth and very lowest circle of Hell, Dante encounters Brother Alberigo de' Manfredi, who is being punished—in a bed of ice that freezes the tears in his eyes—for having invited two kinsmen to a banquet at which he murdered them both. It should be noted that Dante—and presumably God—ranks poor hospitality as a sin worse than mere homicide, which is punished in the comparatively indulgent seventh circle.

Not even the Roman Empire was safe from the seductions of the table. Procopius of Caesaria relates how Alaric the Visigoth finally prevailed against Rome in A.D. 410 after a long and fruitless siege. He sent three hundred attractive and well-bred young men as gifts to the patricians of the city, instructing them to serve their new masters well and to make them comfortable in every possible way. Then one day, when the patricians were relaxing and napping after their lunch—as their descendants continue to do to this day—on a given signal the young Visigoths stole away, converged on the Salarian gate, slew the guards, and opened the city to the invader. Rome fell not to the Visigoths, but to the seductions of a heavy *pranzo*.

Hitler's mountain retreat, the Eagle's Nest in Berchtesgaden, offers us another, even more perverse, perspective on the seductions of hospitality. What breathless Nazi of any rank or age, confronted with the splendor of the setting, the exalted company, and the opportunity to hear an uninterrupted, three-hour, after-dinner jeremiad from the horse's mouth, could come away without falling in love with his Fuhrer all over again? An invitation to the Eagle's Nest was the ultimate *billet doux* in the Third Reich.

> *Good things are for good people; otherwise we should be reduced to the absurd belief that God created them for sinners.*
> —Monsieur de Borose

Even when it works to their own disadvantage, everyone wants to be seduced, to be lulled into a state of *ataraxia* in which, if only for a brief moment, they are able to bask in the illusion of an easier world, an existence free from the need to make choices under a benign controlling authority—a condition we have not fully enjoyed since the expulsion from the Garden of Eden or, at the very least, since youngest infancy. Why do we do it? Why does a poor player return to the poker table again and again? That is for another type of study to consider, but the answer, again, may lie with Epicurus, who reminds us that "the end of all our actions is to be free from pain and fear." Whatever we may do—including giving pleasure to others—we ultimately do to please ourselves, and even friendship is only the most important of those means "which wisdom acquires to ensure happiness throughout the whole of life." This, then, is the crossroads where the cook and the gambler meet, like Robert Johnson and the Devil, each seeking his own advantage, each believing he has come away from the encounter triumphant.

You, as host and chef, are in an unparalleled position to exploit these lessons. This is not an opportunity to be scorned, especially since those you are preparing to fleece are your friends, whom you are constrained to treat respectfully and fairly at other times. By all standards of gaming etiquette, you are constitutionally obligated to sniff out weakness and capitalize on it in every way possible short of cheating. This is your moment: Find the crustiest, most fragrant roll you can; burden it with four generous wedges of brisket; drown them in horseradish gravy; serve with a dill pickle, thick-cut potato chips, and Dutch lager; then watch your friends—who are appropriately suspicious and monitor your every move as the lamb monitors the wolf—abandon all their wise caution and make mistake after reckless mistake at the gaming table. Don't kid yourself—there is nothing unethical about this. They want you to do it to them, they expect you to try, and they hope beyond hope that you can succeed. Being skinned of next month's rent is a small price to pay for this experience, and they know it. That's why they keep coming back.

# Drinking My Inheritance

by Sara Roahen

from *Tin House*

A freelance writer and editor now living in New Orleans, Roahen revisits her Minnesota childhood in this piece from *Tin House*, a smart quarterly literary journal that has encouraged food-and-drink writing as a special sub-genre.

My earliest memory of winter evenings in Wisconsin is of being in a canoe-size toboggan shuttling down the slalom course of Aunt Nancy and Uncle Larry's front yard toward a congregation of evergreens. The grownups would pile on the toboggan with me, their warm-sour brandy breath visible in the pinching cold as they talked incessantly about all the fun we were having. Hours later, my younger sister, Stephanie, and I curled up on a makeshift bed in the living room, listening to faraway yelps and squeals of the grownups as they sprinted, nude, from Uncle Larry's incendiary sauna to a snowbank outside and back again, pausing only to refresh a cocktail. Stephanie dozed off effortlessly, but I lay awake, petrified that a cold-induced heart attack would orphan me at any moment.

Their choice of cocktail was seasonless, but activities at the weekend-long parties changed with the weather. Come summer, the snow melted to reveal a swimming pool surrounded on all sides by overgrown Christmas trees and rented plots of feed corn. The men shot at clay pigeons all day as their women pretended to watch, but Stephanie and I stayed poolside. While she perfected her back dive, I dripped dry beneath the porch with plates of sour cream cucumbers and a prickling sunburn. It was impossible to gauge back then—or now—which was more to blame for my bouts of summer insomnia: the green shag carpeting that poked through Aunt Nancy's satin sheets against my blistered skin; the orchestra of moths searing in the bug light outside; Jefferson County cops triaging drunk drivers over Uncle Larry's radio scanner; or the grownups' howling as they drained the swimming pool in a cannonball contest. Heart attacks didn't worry me in the summertime. Instead, I was sure one of them would crack open a skull on the pool's cement lip.

Occasionally these weekends terminated at Sunday Mass, where we thanked the Lord in person for so much fun. But mostly Stephanie and I feigned sleep when Aunt Nancy woke up on Sunday mornings, praying that instead of rousing us for church she would switch on the Christian radio station she claimed would save our souls. It was a weak substitute for church, she admitted as she shuffled back to bed, but at least it would keep us out of hell for another seven days. If you had asked me at the time to what we owed this stroke of heathen fortune, I would have answered: Uncle Larry's brandy old-fashioned sweets.

These were not the gentlemanly whiskey old-fashioneds of water splashes and sugar cubes and *absolutely nothing carbonated* that cocktail academics believe was invented in the mid-1800s in Kentucky. These old-fashioneds were big and stiff, as generous as the beers sold at Lambeau Field, with a pitch-perfect balance of sweet and bitter, alcoholic warmth and ice cube chill. And they were apparently refreshing enough to drink all night long. Uncle Larry still measures his old-fashioneds in brandy glugs and shakes of bitters and finishes them with 7Up. He stirs them with cinnamon sticks and garnishes them with maraschino cherries. While he is considered the authority on old-fashioneds in our family—his heavily researched recipe is still the platonic ideal for us all—his typically Wisconsin version of the drink is to the original highbrow cocktail what a double espresso latte with whipped cream and cinnamon is to a cup of joe. It's bigger, it's sweeter, it's got more spice. Its smooth base, brandy, is at least as different from whiskey as an espresso shot is from a straight-up French roast. Except around the pool, where only plastic UW-Wisconsin Badger football cups were allowed, these old-fashioneds always came in ice-packed glasses painted with pheasants soaring over marshes and spaniels pointing at flocks of plump, deaf quail.

The garnishes were the greatest thrill for little girls. Phosphorescent, brandy-marinated cherries shimmered under the melting ice in sweating glasses like brightly painted fishing lures. But, like Mom's holiday bourbon balls—which always ended up spit into a poinsettia napkin—the cherries were deceptively harsh. So we gnawed on the cinnamon-sticks, which were never alcoholic, just spicy and wet. To this day, when throwing a cinnamon stick into a pot of black beans, I find myself back in the campfire air of Aunt Nancy and Uncle Larry's wood-heated home.

While I grew up around brandy old-fashioneds, my father's parents hadn't even heard of brandy before eloping from Ohio to Wisconsin in 1939. It became their drink of choice when they found that their new friends kept no other liquor in the house. Brandy consumption in Wisconsin has always been higher per capita than in any other state, but a growing taste for spiced rum, flavored vodka, and specialty martinis among the younger Wisconsin social-drinking circles has led to a sharp decline in statewide brandy sales. This drop is causing panic among brandy producers. Since Wisconsin's bordering states have such similar geographical, socioeconomic and ethnic breakdowns, they have never figured out what originally drove Wisconsinites to covet it. Therefore, they don't know how to ensure that our passion doesn't fizzle out. Says Gary Heck, owner of Korbel Brandy: "It must have been what the wagon had on it when it first got there." It appears that the wagon was brimming. Generations of Wisconsinites have ensured that brandy's uses are boundless. Especially in rural areas, bartenders often use brandy in place of other brown liquors without warning. Natives expect it, but out-of-state customers learn to specify brands when ordering a bourbon and water or a whiskey sour. Most brandy old-fashioned drinkers I know drink them sweet, made with 7Up, but you can also order them made with sour mix (a brandy old-fashioned sour), with water, with seltzer, or with half 7Up, half seltzer. This half-and-half version is called a brandy old-fashioned Press, short for Presbyterian—though no one seems to know the connection between Presbyterians and brandy old-fashioneds.

By the time I landed my first job, brandy old-fashioneds were as embedded in my consciousness as frostbite and fried cheese curds. Most bars wouldn't let kids my age onto the premises to use the pay phone, much less to work, but since the management at private golf clubs in Wisconsin didn't believe in age discrimination, I brought in more cash cocktail-waitressing the summer I turned eighteen than I've made during any three-month period since. I also became unusually attached to the smell of sticky brandy and bitters drying on a cork-lined cocktail tray. I still didn't drink old-fashioneds, preferring Mogan David at the time, but it became clear that a fanatical allegiance to the cocktail was not particular to my family. Thursday's men's nights at the golf club were the rowdiest and most lucrative for me, but it was during Friday night fish fries that my fellow statesmen and women most openly indulged their affections for our regional cherry-brown drink. Friday night fish fries in Wisconsin are as ubiquitous as brats at a Brewers game, and everyone knows the protocol. You always take as much of the family as you can, you always take the good car, and you always show up early for a drink in the bar. Club members whose aperitif preference wasn't a brandy old-fashioned were such a minority that more than a decade later I still remember these anomalies: the retired couple with a powder-blue golf cart who only drank vodka tonics; the Miller Genuine Draft–swilling lout who was an ass pincher on Thursdays and a family man on Fridays; and the leather-skinned golf pro who separated himself from the hacks by drinking whiskey old-fashioneds with olives.

Today there's a very new-millennium martini menu at Club 26, a supper club just south of Fort Atkinson where my parents found the fried cod so superior that they held their wedding reception there on a Friday evening in 1970. Yet the club's bartenders still make so many brandy old-fashioneds that they prepare for Friday evenings by mixing gallons of simple syrup and bitters (not to be confused with the appalling old-fashioned blends sold in Wisconsin liquor stores next to the piña colada, Bloody Mary, and margarita mixes). I doubt a Club 26 bartender has ever made an old-fashioned in that sodaless manner that characterized them in nineteenth-century Kentucky, and that still characterizes them in forty-nine states. If a customer requested one, the staff would probably react with the same confusion that strikes bartenders outside the borders of Wisconsin when you ask for an old-fashioned made with brandy and 7Up even as they're reaching for the whiskey and the sugar cubes. At Club 26, you get an above-average if weak version of Uncle Larry's old-fashioned, minus the wildfowl glasses and the cinnamon stick (both home-made touches). The first one goes down like a Shirley Temple while we pretend to consider Club 26's newer menu items—chicken schnitzel, salmon with sauerkraut—and then agree on the cod.

I've heard it said that a Wisconsin fish fry isn't genuine if it doesn't come with a relish tray of raw vegetables, sour cherry peppers, olives, and little pickles. Club 26 ditched the relish tray for deep-fried dinner rolls long ago, but the centerpiece is still nuggets of firm, bleach-white cod fished from oceans far from the Great Lakes and wrapped in clingy sheaths of brown batter that are more chewy than crisp, but never greasy. A brandy old-fashioned remains the natural accompaniment to fried fish for many of us, but now that Kendall Jackson and his California friends have infiltrated nearly every wood-paneled supper club across the state, even my grandparents occasionally fall for research suggesting that wine will conquer the wicked effects of fried foods.

Nevertheless, there's little other sign of a brandy recession in any generation of my family. The moment we enter the house on a visit, before Mom can set the table with cheddar cheese soup and macaroni salad, Dad asks, "Regular 7Up or diet?" (Some Wisconsinites do count calories.) My cousin's husband, Doug, Uncle Larry's nephew by marriage, is another artisan of the regional cocktail. His patent-worthy technique, the results of which we taste every Christmas Eve before presents, involves holding the glass up to the stained woodwork in the bar he built himself. If the woodwork is darker than the drink, he adds more brandy.

Those panicking brandy makers might also take heart if they saw the solid wall of brandy displayed at a certain truck stop just outside Wisconsin Dells. It's the last place I know of to buy a bottle on the way up to the home where Aunt Nancy and Uncle Larry retired among the osprey and eagles of Lake Castle Rock. Their weekend-long parties have gone the way of Badger football victories, but I have noticed a sauna built suspiciously close to a sliding old-fashioned glass door in the basement. Still the barrel-chested, baritone-voiced man of my youth, Uncle Larry mixes everyone two old-fashioneds before we head out to their favorite local fish fry. I'm the only one who can't finish both. When I was younger, my dad used to stabilize his Friday night old-fashioned-for-the-road between his thighs as he drove. I would fret in the backseat, longing for the day when I could take the wheel. He still protests when I offer to drive—the restaurant is just a few miles down the road, after all, and cars have cup holders now. During dinner I pour my fourth old-fashioned into Aunt Nancy's empty glass, completely undetected. It has always been a combination of thrill and dread trying to keep pace with the grownups.

Most of the family in the generation older than mine is still fairly young, settling down but not nearly ready to give up. They aren't sure yet what part of our family they would pass on if I asked them to. There are no cows to milk, no taffy to make, no shoes to repair in our clan. No law firm. No corner store. But I'm older now than they were when we used to pile on that toboggan, and I have reached an age when finding something to claim as ours before it becomes just me feels crucial. It's a primal impulse, a nostalgic ache for things that aren't gone quite yet— something like the urge to procreate, only in reverse. So I thought about my inheritance options and came to a conclusion that surprises even me: I'm taking the old-fashioned. Taking the garnishes and everything else that comes with it. It was there from the beginning anyhow. I just needed the recipe.

## Uncle Larry's Brandy Old-Fashioned Sweet

Most brandy old-fashioned makers I know are partial to a particular brand (Uncle Larry likes Christian Brothers), but an inexpensive brandy will do. It's essential to make ice in the largest cubes possible; the balance of bitters, brandy, and sweetness is easily diluted, and the kind of nubby ice sold by the bag melts too quickly. Lastly, most store-bought bar syrups are either saccharine-sweet or have a plasticky flavor. After years of empirical research, Uncle Larry found one to fit his taste, Sweet 10, but you can also make your own simple syrup by heating equal parts water and sugar on the stovetop and stirring just until the sugar dissolves. For easy access, store the syrup in a squirt bottle or other covered vessel with a pour spout.

liberal 2 jiggers (3 ounces) brandy
4 or 5 strong dashes Angostura bitters
1 teaspoon simple syrup
½ of one 2-inch cinnamon stick (split it lengthwise)

6 ounces (half a can) cold 7Up
maraschino cherries to taste

Fill a 12-ounce tumbler to the top with ice cubes and pour in brandy. Add bitters and simple syrup; stir with cinnamon stick, leaving stick in glass. Top off the drink with 7Up and stir again with a long-handled bar spoon. Garnish with maraschino cherries, either floating or skewered on a toothpick.

# Fried Butter

by Abe Opincar
from *Fried Butter*

Opincar wanders over a widespread range of food-related topics in his collected columns for the weekly *San Diego Reader*, but he's always armed with a sly, dark wit that stems from his offbeat literary persona: part curmudgeon, part lost romantic.

I pour olive oil into a pan. When the oil is hot I sprinkle into it a tablespoon of turmeric. The yellow powder bubbles and darkens. I crack two eggs into the pan. When the yolks are barely firm, I slide the eggs onto a plate and pour the leftover oil on top. With pita bread I sop up runny yolk and mustardy yellowish oil. There are few moments when I'm happier. Such a simple thing can be enough.

In my odd little immigrant neighborhood everyone knows turmeric. My Indian landlord calls it *haldi* and tells me it's the principal ingredient in curry powder. Patting his big firm belly with both hands, my landlord says, "*Haldi* is quite good for the digestion." The Vietnamese woman next door calls it *nghe*. She says she sometimes makes *nghe* tea, which she claims beautifies her skin. Three blocks away the crabby Chinese herbalist, who has always disliked me, sits in his store and scowls when I walk into his shop. He calls turmeric *wong geung*. He refuses to tell me how it's used in China. The earnest shopkeeper at the Ethiopian market tells me that in his country turmeric is *erd* and is used in a sauce for chicken. The Palestinian owner of the Middle Eastern grocery tells me that in Arabic turmeric is *curcoom,* or in slang *arosh,* which means "yellowish." In the Middle East, as throughout Southeast Asia, turmeric is used to make yellow rice, a symbol of celebration.

Although turmeric is native to India, Marco Polo found it in China where he declared it a reasonable substitute for saffron. Eight hundred years later American and British scientists have discovered that turmeric may be a reasonable substitute for the steroids used to treat arthritis. Curcumin, the chemical compound that gives turmeric its intense yellowness, acts as a powerful anti-inflammatory. Research has also shown that curcumin seems to trick cancer cells into killing themselves. In one study, smokers with mouth cancer, after taking curcumin daily for nine months, saw their lesions disappear. Other studies are investigating curcumin's use in the treatment and prevention of colon and breast cancer. The British press now and again runs stories about "Curry: The New Wonder Drug."

Turmeric, a rhizome, in its fresh state looks like a smaller, scruffier version of ginger, a close relative. Cardamom, a ginger cousin, with its pungent eucalyptus-like aroma, evokes Vick's Vap-o-Rub, childhood bronchitis, my mother, and also the Middle East, where cardamom is added to coffee. Turmeric is neither minty-cool like cardamom, nor spicy-hot like ginger. Turmeric powder, the form in which it's most commonly available, has a rough, slightly bitter astringency, like mustard.

I sometimes find fresh turmeric in Vietnamese and Lao markets. Cut open the small, nubby rhizome and its interior is a brilliant carroty orange. Taste a sliver and you understand every caution you've ever heard about fresh herbs versus dried, about the impossibility of translating poetry. Fresh turmeric's flavor takes a while to bloom on the tongue: a strong and pleasant floweriness gives way to a complicated piney, peppery taste. Turmeric powder gives only a dim, inaccurate hint of the real fresh thing.

Last week I was reading a book of Paul Celan's poems translated from German. In the translator's notes he mentions that when translating one poem, the poem I happened to like best, he used "daydream" instead of "dream" for rhythm's sake. But a daydream isn't a dream. I felt I couldn't trust a single line in the book. I doubted that I'd truly understood any of the poems at all. Ethnic cookbooks often offer similar betrayals.

"If you can't get fresh lemon grass," one Thai cookbook assures me, "the dried kind works just as well. If you can't find that, use dried lemon peel."

I add a tablespoon of grated fresh turmeric to boiling water. I stir in a cupful of rice and place the snug lid onto the pot. The kitchen fills with the smell of fresh turmeric. The phone rings. A friend engages me in a discussion about romance. We disagree. I wait for my rice to be done. My friend tells me that I've never truly been in love, that I've only been in love with the idea of being in love.

This isn't the sort of thing I like to listen to while making dinner. I make an excuse. I hang up. I spoon fluffy bright yellow rice onto a plate. I've made plenty of rice with dried turmeric, and like it just as well, but its taste is entirely different. While I eat my rice and baked chicken, I wonder if my friend was right. I've *thought* I was in love. I've *felt* I was in love. Maybe there's a deeper, tenderer, more vivid love that I can't experience or have never found. My messy bachelor's kitchen is quiet. I hear water drip from faucet into sink. I think I have been in love. It may not have been the real thing, but it was close enough.

Off a small side street in downtown Jerusalem, there was a kosher vegetarian restaurant named Alumah's. In the foyer you often saw a young Orthodox girl seated at a table equipped with a white tablecloth, reading lamp, and free-standing magnifying glass. By her modest dress, you knew the girl was *frum,* or religious, but her manner was provocative. Peering through the magnifying glass, she picked through lentils scattered before her across the white cloth. Her fingers darted through the lentils, flicking—*plink! plink!*—into a bowl in her lap, culling others some into a pile to one side of the table. The girl was a living advertisement for the restaurant's religious rigor. She was searching for bugs.

The Biblical prohibition against eating insects is as unequivocal as the prohibition against eating pork or shellfish—a mealworm or mite being the spiritual equivalent of a minute pig or lobster. Orthodox Jews spend considerable time sifting through flour, picking through walnuts and pulses and rice, examining each leaf in a head of lettuce or bunch of spinach, searching for creatures God has forbidden them to consume. Orthodox Jews who eat only organic insecticide-free vegetables—there are a fair number of Orthodox Jewish-Americans who adopt this additional stricture—keep busy kitchens.

There are exceptions. The Talmud allows Yemenite Jews to eat a certain kind of locust. Jewish law requires no Jew to worry about microscopic insects. Miniscule bugs often burrow beneath the skins of cashews and almonds, but if the nuts are roasted until brown "the intensity of the heat," one rabbi wrote, "will dry out the insects to such an extent that they will be regarded as dust and cease to be forbidden."

To non-Jews, even to secular Jews, this attention to detail appears pathological. But if you've handed over your life to holiness, then spending twenty minutes combing through a head of romaine isn't crazy. It is part of the life you lead. It's an expression of love.

Having spent time in the more rigorous reaches of Orthodox Judaism, I can recognize the tiny blister at the edge of a lentil that means a worm has burrowed inside. I can recognize the fine webs in a package of flour that indicates the presence of weevils or, in Yiddish, *milben.* With a magnifying glass I've scrutinized feathery dill for pinhead-size bug eggs. In the big secular world I'm comfortable with fanatical wine connoisseurs, with purists who use only the most virgin first-cold-pressed olive oil and who insist on the superiority of free-range roasting hens.

I'm familiar with the gamut of reasons people choose to eat or drink some things and refuse others. It's been a long time since Jerusalem was my home. I still can't face a package of lentils without trepidation. I ate so many when I was young and poor and in love with God, or at least young and poor and in love with the idea of being in love with God. Each lentil I ate I inspected by hand.

While I know the secular world's sensitivities to food, I also know the awareness isn't reciprocal. I don't expect a *Gourmet* magazine subscriber to have read the story of Esau and Jacob in the original Hebrew, to know how the muddy, meaty taste of lentils evokes a narrative of betrayal. But I am someone who culled lentils and I know how Jacob, with lentils, cheated hairy Esau of his birthright. Esau and Jacob's story ends with ambiguous kisses and hugs. I sometimes wish my own peculiar family drama would achieve similar resolution. I no longer inspect lentils under a magnifying glass, but in my mind's eye they still are huge.

Poison has fallen out of favor. Criminologists aren't sure why. Some say effective poisons in their purest form aren't as available as they once were. A century ago, arsenic and strychnine were household staples. Housewives soaked flypaper in arsenic. Their husbands pumped strychnine into wasps' nests. Every now and then, in a pest-free home, a husband complained that his soup tasted funny, or a wife died suddenly of unexplained causes. Law enforcement lacked the technology to prove anything shady had happened.

Advances in forensic science have made poisoning unwise; the advent of no-fault divorce and restraining orders have, in almost all instances, made it unnecessary. Intentional poisoning has become so rare in America that there's only one toxicologist I'm aware of who makes it his specialty. This Austin-based gentleman flits about the country advising detectives on hard-to-crack cases. He's man-aged to compose a profile of today's "typical poisoner," a person he describes as "well-educated and immature," in other words, someone much like me.

I've never wanted to kill anyone, but I have wanted to shut someone up. My apprenticeship was slow, my methods simple.

Like most competent cooks, my skills were over time enlisted by family, friends, co-workers. Like most competent cooks, I found myself cooking less often for my own pleasure and more for the pleasure of people I either didn't know well, or knew altogether too well. During many dinners I sat and watched greasy lips pro-nounce banalities, casual insults. I watched people who claimed not to like red meat devour leg of lamb. I watched people who claimed to dislike sweets devour cheesecake. I tried to escape to the kitchen. Shouts of, "What are you doing in there? Come back and sit down!" forced my return. I developed detachment. I noticed that heavy meals had a sedative effect. Pot roast and mashed potatoes, but not baked sole and coleslaw, quieted people down. Pot roast and mashed potatoes followed by pound cake and ice cream lulled people into drowsy silence punctuated by, "Well, it's about time we went home."

For a while I pondered this phenomenon. I browsed medical journals. By the time my father's terminal cancer rolled around, I was well prepared. My father's slow death meant spending weeks in close quarters with my sister-in-law, an opinionated woman with a healthy appetite and a hyena-like laugh. She had a shaky grasp of inheritance law and, while my mother, brother, and I were occupied with my father's care, she'd wander around my parents' home, examining their furniture.

One afternoon she drew me aside. "You know, the only thing of your parents' that I've ever wanted is that cherry-wood china closet."

I explained that my father was dying, that my mother, as far as I knew, was in good health.

I immediately went to the supermarket and bought a couple hundred dollars worth of groceries, including the resentful cook's best friend, several pounds of butter.

At 100 calories per tablespoon, butter is less caloric than other fats. (Canola oil has 130 calories per tablespoon, olive oil 120.) But butter incorporates itself easily into most foods and its "buttery rich goodness" makes almost everything taste better. Years of cooking and quiet observation taught me, for example, that a pot of mashed potatoes containing two tablespoons of butter didn't taste as good as a pot containing eight. A pot containing twenty-four tablespoons—the most I ever attempted—tasted best of all.

In addition to improving flavor, there are two reasons for getting as much butter as possible into food, particularly starches. The human digestive system, struggling with an onslaught of hard-to-digest fatty acids, engorges itself with blood the body would otherwise use to keep the mind alert and chatty. Also, butter contains tryptophan, an amino acid which, when absorbed by the brain, induces sleepiness. The trick is getting tryptophan from the gut to the brain. And starches, for complex reasons, accelerate and enhance this process. In the right hands, mashed potatoes can be as calming as Haldol.

Turkey and bananas are also rich in tryptophan. While my father lay dying and my sister-in-law studied her *Beginner's Guide to Antique Appraisal,* I made many loaves of buttery banana bread. I baked a twenty-pound turkey, first rubbed well with unsalted butter. While I was at it, I made stuffing. My recipe from *Joy of Cooking* called for only one cup of melted butter, but I knew that three cups yielded a superior result. I of course made plenty of mashed potatoes.

My mother, brother, and I were too busy and too tired to eat much of this food. Mostly, my mother drank the Ensure my father left untouched beside his bed. My brother and I drank coffee and, on difficult nights, bourbon. My sister-in-law, who didn't have a good intuitive feel for bedpans, oxygen tanks, or morphine pumps, had a lot of time on her hands. In the morning I'd see her slathering butter on a thick slice of toasted banana bread. In the afternoon and evening she'd heat herself up some turkey and mashed potatoes in the microwave. The house grew quiet. There were days I didn't see her much at all. She always seemed to be taking naps.

# Descent of the Relatives

by Shoba Narayan

from *Monsoon Diary*

Narayan's delicious autobiography is intricately bound up with foods—what she ate in her Indian childhood, what she learned to eat when she moved to the States, and how to navigate the gaps between the two. Having her parents visit only underscored how far she herself had come.

A year into our marriage, my parents decided to pay us a visit. It was traditional for someone from the bride's family to visit and help set up a household, and so they came armed with utensils, cooking vessels, and bed linen. They also smuggled many substances of dubious heritage into the United States. One was *narthangai,* a citrus fruit that makes a delicious sour pickle. Knowing my love for it, Mom packed it in a plastic bag. For good measure, she also brought powders of various kinds: curry-leaf powder, chili powder, *sambar* and *rasam* powder. Since she couldn't wake up in the morning without covering herself in her favorite Pond's sandalwood talcum powder, she packed five containers of this.

Prior to departure, my father opened the suitcase and was appalled. Right on top were packets and packets of white talcum powder, which my father promptly confiscated. "They will think it's some sort of chemical," he said.

Both my parents were cross and testy when I phoned them a

few days before they left India. "Your mother thinks she is traveling to the nearest village," said my father. "The customs officers will never let us enter America carrying all her powders. I haven't been sleeping at night thinking of all that could happen. And your mother blithely keeps packing away."

Mom was equally irritable on the other line. "What can these customs people do?" she asked. "If they ask what it is, I will tell them that I am carrying Indian medicines."

"Ha!" said Dad. "Indian medicines indeed. They will throw everything into the trash can."

"Let them throw," Mom said. "It will reduce my load. Why can't you think of your poor daughter instead of those prying customs officers?"

"What if those prying customs officers jail us indefinitely when we transit through London? What if they deport us back to India? What if they think we're terrorists because of my moustache?"

My parents fought all the way across the Atlantic and arrived without any of the powders, pickles, *papads,* and sweets. The customs people at Kennedy Airport had tossed them all.

In America my father loved going to the grocery store. He derived great pleasure from looking up strange substances in the encyclopedia and seeing if he could spot them at the store. His culinary adventures were innocuous in and of themselves, except that he had no idea about how much to buy. In India my mother did all the shopping. As a result, my father's estimates of quantity were frequently greater than what he—or even we—could eat. To paraphrase an old saying, Dad's eyes were "hungrier than his stomach." Our collective stomachs, I should add.

And so his foods languished, sometimes for weeks, in the fridge. This worried him, for he took it as a sign that none of us shared his passion for new and exotic foods. I know many worriers, but my father's version has all the nuances of a Stradivarius. He worried that he was spending too much money buying stuff that no one else in the family could eat. He worried that the things he bought would go bad and proceeded to ingest them at a rapid rate. Then he worried about their effects on his "tropical body," unused as it was to temperate climes and their food. He worried about what his son-in-law thought of his experiments. He wondered if the grocery-store clerk thought he was senile, or worse, retarded, because he frequently asked for items that nobody had heard of. "You would think someone who works in a grocery store would know how to cook salsify," he said. "But that clerk didn't even know what salsify was, let alone how to cook it. He looked at me like I was from another planet."

I didn't think it was appropriate to tell him at that point that I had frequently wondered the same thing myself.

Since I have inherited my father's penchant for worrying, I was his frequent confidante. "Do you think," he whispered to me one day, "that your mother approves of my shopping trips?" I didn't really know, but I reassured him that if Mom didn't approve, she would make it clear. Unlike my dad, my mom wears her opinions on her sleeve.

After watching a documentary about the virtues of eating soy, my father went on a soy kick. He started with soy milk and bought two gallons. When he discovered that we didn't partake of the beverage, he proceeded to drink it continuously, sometimes diluting it with beer, until he got diarrhea. "It has an expiration date," he said mildly, when I chided him for drinking too much too soon. "Since I bought the stuff, I must drink it."

An American friend unwittingly added fuel to his fire by raving about soy's isoflavonoids and antioxidants and how they had the capacity to confer renewed youth. Encouraged, Dad bought several packets of tofu bologna, tofu ham, and tofu pups, a vegetarian version of hot dogs. He had never eaten hot dogs before, nor was he likely to, given that we are a vegetarian family, but this didn't stop him from exploring America's most famous food. "The French call their hot dogs *chien chaud*," he announced one day.

The tofu version of the *chien chaud,* however, proved to be staggeringly bland, even after we dressed it up with ketchup, salsa, and mustard (all of which were on Dad's list of foods to try). The tofu ham was even worse, and the tofu bologna took the cake for the worst-tasting soy product we had ever eaten. So there we were, left with three packets of tofu slices that nobody wanted to touch.

My father wouldn't admit that he hated the stuff just as much as the rest of us. He took to eating it with breakfast. "Stick a couple of tofu bologna slices inside my toast," he instructed me. "On second thought, make that four slices—I have to finish it up quickly. And smear a generous amount of peanut butter on them."

When my mother asked if this daily devotion to tofu was necessary, Dad retorted, "It is not bad. Quite refreshing, actually. Besides, you are the one who keeps harping on how I should eat healthy foods."

After a few days of this, even Dad got tired. But he couldn't bring himself to throw out the remaining slices. His solution was simple, and in retrospect we all should have expected it. He snuck the tofu into our coconut chutney. With disastrous results.

Coconut chutney is a favorite accompaniment to breakfast in my family. A hearty blend of grated raw coconut, roasted lentils, a couple of green chiles, and some salt, my mother makes it almost daily, since it is easy to prepare and goes well with most Indian dishes. We eat it with *dosas, idlis,* toast, tortilla chips, and anything else we can think of.

There are those who tinker with the traditional coconut chutney recipe, adding a tomato to give it some tartness, or fresh cilantro for some tang, believing—wrongly, in my opinion—that it adds to the taste. I view such digressions harshly. Why mess with a recipe that is five thousand years old? I ask, echoing Ram's sentiments. Why adulterate pure coconut chutney with unnecessary additions? My contention is that cooks who add foreign ingredients to chutneys do so to hide their own ineptitude. I have spent the better part of several afternoons trying to veer lax cooks away from such transgressions. How, then, to account for the fact that my father is the biggest culprit of all in this regard?

Unlike me, my father views the chutney with heretical flexibility. He thinks of it like soup stock, as a base into which he can add whatever he pleases, be it peanuts, leftover rice, or potato chips. He has even added a few chunks of pineapple, which delivered a sweetness that was totally against the chutney's character. When my mother blends her chutneys at home, she keeps an eagle eye on my father, who prowls around the kitchen looking for something imaginative to throw in.

When the tofu bologna began disappearing from the refrigerator, we should have checked the chutney. But Dad showed remarkable restraint in the beginning. All we could detect was a slightly smoky taste. We thought it was because the blender had overheated.

Spurred by his success in escaping detection, my father got bolder. One morning we woke up to find him brandishing a bowl full of chutney. "I couldn't sleep," he explained. "I decided to start breakfast."

My mom got busy making some steaming hot *idlis,* and we all sat down for a hearty Sunday brunch. The fluffy dumplings, soft and bland, are a perfect foil for the spicy chutney that is poured liberally over them. And this is exactly what we did on that fateful morning: grab a handful of *idlis* and pour Dad's chutney on them.

As usual, my mom, who had been up since dawn and was therefore ravenous, was the first to go. She took one bite, made a strangled sound, and stopped chewing, her mouth full. She sat there for a moment, looking slightly stunned, shaking her head slowly from side to side like a woeful elephant. As my husband and I watched, she glanced murderously at my dad and walked purposefully into the bathroom. We heard her cough, retch, spit, then throw up, until finally, mercifully, she turned on the tap.

My father grabbed his grocery bag and left the house.

• • •

After my parents left, Nalla-ma came for a month. Nalla-pa was busy with patients, and she had to occupy herself. So she made a whirlwind tour of America, with us being her first stop.

When I got married, I thought Ram was a picky eater. But Nalla-ma really took the cake. Well, not exactly—she didn't eat cake because it had eggs in it. Not only that, she had a bewildering assortment of food rules that were as irrational as they were inconsistent. And they changed all the time.

Upon arrival, Nalla-ma announced dramatically that she wouldn't eat anything she hadn't cooked with her bare hands. This was a foreign land, she said, and one never knew if errant cooks had accidentally dumped lard in the supposedly vegetarian items. When we traveled, Nalla-ma came armed with little packets of food. Trips with her were like Arctic expeditions, with every food contingency examined and prepared for.

The weekend music classes that I taught in New Jersey turned into complicated affairs. Before Nalla-ma came, Ram and I would drive on Friday evening to the Comfort Inn, spend all day Saturday and Sunday there, and return Sunday night. We grabbed a sandwich here, a pizza there, and that was it. No longer.

On Saturday morning Nalla-ma went into the kitchen at dawn and didn't emerge until she had cooked enough food for the weekend. We would fill empty yogurt containers with fragrant curries and head out to New Jersey. We stayed in a corner suite so that the other hotel guests wouldn't complain about the sound of music and the smell of food that wafted from our room. Between classes, we ate whatever Nalla-ma had cooked—for breakfast, lunch, and dinner.

Then Nalla-ma heard that breakfast was included with the cost of the room. She couldn't bear the thought of three free breakfasts going to waste and insisted that we go down to the hotel's dining room for breakfast.

Ram and I would help ourselves to the cereal, bagels, and coffee from the buffet. Nalla-ma would sit discreetly in a corner and eat the glutinous rice porridge that she'd brought with her. She'd hide the container on her lap because she thought that the management would throw her out for bringing her own food. Periodically, a spoon would emerge from under the table and transport the food into her mouth. Whenever a waiter passed by, Nalla-ma would stop chewing, take a sip of water, and smile brightly.

Nalla-ma usually filled a tray for herself from the breakfast buffet as a ploy to distract the waiters. When nobody was watching, she would quickly pack the bread and dry cereal into a Ziploc bag "just in case one of you wants to eat it for lunch." When she discovered that she couldn't get Ram or me to eat the cold bagel or cereal, she was in a quandary. She couldn't bear to throw the food away, but she didn't want to leave the bagel and cereal behind. "After all, we are paying for the breakfast," she said judiciously.

At lunchtime Nalla-ma would graciously offer the bagel to one of my students. If they refused, she would carry the bagel and cereal all the way back home in the hope that I would eat them during the week. Sometimes I did, just to put her mind at rest, and sometimes I threw the bagel away when Nalla-ma wasn't looking.

Lunch and dinner in Edison were more relaxed. In fact, they were scrumptious compared with our previous forays to the local pizza parlor. Nalla-ma would spread a newspaper on the bed and lay out a series of yogurt containers. Inside were spicy vegetable curries, rice, *rasam, pongal,* and pickles. She took great pleasure in rationing the food with the precision of a military general so that the last morsel was finished by the time we were ready to drive back home on Sunday evening.

It was our annual cross-country trip that caused Nalla-ma to finally eat food prepared by others. We started in New York and New Jersey and then drove to Cleveland, Chicago, St. Louis, Memphis, Oklahoma City, Albuquerque, and Los Angeles. The whole trip took ten days.

When Nalla-ma realized that there was no way she could cook

and carry her rations for the duration of the trip, she refused to go with us. But Ram wouldn't hear of her staying home.

"You must come," he said. "This is a great chance for you to see the country."

"Why should I see the country, old woman that I am?" Nalla-ma said. "Why don't you youngsters go along, unencumbered by old people like me? I'll stay back and watch the house."

"The house doesn't need watching, and I don't need to be worrying about you all alone at home," Ram said. "You are going with us and that's final. If you are worried about food, we can work something out."

After much research and inquiry, we reached a solution. Nalla-ma would take her rice cooker, a bag of rice, and a tall bottle containing the spicy tamarind relish (*puli-kaachal*) that she had concocted. She would cook her own rice in the rice cooker and subsist on that and the *puli-kaachal* during the trip. That was the plan, anyway.

The upheaval happened when we reached Bloomsburg, Pennsylvania. Nalla-ma discovered that she had left the rice cooker at home. After that, it was pandemonium. She was almost in tears, begging us to turn back or at least drop her at a train station where she could take a train back to New York. I tried to pacify her by saying that I would buy her a new rice cooker in Chicago. She got mad because I was thinking of waiting until Chicago to buy it. What was she supposed to eat in the meantime? Then Ram had an idea.

"Why not buy rice at a Chinese restaurant?" he suggested. "After all, they sell plain rice as a side order."

"Don't worry about me," Nalla-ma sniffed her annoyance. "I'll starve."

"Come on, Nalla-ma!" I said impatiently. "How will you manage on tamarind chutney alone? Why don't you eat some fruit at least? It hasn't been cooked or anything. How much purer can food get? And what about drinking some milk, huh? After all, our scriptures call it the holiest of foods."

Nalla-ma examined the milk bottle that I handed her. "What does *pasteurized* mean?" she asked finally.

"It means that they have boiled it so that all the germs have been killed," I said.

In Du Bois, Pennsylvania, Nalla-ma accompanied me to a grocery store. After much deliberation, she picked out a carton of 2 percent milk and some fruits.

In Cleveland she tasted strawberry yogurt for the first time and decided that she liked it. We went to the Kroger's and stood in the dairy aisle for fifteen minutes. I read the labels of the various-flavored yogurts to make sure they didn't contain lard or any other questionable substance.

In South Bend, Indiana, Nalla-ma declared that Dunkin' Donuts coffee tasted just like the filter coffee back home. For the rest of the trip we had to stop every time we saw a Dunkin' Donuts so that Nalla-ma could have a large coffee accompanied by a French cruller, which, according to her, tasted just like *jilebi*. By the time we reached Chicago, Nalla-ma was eating rice from Chinese restaurants.

Every night we stopped briefly at a Chinese restaurant. I went in and asked for two servings of plain rice. Then we went to the local Italian restaurant, since Ram and I loved Italian food. While we ate our pastas or pizzas, Nalla-ma mixed the Chinese rice with her tamarind relish and ate it for dinner. "My grandmother can't eat Italian food," I told the waitress. "It's against her religion."

Once, the waitress at a Mexican restaurant offered to bring some potato chips for Nalla-ma when she saw the rice mixture she was eating. Too polite to refuse, Nalla-ma tried some potato chips with her meal. The next time we were at a grocery store, I read her the potato chip labels. We consulted with the store manager, who assured us that yeast wasn't an animal product. Satisfied, Nalla-ma decided to patronize Wise and began with a packet of lightly salted potato chips.

She started eating ice cream while driving in the blistering heat of Texas. She wouldn't eat Häagen-Dazs, since it contained egg, but favored Edy's No Sugar Added ice cream. That phrase gave her the license to eat as much of the stuff as she wanted without having to worry about gaining weight or worsening her diabetes.

In Albuquerque, while I was buying a sandwich at Wendy's, Nalla-ma discovered that mixing their ketchup with hot water gave her a fluid that tasted like Indian *rasam*. When she learned that the ketchup packets were free, she took about twenty of them, which lasted her until Los Angeles, where we went to Wendy's again.

I became an expert at quizzing waiters about what their food contained. I would begin with meat, the big no-no. Once I made sure that the food didn't contain any meat, fish, chicken, lard, or garlic (denigrated by yogis), I got to her likes and dislikes. She disliked mushrooms—"too slimy"—and artichokes—"too tart. What is it anyway? A flower, fruit, or vegetable?" She would take salad without the dressing, pasta without the garlic, Mexican food without the cheese, and Thai food without the lemongrass. Once a week she insisted on Indian food, particularly *pongal,* her favorite dish. But at least she ate "outside" food. We had come a long way.

## Pongal

*Serves 4*

I usually make *pongal* when we return from vacation, since it's a one-dish dinner that is easy to prepare. Besides, after a week of eating at restaurants, I like to serve my family a wholesome, cleansing food that is light on the stomach. My daughter eats this *pongal* with brown sugar, while my husband favors lime pickles as an accompaniment. I eat it piping hot and plain, with a dash of ghee on top.

1 cup split *mung* dal
1 cup white rice

1 teaspoon salt
1 teaspoon whole peppercorns
1 tablespoon ghee or canola oil
1 teaspoon cumin seeds
½ cup roasted cashews

1. Roast the split *mung* dal, then mix it with the white rice in a pressure cooker or a heavy pot with a tight-fitting lid, and cover with 5 cups water. Add the salt and cook until the rice is soft and squishy.

2. Using a mortar and pestle, coarsely grind the peppercorns and set aside. In a sauté pan, heat the ghee and add the cumin seeds. When they start popping, add the cashews and sauté until golden. Add the pepper, then pour in the semisolid, cooked *pongal* from the pressure cooker and mix well. Top with a dollop of ghee.

# Fair Shares for All

by John Haney
from *Gourmet*

Food cues are powerful indeed, as every traveler knows who's felt the telltale stab of nostalgia for home foods while on the road. *Gourmet* copy editor Haney's mini-memoir, however, describes a subtle variant—nostalgia for foods that define one's former social class.

O n those Sundays when he wasn't working an extra shift to keep up the mortgage payments on a house he'd never expected to own—his mother actually called him a "traitor to the working class" when he announced that he was planning to become a homeowner—my dad, a telegraphist by trade, did the prep work for Sunday dinner. (Dinner, for those unfamiliar with a fading British vernacular, is the meal referred to as lunch in superior circles; breakfast is breakfast both above and below stairs; and the feast known as dinner by those who hunt foxes is known as tea by those who race pigeons.) Within the bounds of a cuisine that pretty much consisted, in British working-class households during the 1950s and '60s, of meat and two veg followed by "sweet," or "afters," in the form of some kind of spongy pudding leaking strawberry jam into a lake of custard, my parents, Denis and Kitty, were excellent cooks. And they both considered the fact that we had enough to eat a direct reflection of the principle of "fair shares for all," first introduced into British politics in 1945 only to be demolished by repeated blows from an iron handbag four decades later.

The absence of fair shares from my father's life prior to 1945 had been particularly acute. My paternal grandfather died when Denis was three years old, plunging Florence ("Flo") Haney into poverty—and into the rougher parts of the East End, like Canning Town—virtually overnight. Three of her four sons were sent to the Alexandra Orphanage, in North London, the fourth to an aunt and uncle who could afford to feed him. For the first few years, my father once recalled, the food at the orphanage was only a marginal improvement on the gruel immortalized by Dickens. "In the early days, when I was a little child, it was bloody awful," he said. "Just bread and marmalade for breakfast, sometimes cocoa instead, which came in a basin, and you ate it with a spoon. If you were lucky, there'd be some bits of bread in it. And on a plate beside that, there'd be marmalade again, maybe a dab of Marmite, a bit more bread and butter. And that was your breakfast. Unless you were spindly, like I was, in which case you'd be put on the porridge list."

As the orphanage contingent trickled home at the age of fourteen and found employment with the Commercial Cable Company, where their father had worked, life became a bit less desperate for Flo, who, in the wake of a short-lived relationship, was now a mother for the fifth time. Even so, circumstances still made moonlight flits and skimpy meals unavoidable. Food had to be stretched. Senile bread could be rejuvenated by immersion in milk. A slice of fresh bread packed an increased calorific punch when smeared with condensed milk. Or you could daub it with a farthing's worth of beef dripping and add a dash of salt. Any bread surviving this onslaught of frugality and resourcefulness became bread pudding. Spotted dick (suet pudding spiffed up with a couple of currants) was usually made on a Sunday and then rationed out to provide no-frills teas (that's dinners, remember) for a week. Saturdays saw

Flo pushing the economic envelope with the purchase of eels, bought from the bucket and chopped up still squirming, or, in a very good week, rabbit, bought off the hook and skinned at home.

This was food keyed to subsistence, to survival. In a down-at-heel corner of a dithering empire, it attracted no adjectives. Perversely, however, I came to develop such an affection for this utilitarian fare, which has very little to commend it nutritionally and absolutely nothing to commend it aesthetically, that from an early age I would sometimes actually feel shortchanged when, for instance, my mother handed me a bowl of peaches, sweet wafers, and ice cream. Why? Because what I really wanted at that moment was a slice of spotted dick. Or a wedge of my dad's take on canary pudding, which was about as simple as afters could get—a deliciously yellow hemisphere of sweet sponge topped with a plop of treacle. Or maybe, instead of dessert, some bread and beef dripping.

My discovery that in some circles an addiction to the lowlier comestibles is viewed as a character deficiency came at the age of eleven, when I gained a place at a nearby grammar school. There, I quickly learned that I was being trained, despite my unquestionably plebeian background, to disguise myself as a member of the class (middle) into which a fair proportion of my companions in academic adversity had been born. Never again would I even dream of evincing in public a passion for condensed-milk sandwiches. Never again would I boast of the ecstasy occasioned in my ancestors by the sight of stewed eels encircling an archipelago of severely mashed spuds. My natural selectivity would go unremarked except within the confines of my own social subspecies; circumstances forced me to acknowledge the inadvisability of revealing myself, at an institution chartered by King Edward VI, to be the progeny of East Enders. For that's a stratum in which I was—and, churlish though it may seem, still am—thoroughly content to be classified.

Oddly, some of my most vivid memories of the food I enjoyed

when very young relate not to meals I devoured in my own home but to those dished up during ritual Saturday visits to my maternal grandparents and my aunt Jackie, who lived in a cavernous house in the northeast London borough of Redbridge. A major source of warmth for the entire building was the stove, from which my grandmother would triumphantly extract glistening platefuls of kippers, mackerel, and impossibly yellow haddock—or, every other week or so, supremely portly bangers (sausages). The customary accompaniment to this steaming cascade was outsize slices of white bread (fondly referred to as doorsteps) slathered with margarine, along with multiple mugs of murderously hot and tooth-dissolvingly sweet tea necessitating numerous trips to the outside lavatory.

An occasional highlight of these excursions to Redbridge was the narrative with which my sister and I were regaled during the afternoon by my grandfather, Harry Augustus Bush, a veteran of both world wars, sometime cavalryman and twice-torpedoed sailor. In between puffs on a Cuban cigar and sips of 80-proof rum, he'd give us a guided tour of a half century of hard times. For example . . . as a boy growing up in Limehouse, one of the poorest parts of the East End, he often scavenged family meals from the gutter when the street markets closed. Between the wars, he'd worked at a variety of jobs that my sister and I found bewilderingly unlikely—tap dancer, journeyman butcher, ship's steward, docker.

At about six o'clock, we'd take a break from the story of our grandfather's journey through conflict and its absences. The time had come to focus on food, whose arrival would be announced on what I called banger weekends by a crescendo of sizzling and popping signifying that the next hour would be spent disposing of sausage after sausage after sausage—the Englishman's favorite form of pork. My grandmother would scoop the tubby tubes, as plump as the pig they came from and perfectly browned, straight from her enormous frying pan onto superheated plates. We'd hack at them while they were still almost too hot to eat, still shimmering with the lard in which they'd been cooked. The savory sauce we used as a condiment mixed splendidly with the golden yolk of the accompanying eggs. Relishing every last speck of grease, we mopped up the resulting runniness with yet more doorsteps. And then we'd have more doorsteps, this time painted with the super-salty yeast extract called Marmite, a substance guaranteed to disgust anyone who didn't acquire a taste for it within a few weeks of leaving the womb. (An American acquaintance of mine who once made the mistake of sampling a mere dot of the stuff pulled a face indicative of terminal perplexity, tried hard not to gag, and yelped, "This isn't food. It can't be. It just can't be.")

At the end of a day at Harry's, my parents usually had a tough time dragging me out to our third-hand car for the ride home—particularly on wintry sausage nights, when I'd be begging for one last warming banger as my father, cursing the cold beneath his breath, scraped the ice from the windshield with a copy of the *Evening Standard* and then struggled for a few tense minutes with the conveyance's refractory ignition. I'd remind myself that next Saturday night would be fish night, alright in its own way, and that two Saturdays from now I'd once again sit down to the best food, the very best food, in the world.

In November 1998, I visited my father for what I realized, the moment I set down my suitcase and embraced him, would be the last time. (He and my mum had divorced in the late '70s.) Dad was all skin and dry bones, suffering from a serious lung disease, and the effort of eating left him prostrate for an hour. His half-brother, Don—bus driver, accomplished darts player, lifelong East Ender—had passed away two days earlier.

I found Don's departure from this world particularly significant. I had always thought of him as an exceptionally forceful reminder of my father's side of the family, not least because—unlike the rest of the Haney brothers, who moved to suburbs or to the country just as soon as they could in the years following the war—Don chose to spend his entire life in the East End. He had once had his doubts about the durability of my allegiance to the class of which he was, so very indisputably, a fully paid-up member. His misgivings in this regard may have originated in the fact that I went to university—a family first—and therefore might have come to consider myself a cut above the rest of the clan. In 1981, at his eldest daughter's engagement party, he came straight to the point and asked me if I thought I was "better than us"—better than his family, his friends, his neighbors. This was one of the saddest questions I have ever been asked. Taking a shaky sip of the few drops of beer I'd managed not to spill from sheer surprise, I gave him the benefit of a very firm "No." Thus reassured, he bought me another pint. The party continued, and people belted out songs I'd first heard as a hysterically excited five-year-old at jubilantly crowded Christmas parties in Don's postage stamp of a living room in a tiny terraced house in a section of the East End known as the Isle of Dogs (in a part of the world that's now known as Docklands and bears little relation to the way it was, to the lives that were lived there, before money moved in).

Frankly, I've never had that much fun at parties again. What do I see when I repeat my own memories to myself? Torrents of cigarette smoke, Sherry, and stout. The younger men in navy V-necks, the younger women in gray pencil skirts. The older men enormously beery in ill-fitting two-piece suits, waistbands suspendered to their sternums, constantly brushing fag ash from their crumpled synthetic ties. The older women in voluminous black dresses, trailing their daughters' hiccuping, half-naked babies and a couple of feet of imitation pearls, A kitchen table crammed with squadrons of cocktail sausages, hulking wedges of Cheddar, precipices of ham, mountains of mince pies, piles of piccalilli, stacks of thick-sliced bread, and a teapot capable of accommodating the Mad Hatter and every last one of his lunatic friends. All this, and infinite kindness. Such were some of the happiest times I knew as the constellations wheeled above the bedlam of my infancy.

• • •

The visit with my father was preceded by a sojourn with my sister, Joy—an artistic type and sometime vegan who plays the part of patient vegetarian whenever her unrepentantly carnivorous brother drops in—and her husband, who were kind enough to pick me up at Heathrow. Traveling with little luggage other than a funeral suit, I asked to be escorted to the nearest concession offering what Brits of my background regard as a classic "stoke-up." My sister's partiality (despite the general refinement of her tastes in food) to any chip (french fry) presenting itself for hasty ingestion made this a more reasonable request than the average purist might expect.

Having received the fix I craved—egg, sausage, bacon, baked beans, fried bread, fried mushrooms, fried tomatoes—I resigned myself to a couple of days of wholesomeness relieved only by solitary excursions to a cafe near the bookstore where my sister works. Run by a Spanish socialist with a penchant for Che Guevara posters, it's a spotless hole-in-the-wall sporting a blackboard that speaks my language—pork, pork, and more pork—with, in one instance, an amusingly Continental twist: a bacon sandwich that substitutes *ciabatta* for Wonderloaf. (This, I think, is about as far as British integration into Europe really needs to go.) Although I was genuinely grateful for the two excellent dinners my sister cooked for me—fresh organic pasta with Swiss chard; moussaka with Puy lentils and eggplant—I was basically looking forward to the culinary monstrosities awaiting me at my father's apartment. There, I knew, I could safely revert to being the viscerally pork-oriented tot who always found the traditional string of sausages the most alluring element of a Punch & Judy show.

I wasn't disappointed. Lunch (dinner) on my first day at my father's was, oddly enough for a Sunday, a childhood midweek standard: sausages with onion gravy (meaning a viscous slurry of lifeless onions and irrigated Bisto), mashed potatoes containing an infusion of butter that even Fernand Point might have found excessive, and the soggy tinned legumes commonly referred to by generations of English schoolchildren as cannonball peas. This deadweight of pork, starch, and distressed chlorophyll was followed by a ready-made treacle pudding disgorged from a plastic tub. The whole repast took my father more than an hour to prepare and cook as he moved at a snail's pace around his minuscule kitchen. And it tasted just as good to me as it had forty years earlier, when Denis could put together the very same meal in a matter of minutes. The following day, he produced (on a Monday) the lunch that will always remind me of childhood winter Sundays—chicken injected with a pound of butter, quartered potatoes roasted in the pan juices, carrot slices the size of silver dollars, and tepid broad beans as big as a bulldog's testicles. Tea (eggs, bacon, baked beans, and a hefty slice of two-day-old bread pudding with a bottom crust the consistency of cardboard) followed barely three hours later. My father then retired for the night, a little more breathless than usual. I sat alone, a little sadder than usual, pondering the prospect of Don's send-off.

The surge of grief attendant upon this soliloquy was leavened (incongruously, inappropriately, and, for a Brit accustomed to three- to four-year intervals between trips home, perhaps understandably) with sporadic speculation as to what—apart from tea, Sherry, and stout—Don's widow, Aunt Rose, might be planning for the menu at the wake. Pickled onions, probably. Cocktail sausages, hopefully. A sausage roll or six. Pork pies. A hillock of ham . . . in which case . . . piccalilli.

That wasn't quite how it worked out. After a tearful service in an unheated Anglican church overseen by an annoyingly upbeat lady vicar who was disturbingly forthcoming about her professional unwillingness to second-guess the nature of the afterlife, Don's remains were borne beneath a magnificent floral arrangement in the form of a dartboard to the City of London Cemetery. By the time we arrived back at Aunt Rose's, we were all emotionally exhausted and extremely cold. After settling my father, now speechless from fatigue, in an armchair next to his last surviving brother, Ray, I accepted a cup of tea from my cousin Diane. Next, I headed for the kitchen table, which, to my amazement, was groaning with six different kinds of quiche and not much else. Gone were the pickles and pork of yesteryear. I found this most depressing. My sister, on the other hand, was delighted. Her most recent confrontation with East End fare had been at Uncle Dave's funeral, where, in response to her inquiry as to the availability of something a vegetarian could safely swallow, she was told: "We've only got tomatoes. How about tomatoes? You're sure you don't want a nice bit of pork pie?"

It quickly became apparent, however, that the kind of vegetable quiche allowed onto the Isle of Dogs bears no resemblance to its buttercup-complexioned cousins from Hampstead.

"Diane," said Joy, "are any of these meatless?" (My sister had by now discerned that one of the quiches on offer was conspicuously sausage-laden.)

"Oh dear," said Diane. "We've forgotten you again, haven't we. Let's have a look. This one. This one looks like cheese only. But you'll have to pick the bacon bits off the top."

"Maybe I'll just have a cup of tea."

"Milk and sugar?"

"Er, no thanks."

"What? Nothing?"

"A slice of lemon would be nice if you've got any."

"Oh dear. I'm afraid we don't."

A few days later, I stumbled into a taxi to Heathrow at six in the morning with my wife, Pam, who had joined me later in the trip. My father, who had risen at four to begin making breakfast for us—watery scrambled eggs, bacon, toast, marmalade (for Pam), Marmite (for me)—waved good-bye from the kitchen window. It was the last time I saw him.

• • •

The following May, my wife and I flew to London for my father's funeral. Pam, determined to wangle us an upgrade to business class on the strength of my bereavement, gave the British Airways ticketing clerk two passports and a sob story. Embarrassed, I immediately shuffled away with the carry-on luggage. (To someone with my social DNA, the mere thought of an upgrade from economy is tantamount to getting ideas above one's station. In 1995, I was offered a seat in business class at no extra charge on an underbooked flight to Britain and turned it down.) My wife's entreaties failed—or so I thought until we were summoned forward to a much nicer part of the plane as the great machine began grumbling toward the runway. Once aloft, we speedily revealed our minimal acquaintance with the finer things in life, having to be shown by the flight attendant how to extract a video unit from beneath the armrest. Thus was humiliation added to grief. I was definitely ready for breakfast. Would the reality match the quality promised by the commercials? Well, almost. Everything was edible except the scrambled eggs, which were watery. As watery, in fact, as the scrambled eggs my father had cooked for me that Sunday morning six months earlier. My appetite fled.

During the two days immediately preceding the funeral, Pam and Joy prepared a huge amount of forbiddingly healthful food for the prospective mourners. My brother-in-law scoured the suburbs for reasonably priced stemware. Armed with several bottles of Sancerre, I retreated to my sister's studio to pen a funeral oration. The wine disappeared, the speech got written, the funeral came and went. Disbelief and desperation grappled with the gratitude I felt for the love my father had always shown me.

The day after the funeral, I forsook the Sancerre, if only temporarily, in favor of a wander through Crystal Palace Park, a constitutional of which, thanks to the wine, I was more in need than my companions in dejection were. It's an unusual place, containing as it does odds and ends of the landscaping and stonework relating to the enormous glass edifice that housed the Great Exhibition of

1851 and burned down in 1936. On its fringe stands the fabled (in England, at any rate) Crystal Palace television-transmitter mast, a structure that quickened the pulse of every communications engineer of my father's generation. Also in the park is a lake whose banks are infested with statues representing early Victorian paleontology's best stab at the likely appearance of a number of prehistoric reptiles. Toward the end of my mildly hungover circumnavigation of this improbable environment that blends so very queerly apparitions ancient and modern, I came across a brightly painted van reeking of cheap meat and displaying a menu blackboard headed by the two words that mean more to me when conjoined than any others in the English language—"bacon" and "sandwiches." In response to my order, the proprietor hauled several ribbons of scrag end of porker from a stainless-steel trough loosely covered with a piece of grubby polythene. Wearing as disproportionately toothy a grin as that of a ravenous tyrannosaur suddenly confronted with a dying pterodactyl, I looked on joyfully as the grill spat and smoked. A moment or two later—it seemed an eternity—I was handed a steaming heap of pig and squashy bread. To sever the rind as surgically as possible and thus prevent it from stretching and snapping and scattering spots of grease several feet in all directions, I bit down very hard. As I did so, a British Airways Concorde whistled overhead, shattering my concentration for a split second during which I felt as nervous as an antisocial caveman surprised by an intruder with a bigger and better club. Instinct then reasserted itself. I chomped on grimly. The park began to empty. Another sandwich, then another. Grief, greed, and the need for another shot of Sancerre achieved perfect equilibrium. It was time to head home for zucchini.

Two years later, I returned to London for a nonfunereal visit with my sister. Time had turned out not to be a great healer, but I was determined to squeeze as much pleasure out of my trip as a continuing sense of loss might allow. Food, of course, would be foundational to this endeavor. Upon my arrival, Joy, guessing quite correctly that green tea and tempeh would not be at the top of my want list for the next few days, announced that a new and reputedly halfway decent café had opened in her neighborhood. Two seconds later, we were on our way.

The café turned out to be so new that the cooking was taking place amid the residual debris of hasty construction. Undeterred by jet lag and the jury-rigged look of the joint, I skimmed the blackboard and promptly sprang at the counter as eagerly as a puppy distracted by offal, ordering two fried eggs, chips, bacon, baked beans, sausage, tomatoes, mushrooms, and fried bread. Plus a cup of tea, no milk, no sugar. This was a gluttonous amount of food for one person—and a most un-British approach to tea. The proprietress barely flinched.

The weather being warm, my sister suggested that we sit outside in the establishment's "garden," which turned out to be a square of cement with a pile of wood shavings in one corner, a handful of weeds in the other, and, in the middle, a single plastic table with a bent umbrella. Eden it wasn't. The food, however, was divine—the eggs radiant, the chips uniformly golden, the bacon pleasingly pink and rimmed with an appropriate amount of fat, the beans properly steeped in their pallid tomato-flavored sauce, the sausages a scintillating shade of brown and speckled with a spot or two of mustard, the tinned skinned tomatoes a study in scarlet, the mushrooms ragged at the edges and oozing dark juices, the fried bread as crisp as a crouton. The tea was as bitter as hops. I was home again. (Joy made do with a couple of chips.)

The week that followed was my idea of idyllic. Sadness was tempered by the fondest of memories, and my sister and I grew closer than ever. She admitted that it was only recently that she had begun to be able to think of Denis without bursting into tears. I owned up to feeling perpetually waterlogged. She fed me massive quantities of expertly prepared organic food and never complained when I disappeared to dispose of a sausage or two amid the sawdust.

On the Monday on which I departed, we sat down in her cement-floored backyard to a lunch that we had put together as a fairly authoritative recreation of the teas we had eaten as children on summer Sundays. My sister avoided the meat, of course, but appreciated the historical accuracy of the pile of cold baked ham and the hatbox of a pork pie (with a hard-boiled egg imprisoned at its core) that I had purchased at the supermarket that morning. The fruits of the sty were accompanied by good crisp lettuce, quartered tomatoes, spring onions, cold new potatoes, and dollops of an organic mayonnaise that bore a striking resemblance, both in taste and in texture, to the "salad cream" without which no basic British salad was complete four decades ago. In between bites, I gazed at my sister's beautiful container garden and conjured the time and the place in which we had first enjoyed meals like this one.

It's late on a summer Sunday afternoon in rural Essex, circa 1961. I'm looking at a small garden, plus vegetable patch, situated behind a modest semidetached house. There's a rabbit dozing in its hutch. Butterflies bask on a ramshackle rockery. A hedgehog is tottering through the daffodils. The family cat seems frightfully proud of the sparrow between its teeth. The local crow population is making its habitually raucous return to a stand of enormous elms. The bells of the Anglican churches are sounding for Evensong. (I'm not making any of this up.) In the neighboring gardens, similar sights, similar sounds. Cutlery clinking on cheap china. Teaspoons clonking in mugs full of sweet, milky tea. My sister and I are sitting on our back-door steps next to a tank full of tadpoles. My father is eating his tea in a rush before leaving for a night shift, hunched over his salad in shirt and tie. My mother asks us if we want any more before she starts putting leftovers in the fridge. My sister, daydreaming, says nothing. And I hear myself saying, in a hopeful tone, "Bit more ham, please, Mum."

And now Joy is asking me, almost inaudibly it seems, if I'd like a bit more to eat before the taxi to the airport arrives. What I'm hearing very clearly is ghosts, ghosts whose vanished voices have momentarily obscured the sounds emanating from what is, supposedly, the real world. Suddenly, the scent of cigar smoke and kippers overwhelms the fragrance of my sister's lavender. Maybe the healing has begun. I cut myself one last wedge of pork pie.

# Remembering Daddy

by Miriam Sauls

from *Gastronomica*

If Atticus Finch had been a cooking man, surely he would have been like Miriam Sauls' father, a North Carolina lawyer who raised cooking to the status of art. Sauls' evocative writing not only dishes up his down-home specialties but also draws us into his vibrant family gatherings.

If someone asked me how I knew my Daddy loved me, I would probably describe the times he passed out bites of apples or candy to his children. We would gather in the den, and he would take out his pocketknife and peel an apple in one continuous spiral with the care that a sculptor takes with his clay. Then he would cut the peeled apple piece by piece and, with the tip of his blade, pass each bite to my two siblings and me in turn, with the love that only a man who adores both his offspring and fresh food could muster. He would perform a similar ritual with a large Baby Ruth, making sure he kept the portions perfectly equal.

Mother did most of the day-to-day cooking, the thankless kind no one gets excited about, least of all the cook, but when Daddy did the cooking, he handled food with reverence. I can still see him cutting up the potatoes for his French fries, a Saturday night special. There was no chopping board for his potatoes—no sir; he custom-cut every single fry as if it was the one that might be served to the President of the United States. Being a man of the South, he fried a lot; the fact that I never fry anything now doesn't reflect good eating habits so much as the truth that I simply can't fry as he did. Having tasted fried perfection, I won't settle for less.

On Sunday mornings, if Daddy got up early to fry chicken for Sunday dinner after church, he would make us critchie crunchies (surely he should have patented the recipe or at least taken out a copyright on the name). He would crack an egg into the hot grease after the chicken was pulled out and flick all the left-behind crumbs up onto the egg so that the dish was a masterpiece of beauty and flavor. If we didn't have a critchie crunchie, chances are we would get a drippie droolie, a soft-boiled egg with salt and butter.

If you wanted something really extra special with your eggs, he would scramble them with fish roe harvested in the spring when the herrings were running in the Roanoke River that flowed through town. Then you'd have the fish itself fried up real crispy later that evening for supper. Or when the rock fish were running, Daddy would make a rock muddle. He would place the fish in the middle of his oblong pan and surround it with eggs and potatoes and onions placed just so and then covered with a lattice of bacon, creating his own still life.

On winter mornings, we were likely to start the day with biscuits left over from the night before (Mother gets credit for the biscuits) and sausage fresh from a hog killing. Daddy grew up in Farm Life, a rural community down east in North Carolina outside Williamston, our thriving town of seven thousand people, so he still got invitations to the hog killings and always walked away with at least a yard or two of sausage. He would hang the sausage links on a bamboo rod in our pantry beside the ham that would be hanging there in payment for his lawyering, from a farmer who had more money in the barnyard than in the bank.

And he might bring home souse and chittlins, too, the foods made from what's left of the pig just before they sweep the floor. They say everything from the pig is used but the squeal, and it's true. We always managed to have a pig's foot or two on New Year's Day along with the collards and black-eyed peas, to enhance our good fortune for the coming year. One time Daddy came home with an entire half of a pig (he must have kept somebody out of jail), which he proceeded to butcher on our kitchen table. I was thrilled to be able to take the pig's eye to my fifth-grade class the next day, suspended in rubbing alcohol in a Jif peanut butter jar.

Daddy always made it a point to come home from a killing with some cracklins, the crispy residue of rendered hog fat. Cracklins found their way into the cornbread we had on Saturdays at midday along with the greens and boiled Irish potatoes and baked sweet potatoes. But some cracklins had to be saved for the pot of squirrels he cooked every Friday night after Thanksgiving for our wild game dinner.

Through most of my childhood the game dinner was held at the town water plant. My Uncle Bob was the utilities manager for the town, so we had access to the cavernous plant, a place of intrigue and wonder with open space for indoor tag and creepy dark corners for hide-and-seek. In late November it was chilly, but not yet freezing cold, so the one pot-bellied stove served us fine, both for heat and as a cook-top for the squirrel stew.

If there weren't enough squirrels on hand for the stew, my brother Chuck and cousin Sam would go out Thanksgiving afternoon and bag a few more. It was a hungry man who first thought of eating squirrels. After they're skinned, they look like nothing more than a small bag of bones.

There was an electric stove at the water plant for the venison Daddy fried and gravied up, country style. Our bread course was always soda crackers crumbled up and thrown in the pot liquor left from the squirrels—a delicacy known as chowder. Nothing else from the food pyramid was likely to appear at a game dinner besides meat and mushy crackers, although a new meat course emerged during my teenage years.

It seems a friend had killed a raccoon while he was out squirrel hunting and thought of Daddy because he knew he liked to cook. So Daddy decided to barbecue up the coon. It happened to be the same weekend as the annual ladies night at the Ptomaine Club, the hunting men's supper club. Daddy and Gabel Himmelwright, the local surgeon, decided it would be fun to fool their wives into eating coon, a creature only one notch above possum on the food chain. So Daddy mixed up his vinegar, salt, and Texas Pete sauce and basted and baked it until it didn't taste so wild anymore.

Gabel first offered it to his wife, Margaret. "Here, Peachy Belle, try this," he said, without telling her what it was. After Margaret had scolded him for using her pet name in public, she allowed that it was pretty good. Then Daddy offered Mother some, and she agreed it was tasty. Then the wives asked what it was. I've heard that some words flew that night that were maybe okay inside the Ptomaine Club, but they wouldn't have been proper elsewhere.

After Mother asked how he could have fed her such common food ("common" being the term used for anything low-class), Daddy pointed out that raccoons were the cleanest animals in the woods—they always washed their food. And why didn't she keep that question in mind next time she cooked a pork loin or added fatback to the boiled pot? After the platter was licked clean and everyone confessed pleasure, coon became an official part of the wild game menu each Thanksgiving.

It's no surprise that we didn't have a lot of fruits and vegetables at our late fall dinner, because family feasts tended to celebrate what was in season. Summers were the time when a riot of vegetables appeared on the table. Daddy had started a tradition before I was born of inviting all his family to our house on the Pamlico River for the Fourth of July. With most of the older cousins coming down the night before, that meant upwards of thirty people any given year in our little cottage, which he had hand-built as a young man.

There would be bodies strewn on sofas in the living room and on pallets on the kitchen floor and on cots or in hammocks on the porch. And anybody not willing to work might as well stay home, because at 5:00 A.M. Daddy was handing out kitchen utensils to start the corn shucking and bean stringing and butterbean shelling and the peach and potato and cucumber and tomato peeling and the chicken frying.

The assembly line around the bushels of corn was especially lively as sleepy-eyed boys shucked and passed the ears to the next workers for silking and then on to Daddy to cut the corn from the cob for the big pot of stewed corn. An even bigger pot would hold the corn to be eaten off the cob. Daddy would have a particular look of satisfaction on his face as he cut the corn, because he was always anxious that the Silver Queen wouldn't be ready by the Fourth, though in my whole childhood, that never came to pass. He would walk around the rest of the day with corn milk spattered across his glasses and we would all marvel and see how long it would take him to realize his vision was blurred.

By then it was time to take a swim. We would load the vegetables in Elder Hall, our overflow refrigerator named after a rental-house tenant who had left a note on his door one day that said, "Be rat back," but he never turned up and neither did his back rent. So Elder Hall moved to the corner of our kitchen at Pamlico and cooled our bounty until it was time to start the pots boiling.

On those hot July days we had to have two seatings for dinner. The kids ate first with the grown-ups waiting on us, and then we returned the favor. The kids and grown-ups alike never failed to play "pig," the game invented at that very table, where one person puts a finger on his or her nose and everyone follows suit until only the "pig" is left, still too absorbed in his food to see that everyone else is convulsing with laughter.

While Daddy and all my uncles took naps in the lounge chairs and hammocks in the front yard under the pine trees, with the river lapping at the shore a few feet away, Mother and my aunts prepared the custard for the homemade ice cream. There was always a freezer of vanilla and one of fresh peach and sometimes a third kind would slip in, like strawberry, if someone had frozen some berries in May. Daddy would have driven down to Earl Guthrie's store to buy a big block of ice sometime earlier in the day, and the production would begin when the custard made its way to the front yard.

The little kids would crank the freezers first while they were still easy to turn, and we would work our way up the muscle ladder until we got to whoever was feeling most macho that day to do the final arm-aching churns. Small cousins would take turns sitting on the freezers to keep them stable, rotating when their cold little bathing-suited bottoms couldn't stand it any more. Meanwhile Daddy kept the freezers supplied with rock salt and ice chips. When the crank wouldn't budge another inch, the beaters were carefully removed to great oohs and aahs. The toughest thing in life at that point was deciding whether to have Aunt Marie's chocolate cake or Aunt Grace's pound cake or Aunt Emma's orange blossoms or Aunt Nell's cookies, and of course which kind of ice cream to try first.

After the satiated relatives drove off, we settled in for the rest of our idyllic summer. Daddy would drive the hour to town to work on Mondays and Fridays, and we would fish and crab and swim and water-ski the days away, only stopping long enough to eat a bacon, lettuce, and tomato sandwich. We would walk to Miss Annie Moore's store for dip ice cream and stand in front of the cooler, holding our breath, praying that the drop of sweat dangling from the tip of her nose in the one-hundred-degree store wouldn't let go as she got to our cone. We only went back to town when it was time to put up pints of corn and quarts of tomatoes and jars of pear preserves for the pantry shelf, and my favorite bread-and-butter pickles. The hardest thing of all was waiting several days for the pickles to "strike" before we could open one jar and taste Mother and Daddy's handiwork.

The corn and pickles made their next appearance at our Christmas feast. On Christmas day we had at least one and sometimes two other families of relatives at our dinner table. Preparation began early, not just in the day, but in the week, because Daddy would save every scrap of bread for days leading up to Christmas so his dressing would have a variety of colors and flavors. He might even throw in a few cheese tidbits. According to Daddy, hens were best for the turkey dinner; toms were too tough. He would dress "Lurkey" (as he called the turkey) and put her into the oven in time to move on to his next work of art—seven dozen eggs' worth of eggnog for the party that would begin around 11:00 A.M.

Not only did Daddy's brothers and sisters and all my first cousins attend, his cousins and their children and all our neighbors dropped by, too. So our house was a swarm of folks, drinking eggnog and eating fried peanuts and Christmas candy and date bars and "moons"—nutty shortbread cookies—as all the kids showed off their toys. I could never understand how some of these otherwise dull neighbors became so lively until I was old enough to look at the eggnog recipe.

> Take a dozen eggs, separated and brought to room temperature; a dozen tablespoons of sugar; a pint of whipping cream; and a pint of corn liquor (Daddy always increased the recipe six- or seven-fold; he would use apple brandy for added flavor for at least one of his pints). Beat the egg yolks till creamy, slowly adding the alcohol to cook them, then add in the sugar slowly. Set the yolk mixture aside and clean bowl thoroughly. Beat egg whites to stiff peaks and set aside. Then whip the cream till firm. Fold the whipped cream and egg whites into the yolk mixture and blend well. Serve with a sprinkle of fresh nutmeg and prepare for nirvana.

After the morning crowd cleared out, the table was cleaned of party food and set with the silver, crystal, and china. And after a sumptuous Christmas dinner, the storytelling began. There was always the latest funny thing Cud'n Fanny Mert had said and how long Uncle Henry might have to stay in the hospital, and talk like that, but the story we asked to hear again and again was the one about our great-grandfather John coming home from the Civil War.

John Manning was "mustered out" in Wilmington and walked the more than one hundred miles home to Martin County, where he passed the home of his sweetheart, Sarah Margaret, whom he had left behind several years before. Finding her rocking on the front porch as he passed her house, he nodded and said, "Hey, Miss Sarah Margaret, I'm home." And she said, "I'm glad, John." And he said, "See you Saturday night." And she nodded, and that was it. As we shook our heads at the subtlety of it all, it was time for dessert— coconut cake and wine jelly and whipped cream. Even the children were allowed to sample the wine jelly, and we must have cultivated a taste early, because it appears without fail at all family Thanksgiving and Christmas dinners to this day.

> Take one box (4 envelopes) of gelatin and dissolve in a pint of cold water. Once dissolved, add 1 quart of boiling water, 2 cups of sugar, 1 pint of sweet white wine, the juice of 4 lemons, and 2—3 cinnamon sticks, and bring back to boil. As soon as it boils, remove from heat and let it sit a few minutes. Remove cinnamon sticks and pour into container to chill. Serve with slightly sweetened whipped cream.

Now that would be enough food and entertaining for most anybody for one day, but not Daddy. He brought all the relatives back for ham biscuits and home movies in the evening, which meant that as soon as he and Mother had stood up from the dinner table, she started mixing lard and flour and buttermilk and rolling out biscuits, and he started slicing the country ham. And if there was leftover eggnog, everyone got jolly all over again.

It must be said Mother was a good sport about these gatherings.

All the guests were Daddy's family. She was an only child and didn't even have any first cousins, so she had to learn early to cope with this big crowd. It wasn't that all these relatives were strangers to her; in fact, she and Daddy were kin, so she had met them all at childhood family reunions. But this kind of food in large quantities and entertaining in bulk was a learned response to life with Daddy.

In later life, Daddy was appointed District Court judge, a job that allowed him to slow down professionally. His district happened to cover five counties in eastern North Carolina, low in crime but high in seafood. After an hour of court cases in Hyde County, he would take off his robe and go fishing with the sheriff for the rest of the day. It was not uncommon for him to come home with a mess of mackerel or a bushel of oysters or scallops after a "hard day's work." The ensuing feast would renew your faith in the justice system.

In his seventies Daddy was diagnosed with cancer. Like many Americans by the 1980s, he had changed his eating habits—less fried food, less beef and pork, less eggs and cheese and salt. He had done all this to protect his heart, and he was totally outdone when it was cancer that got him instead of a heart attack—all that deprivation for nothing. His loss of appetite at the end was as disheartening to the family as his general decline. But the cancer had given him time to write his own funeral service. A friend of mine came up to me afterwards and said, "I've never laughed so much at a funeral"—a fine testimony to his humor and creativity.

I went through years of boarding school and college and graduate school tempted to disown my rural heritage, but I never really got over wanting to be at that game dinner or around that Christmas table. The Fourth of July festivities eventually wound down as the aunts and uncles got too old to travel and cousins spread out across the country. But before I knew it, I found myself entertaining scores of friends on the little Christmas-tree farm my husband and I bought (with Daddy's help) right after we got married, inviting them out to cut a tree and feeding them venison stew by the barrel and cakes made with persimmons from the tree in front of the house.

And when my kids attended a Montessori School, where they were invariably fed ethnic food by classmates' mothers every time a Hindu or Muslim or Jewish holiday rolled around, I realized that although I had moved only a hundred miles from where I grew up, my heritage was just as exotic as theirs. So I fed my kids' classmates venison stew at Thanksgiving and in early summer took them on field trips to the vegetable stand out in the country to choose cabbages and squash and tomatoes to cook up with a pan of cornbread.

I spent my young adult life lamenting the fact that no one in my family was artistic. It slowly dawned on me, however, that I had grown up in the shadow of an artist—one who didn't paint or write or sculpt but who cooked and held feasts and told stories. As a child, I'd been transfixed by Daddy's tales. Stories and food, love and self-expression, were bound together and led to my becoming a "good knife-and-fork girl," Daddy's highest compliment, and a writer, my profession. Today, when I prepare my holiday feast with a passion for what will be served, when tales old and new are told around the table; when I write a story inspired by the particular brand of quirky humor that surrounded me as a child or when I interview an old-timer who's passionate about his ways, I give silent thanks to the man who taught me not only how to hear stories but also how to prepare a meal that inspires their telling. And when I see hunters in their camouflage suits on a crisp fall day in rural North Carolina, I don't think they are cruel or mindless. I know that before the day is over there might be a work of art placed in front of a child who will someday recognize it for what it is.

# A Passage to Pakistan

by Madhur Jaffrey

from *Saveur*

> Food can carry a politically loaded message, especially when religious dietary restrictions come to the fore. Author of definitive Indian cookbooks, Jaffrey has a wistful perspective on how the divide between India and Pakistan translates into culinary terms.

I was born in colonial India. Before our erstwhile British rulers gave us independence half a century ago, they split our nation into two countries, India and Pakistan. We started our new "independent" lives by trying to massacre as many of one another as possible and have continued in a constant state of belligerence. We have fought two wars over Kashmir, a region we both claim. Now, as another conflict looms and fades, I want to tell my own Pakistan story—punctuated with food, as I simply do not know how to write any other way.

1945. Delhi, Colonial India. We are a gang of twelve-year-old school friends, racing out of our classrooms at recess, pigtails flying, tiered tiffin carriers in hand. Abida and Zahida—gentle, kind Muslim twins—have brought chukandar gosht, a dish of cardamom-flavored meat with beets. We suck the marrow from the bones. Manjeet is a Sikh. She has brought parathas—flat, flaky breads stuffed with grated cauliflower. I, a Hindu, have rather humble potatoes cooked with cumin and ginger, to be devoured with phulkas—small, delicate flatbreads. We all eat with gusto, dipping into one another's containers.

1946. Delhi, Colonial India. Independence and Partition have been announced. Our class, symptomatic of all India, has split into two warring factions, Hindus on one side, Muslims on the other. Fingers point, accusations are hurled. I am the only one who refuses to participate in this growing horror. I plead with each side to see the humanity in the other. One girl, from the Hindu faction, spits out her ultimate condemnation: "You are just the kind of Hindu that will end up marrying a Muslim." No more common lunches. Each hostile side now takes its tiffin carriers sullenly to different ends of the playground. I am viewed with slight suspicion by both. I cannot bear to see my India being broken up this way.

1947. Delhi, Independent India. The British rulers have departed from our paradise, but not before creating an Eve—Pakistan—out of India's ribs. They have not left behind a happy couple. Half of Manjeet's family has died in the religious riots that followed the announcement of Partition. Abida and Zahida are gone. Indeed, most of our family's Muslim friends have moved to the newly formed Pakistan—my father's hunting companions and old college mates, my brothers' bridge partners, my bosom pals. Many of us remaining in secular India are bereft. We've watched the dismemberment of all that we know and hold dear. How are we going to split our shared history and culture? Delhi is filling up with refugees.

2001. Lahore, Pakistan. When I was little, one of my cousins lived in Lahore. (She was later to become a refugee.) It was she who enlightened us about the birds and the bees and who made the unforgettable statement "Lahore is the Paris of India. You haven't lived until you have been there." I have always wanted to visit Pakistan but have held back, mostly owing to prevailing belligerence but sometimes because of an undefinable unease. Yet we are the same people, I have been saying to myself for more than fifty years. Finally, I have deliberately arranged to begin a new cookbook—a project that will take me there.

Upon arriving in Lahore, I am whisked to the home of Iqbal Ahmad, the brother of friends from the United Nations. My heart lurches when I see my hostess, Saira Ahmad. She is, right down to her porcelain skin, the spitting image of my mother. At all family meals, Saira flits in and out of the kitchen, quietly supervising the cook, just as my mother would have done.

One chilly morning we are served pasanda kebab (grilled skewered ribbons of lamb), dahi roti (flatbreads made with yogurt), and bihari bhujia (potatoes seasoned with red chiles and a crumble of crisply browned onions). This breakfast thrills me with its new inflections, particularly the presence of meat so early in the morning. The nation as a whole, I will discover, thrives on meat—from beef (charmingly called "big meat") to game birds. I am reminded how, years ago, while dining with a Pakistani gentleman who had opened a restaurant under the Paris cinema in Manhattan, I remarked on the dearth of vegetables on his menu. He replied disarmingly in Urdu, "Bibi [lady], what can I say? We are Muslims, and meat is what we eat!"

Lahore has always been the heart of Punjab, the state through which one of the lines of Partition was drawn, and people on both sides of the border still speak Punjabi. Much of the cuisine in and around Lahore has the same Punjabi core found on the Indian side, twenty-six miles away—mustard greens pungent with green chiles; corn flatbreads dripping with butter; black beans cooked overnight in the embers of a tandoor oven.

But the city shows other influences as well, common to much of northern India. It was repeatedly conquered by foreigners, including Genghis Khan and Tamerlane. In A.D. 1526, Babur, a descendant of those marauding warriors, came roaring through the Khyber Pass to the north. Unlike his loot-and-run ancestors, he stayed in India long enough to found the powerful Mughal dynasty. With Delhi as their capital and Lahore as their much loved western command post, the Mughals retained a firm grip on the subcontinent until they were dislodged by the British three hundred years later. It was in those royal courts that Mughal cuisine, a mixture of Persian techniques and Indian spices, was born—the pilafs, biriyanis, and kebabs that delight Indians and Pakistanis to this day.

My own ancestors were intricately tied to the Mughal emperors, having helped run their courts as prime ministers and finance ministers and, in humbler capacities, as historians, translators, and lawyers since the sixteenth century. Partly because of this familial connection, I am eager to start exploring Lahore's Mughal monuments and gardens, but invitations for tempting meals are pouring in and I cannot resist. I do not know most of my hosts; they are friends of friends. Pakistan is like that. As I dine in one home after another, I realize that hospitality here has been refined to a fine art, combining grace, duty, and an almost ennobling sense of etiquette. Any recipient of this largesse can thank his or her lucky stars.

I start with "Auntie Tari" (Tahira Mazhar Ali), the aunt of London friends and a wise, elegant member of a distinguished literary family. As I enter her walled compound, I am instantly at home. The single-story whitewashed structure, set in a lush garden, is of the same period and aspect as the house I grew up in—a sprawling turn-of-the-century British-style bungalow complete with a long, sun-drenched veranda. Lunch has been set out here, and we are treated to all the dishes I have especially requested: slow-cooked harissa (a soothing, savory porridge of pounded meat, wheat, dried beans, and spices); magaz (goat-brain curry), which I never cook at home, as my American husband will not even glance at it; dal gosht (split mung beans with chicken); and yogurt sweetened with jaggery (raw cane sugar). There are also pistachios from Iran and almonds from Baluchistan—both of which I ate as a child but are now, like the Afghan grapes from which my grandfather used to make wine, lost to India because of politics.

The next day I am feted by "Auntie Sarwat" (Sarwat Akhtar) with a sixteen-dish meal starring bater (wild quail braised with ginger, garlic, yellow onion, green chiles, and coriander seeds). The servants bring the food from the kitchen across the courtyard, stopping to pick up fresh nan (whole wheat flatbread) from a bread maker who works the tandoor ovens buried in the walkway floor. We sop up the quail juices with the bread.

That way of entertaining harks back to genteel Anglo-Indian times, but Yousaf Salahuddin, Lahore's premier party giver and the grandson of the great Urdu poet Iqbal, is all stylish new Pakistan. In Salahuddin's refurbished 250-year-old fortress-cum-mansion, his cook, Samina, has prepared goat with spinach, chicken with garlic, gosht biriyani (kid goat baked with rice), and keema nan (tandoor bread with ground lamb) for the visitors attending his Basant (Spring Festival) party. The guests drink Pepsi and green tea—liquor, of course, being barred, at least officially. I see many men holding suspicious-looking glasses, but I dare not ask for whiskey, which I am just dying for. Daily papers carry reports of orthodox Muslims' condemning the Basant festival as "too Hindu", as that is where its roots lie. But the partygoers here—indeed, Basant revelers throughout the city—defiantly fill the sky with the traditional kites, which swoop and dive in mock combat.

Salahuddin tells me a story. Two centuries ago, his ancestors were Kashmiri Hindus, he says. When one of them got into trouble with the law, he saved himself from the wrath of the Hindu maharaja by converting to Islam and fleeing. A branch of Salahuddin's family remains Kashmiri Hindu to this day. I hear the story and let it lie there.

I am treading carefully, diplomatically. My hosts are over-whelming me with kindnesses. "We must take you to Food Street tonight," they say. This is in the old, walled city and is given the breath of life at dusk, when the eighteenth- and nineteenth-century buildings are floodlit, cars are banned, and the street is set up with long tables. We go and amble up and down for hours, picking up fried river fish here, a savory meat-stuffed pastry there, all the while inhaling Lahore's own brand of nightlife.

From the moment I arrived in Pakistan, I have been asking, begging, for a childhood dream to be fulfilled: to be taken through the historic Khyber Pass to the wild Afghan border. When I was a child, a cousin of my fathers, perhaps inspired by his own romantic dream, went on a trip to the Pass. Somewhere along that lawless route he was kidnapped and held for ransom. The ransom was paid, but he never returned. His wife and children were henceforth known to us as the family of the uncle who had been kidnapped at the Khyber Pass.

The Pass is just as dangerous now, but I have a desperate desire to see it. To get there, I need to go through Peshawar, capital of the North-West Frontier Province. My ever obliging hosts first arrange for the army to provide an escort for me from Peshawar to the Pass; then they pack me into a car, with their son as my escort and a picnic basket filled with egg sandwiches and sweet corn flatbreads.

2001. Peshawar, Pakistan. Standing in the narrow-laned inner city, I am mesmerized. Hollywood could not dream up this place. Built inside a bowl of mountains, it has remained a rough, tough, gun-ridden border town for centuries. In Qissa Khawni (Bazaar of Storytellers), where international intrigue and rumor are one kind of currency, we see mostly bearded men in long, earth-colored shirts and baggy *salwars* (pants), their bodies draped in rough shawls against the cold. Rickshaws, bicycles, and donkey carts ride roughshod over all that gets in their way. Do I want to buy spices? There are small hillocks of yellow and red and brown powders ready to be measured into small newspaper packages. Or do I want blood oranges, sliced and eaten with black pepper? I decide to step into the Khan Klub hotel, loll on its red-cushioned dining-room floor, and devour a plate of boorani banjan—spicy fried eggplant slices resting on seasoned yogurt. Outside again, I turn a corner and see stalls of gold jewelry. I turn right into a dark courtyard and find stashes of lapis lazuli, Russian cups, and Chinese vases. The few women to be glimpsed here drift through Meena Bazaar, the women's market, keeping to their ghostlike selves in head-to-toe burkas.

All business is conducted over tea. There are tea shops everywhere—tiny stalls filling dozens of orders a minute: "Three cups green." "Two cups black." "Six cups green." The Afghans, mostly refugees, drink only green tea, flavored with cardamom and sugar. The Peshawaris drink both black and green, flavored with wisps of shady deals.

We must move on now. The Pass is about an hour away by car. We are to travel with an armed military escort. At a roadblock by a big sign declaring WELCOME TO THE KHYBER AGENCY, we are joined by a convoy of jeeps with mounted machine guns that will take us into the Khyber administrative zone. As we proceed, I see the high adobe walls of Afridi tribal houses, which seem to melt into the rising brown mountains beyond. For many centuries now, the Afridis have specialized in the making, restoring, and selling of guns.

Could I not visit one of their homes? There is much consultation. I am told that someone in our convoy knows an Afridi sergeant whose home is around the corner. A set of metal gates is opened, and our convoy drives through. The adobe walls hide a palatial residence, all marble and velvet. In the open courtyard, the sergeant's wife is sautéing round squash with tomatoes, onion, garlic, ginger, turmeric, crushed coriander seeds, chiles, and lots of black cumin. The tannoor (the same as tandoor) bread is made near the cowshed with a ball of dough about six inches in diameter. Some of us will enjoy this large, unbelievably delicious whole wheat bread, called tikkala, in the car all the way to the Khyber Pass.

The Khyber Pass winds precariously along craggy cliffs for about fourteen miles and comes to an abrupt end at Michni Post, a lookout point 3,600 feet above sea level. From there we look down into the valley and make out Torkham, the town astride the Afghan border. I want to go down but am seriously discouraged. I have come all this way, I plead. The army officers, under instructions both to please us and to keep us safe, finally compromise: "We will do it," they agree. "But very fast."

At the border gates, refugees from the Afghan side are pushing hard to get across into Pakistan. It is like the last days of Saigon. We are ordered to get back into our cars immediately so that we can leave. We do, but halfway through the town I see a kebab maker selling the famous local hamburger, chappli kebab. I stop our car and leap out. The kebab maker is sprinkling ground beef with chickpea flour. He adds chopped tomato, onion, crushed coriander seeds, chiles, and cumin seeds, then forms a patty and slides it into a pan sizzling with lard from a *dumba,* a fat-tailed sheep. There are cries from the front of the convoy: "Get back into the car!" I have seen enough; I have the recipe in my head. I jump back into the car, and our convoy takes off again.

Oh, yes, I do search for Abida and Zahida, the companions of my childhood, but I am unable to trace them. Perhaps they are married and living happily under new names. I hope so. And while I cannot help dwelling on the power of religion to divide people, I think also of my new friendships, which have overcome politics completely. I remind myself that although our nations have long since parted, we can still speak to one another in mutual languages—Punjabi, Urdu—and still enjoy foods in common: nans, kebabs, biriyanis, and mustard greens. Surely there is some good in that.

# A Slice of Life

## by Rick Nichols

from the *Philadelphia Inquirer*

The bond between a newspaper columnist and his readers develops over time into a kind of personal friendship. In these three columns—published months apart—Nichols deepens that bond by sharing snatches of his personal history with his Philadelphia audience.

### June 19, 2002

#### A MOTHER SAVORS ONE LAST SLICE OF LIFE

My mother, bless her heart, never got to have her last supper.

It was still on the kitchen counter the next morning when we found her, the stove's exhaust fan dutifully spinning. It was going to be one of the standards; a thin, skinless chicken cutlet was set to one side. Two red-skinned new potatoes were in the pot, and in a stainless steel bowl of water, the salad lettuce was crisping.

I don't think she'd mind seeing that menu in print. She would skimp sometimes, have odd mixtures of leftover cooked carrots and cheese. Or, on occasion, breakfast-for-dinner or some warmed-up scrap left from a foray to a restaurant.

She was eighty-eight—thousands upon thousands of meals served to her late husband and children. They were, on the whole, good and decent fare. But we teased her about the fallbacks—

suppers of chopped hot dogs in a simple white sauce, "gravy bread," and once, when my father was briefly out of work, a panicky recourse to fried bananas.

Her background was Pennsylvania Dutch; her maiden name was Esbenshade. So she had a small repertoire of Lancaster County specialties—magically magenta pickled eggs; supremely flaky, big-pan chicken pies; some sort of thin flank steak (I think it was) rolled around a filling of chopped onion and suet and secured with a long needle. "Roly-polys," we called them—cried out for them.

It may have been suet guilt or perhaps some food-page article in the late '50s, but there was also a hellish health-food phase. Each morning's regimen was rugged and unvarying: a tablespoon of honey, a tablespoon of dust-dry wheat germ, bowls of yogurt. As I remember it, there were also occasional forced shots of blackstrap molasses. These were, I am sure, the recommendations of the day on how to make your kids grow up big and strong. (She'd also read somewhere that water for infants should be distilled, and later feared she'd starved my teeth.) So she tried—as mothers have always tried—to navigate the contradictory agendas that land on the table at every mealtime: How to satisfy the appetite for the soul foods of tradition? How to accommodate the latest data on healthful eating? How to get the family fed after a hectic drive home from the Shore?  You can't please all the people all the time. But my mother had just enough moves in the kitchen to leave me fond memories of vinegary German potato salad and rhubarb pie, meatloaf studded with chunked onion and bread, Sunday pot roast with roasted carrots, and snowy mashed potatoes that came with a well pressed in the top for the gravy. She made a beef-vegetable soup, thin and brothy and full of flavor, that I've never been able to approximate. For years we helped make fragile little pastry cups that she'd fill with exquisite chicken a la king every time my Uncle Tom came for dinner. But that stopped abruptly when my mother discovered—to her enduring horror—that Uncle Tom had always detested chicken a la king.

Then about twelve years ago something happened. Part of it was simply the empty nest syndrome, part of it was my father's death, part of it her own health. My mother put down her smooth wooden spoon and started eating like a bird, uninterested in cooking, fearful of the havoc that "experts" told her seeds and skins and nuts and corn might visit on her digestive tract. A doctor gave me a name for the aging widows in her boat. He called them "toast and tea ladies." Ladies, in other words, for whom not only cooking, but eating itself had lost its thrill. And so I feared my mother would end her days, slowly waning, fading, the gusto ebbing, and her appetite gone along with it.

But in the last few years her health stabilized. Dire predictions didn't come true. She relaxed a little. She got hungry again—famished, in fact. She kept to a daily regimen, eating her oat flakes, watching fluids, swallowing her prune juice. But she loved it when I came to cook—wolfing down green salads topped with strips of grilled lamb; warm Italian rolls with carrot soup; and pasta with black olives and the pan-seared New York strip steaks. She couldn't keep her hands off the delicacies my California and Minnesota sisters would leave stuffed in the freezer after their visits. We ate at an Italian cafe and a Japanese steak house with early-bird specials. We ate Vietnamese. We ate Indian vegetarian. We ate at country inns with old-fashioned favorites. But what my mother really enjoyed—coveted—were big diner breakfasts. And crisp pizza. And a good wedge of homemade pie. She had an out-of-control sweet tooth, as I have written before. I took to rationing her chocolate-covered jellies or dark Wilbur Buds. I'd dole out the teaberry ice cream by the teaspoon. You couldn't leave her alone with the dessert: She'd sneak it before dinner.

The woman weighed 108 pounds, for goodness' sake. Yet in her last few years she'd rediscovered—at least among friends and family—the joy of robust eating. She'd conquered the fear of consuming the wrong thing. She'd sip a glass of red wine in the afternoon. She ordered a pizza with her home health-care aide. After a haircut a few weeks ago, her young friend took her to a local eatery where they couldn't decide on dessert. The two of them finally ordered—without much agonizing—the sampler platter, a tiny portion of every confection on the menu.

The day she died last week, my mother didn't get to eat her last supper.But she did get to eat dessert.

A kind neighbor from across the street had scurried over that afternoon with a wedge of fresh fruit pie. The next morning, when we found her, she had an air of serenity about her, of peace and perhaps—though I may be projecting—contentment. The skinless chicken cutlet and new potatoes were still uncooked on the counter. But the slice of pie, bless her heart, was gone.

## NOVEMBER 27, 2002
### OVER THE RIVER AND THROUGH THE WOODS . . .

My foraging got off to a bit-too-early start this season, so by last weekend the refrigerator's boundaries had been badly overrun. On the cedar landing just outside the back-room door, the old Coleman cooler has been pressed into service, oak leaves mounding in drifts against its side. The stubby carrots are in there, and fresh soft bunches of flat-leaf parsley, and bowlegged stalks of what in Amish country is called "golden" or "bleached" celery. It is certainly cool enough outside, or has been so far. (To be safe, though, I've moved the bags of cherry-size baby Brussels sprouts inside to the crisper.)

My own roots—or half of them, at least—are in Lancaster County and, though I didn't grow up there, I have a partly learned, and partly genetic, predisposition for its specialties, especially when the frost is on the windshield.

There is another imperative this Thanksgiving. My mother, who passed away this summer, will not be with us for the first time. But for the first time in years, both of our sons are coming, and their lovely wives and the gaggle of grandchildren. We are, I finally realize, grandmother's house now, and there is much care and feeding to be done—and pliable young dispositions to be properly bent.

So the cider for my famous (*Frog Commissary Cookbook* recipe) cider vinaigrette will come from a particularly fragrant blend of apples pressed in Bird-in-Hand. (The cider vinegar is special, too—a fruity vinegar from Sterling Orchards in the Virginia hill country. And the walnut oil, forgive me, has a vintage: It's from the 2001 crop harvested—right along with the grapes—in France's western Poitou region, the nuts hand-cracked during long winter nights, roasted over wood fires, and ground with some sort of magical millstones.) The pumpkin—actually, it's butternut squash—has been honey-roasted already and is waiting to become a silky squash soup. The cranberries are foreign imports: Nova Scotians. New Jersey's bogs are harvested rather roughly, which is why its berries—from just forty miles away—tend to head for juice mills, not the fresh trade. But we'll have unfussy cranberry-orange relish, never improved upon, as far as I'm concerned, by far fancier preparations. Sometime today we will pick up the Eberly turkey—an organic (I think) twenty-pounder my wife likes to roast upside-down—jaw-droppingly priced at $2.99 a pound.

Tradition is a stern cop, handcuffing us, making us walk the straight and well-rutted—to pay any price, to stop time, to summon, if just for a moment, the past back to life. I don't want salty, stringy, metallic celery. I want celery that has been coddled and cooled and then buried out of the sunlight until its heart has been rendered sweet and tender, the pastel yellow of Belgian endive. I don't want canned corn or frozen corn. I want Cope's corn, still made in Rheems, out near Harrisburg, the last dried, sweet, white corn left, so authentic and so intensely nutty that it's coveted not only by the Pennsylvania Dutch, but by the far-flung descendants of America's original settlers who once preserved corn the slow-drying same way.

No, I do not expect to hear from the six-year-old, "Is that wood-roasted, French walnut oil in your famous vinaigrette,

Grandpa?" or "More celery, please. This is extraordinary!" More likely, there may be a fleeting request for Annie's bunny-shaped pasta or a run on the pyramid of clementines. But with her younger sister and brother, she will have tasted a little more of the land of her forebears and breathed in the unforgettable scent of Cope's toasty corn and fruity Bird-in-Hand cider.

For the following day, I plan instruction in the sturdy art of baking (and icing) gingerbread men. We will use, as per custom, the red-plastic cookie cutter that my mother always used. And we will test—with a touch of ginger and molasses—whether we can summon, for a moment, the past back to life.

## FEBRUARY 13, 2003
### A SEASON OF LOVE, AND MAYBE WAR

I have retreated in this icy mid-February to my heaviest copper pot, building in it redoubts of beef stew and bouillabaisse, sauerkraut and rippling chicken soup.

It is a wrenching moment, this week, poised between love and war, the air filled with tales of Valentine devotion and renewed vows that Baghdad—or the White House—is eager to unleash punishing destruction.

At my cutting board, I chop the onions. For the stew, I double the root vegetables, fill it with parsnips and turnips, carrots and potatoes: I want to have my meat but like to think I can be a partial vegetarian.

It is not the dinners themselves that are a comfort. In fact, it is hard to relax entirely, eating them. I know I've tossed butter in the mashed potatoes, even an egg yolk, to bind and enrich them. These are not substances—from a coronary viewpoint—I ought to be fiddling with. They are heavy with love and, I know full well, intimations of death.

No, the more unalloyed comfort comes more from hunting and gathering—getting the free-range fryer hacked up at the farmers' market, finding my Lancaster County saffron, discussing the freshness of the scrod, the technique for defanging the sauerkraut. I try a tip from Chef Tell in Upper Black Eddy: I blanch the kraut for five minutes in boiling water, dialing down the salt and sour before adding it to the apples and onions, the white wine and juniper berries.

There is, of course, the joy of the cooking, too. The solid bite of the knife striking wood, the fragrant sizzle of the mirepoix, the chicken stock's endless simmer. There is the dull clang of my mother's old wooden spoon against thick copper, a familiar rapping before I pull it from the stew, the clap of a distant bell.

So I have been enduring February's unnerving siege— perfuming the house with cornmeal mush frying in the morning, with orange zest in the evening and hints of saffron. I've gravitated to solid ground—chopping on wood and banging on pots, trying to keep the demons at bay (at mealtime, at least), brandishing garlic against the encroaching ghouls.

There is no real retreat, of course, only momentary respite, our hearts in our hand, our fingers on the trigger.

I have a cache of French chocolates hidden. I will pick up the heart tarts I've ordered after noon tomorrow.

But the element of surprise already has served me well. One evening, as my wife and a friend from the snow-blown north sit in front of the fire after dinner, I spot three bananas in the kitchen basket. I split them cleanly on the cutting board; fry them in bubbling butter and brown sugar. I sprinkle them with cinnamon, and bathe them in steamy banana liquor and the last of our summer's white rum. The vapor bursts into wild blue flame when I touch a match to it, sweet catharsis on the eve of destruction.

We eat them, to our heart's content, hot over ice cream as the embers snap.

# Simple

by Jeanne B. McManus

from the *Washington Post*

Putting together a newspaper's food section, week after week, can become a
mechanical exercise—until a moment of
clarity throws everything into perspective.
Jeanne B. McManus has the wisdom and
talent to take that moment of clarity and
do something with it.

This was supposed to be a piece about a fabulous Christmas
dinner, an elegant roast with a delicious demi-glace that
then became the basis for a variety of sauces made from expensive
ingredients. The original piece was written not by me but by one
of our most reliable and sophisticated contributors, an excellent
cook, and when the recipe was completed it would have been the
star of any Christmas table.

But as I stood in my kitchen two weeks ago testing the recipe,
as the smoke from the splattered drippings poured from the oven,
as the complicated stock simmered on the burner for more than
ninety minutes, as I poured an inch of hot fat from the bottom of
the roasting pan into the separator cup so that I could drain off the
drippings to make that fabulous sauce, it occurred to me that no
one in his right mind was going to make this particular roast on
Christmas Day. Even I, with my relatively unencumbered life and
minimal obligations on December 25, was not going to stand in

the kitchen monitoring the internal temperature of the roast, making the roux from the fat, pouring brandy and wine into a skillet while my family in the living room enjoyed the fire and the tree and the sun slowly setting, dusk arriving.

I began to feel the kind of loneliness that often burdens the cook on the holidays, as he or she stands, obligated, in front of the hot stove, listening to the sounds of family, the roll of laughter coming from another room that suddenly seems very, very far away.

It resembled too closely the kind of gray dread that often descended on me as an adolescent every Christmas afternoon: the presents were open, the event was over, and winter stretched ahead with unmitigated bleakness.

I enjoy the role of cook on Thanksgiving. I choose the inevitable turkey and bring it to its inevitable conclusion. The meal is the event, the day liberated, strangely, by its very limitations, its singleness of purpose: to share and eat.

Christmas is a tangle of hopes and expectations. First, of course, it is a religious feast observed often in the morning, if not the midnight before. It too quickly becomes material, complicated with presents stripped open, often far too quickly, boxes of bounty shoved into oblivion far under the tree, black plastic bags lined up at the kitchen door, stuffed with shreds of the day, too quickly turned to trash.

With those gifts and their consequences, with all they represent, the day is always jagged and a bit raw. The presents that as a girl were disappointments, or the ones that never materialized, now have been replaced by losses far more profound: the friends, the family that no longer are here to sit around the tree, the knowledge that comes with adulthood that makes one wary of success and expectant of disappointment. Christmas now does not seem to be the day to put my loved ones far away in another room, while I struggle over a demi-glace.

And so the recipe for elegant roast is in the back of my notebook, to be included here another day when all of us have more time. And instead I devised a simple plan, the plain and pleasant rarebit that my mother often made for us on Friday nights. (And please: we called it rarebit. Let's not renew here the debate as to whether it's "rabbit" or "rarebit." After all, this is the season of peace.)

A combination of cheddar cheese and cream, redolent of beer, rarebit was commonplace partly because we didn't eat meat on Fridays but also because Friday nights at our house were the most hectic, and it could be prepared in the double boiler and kept warm until we all landed together at the dining room table.

In the rows of cookbooks that line my shelf, I started my search. And when I picked up the *Fannie Farmer Cookbook* that my mother had given me when I first moved out on my own, I saw one page was bookmarked—with my one-page telephone bill from 1977 (monthly charge: $12.57), the year that I lived in a basement apartment in Glover Park and the year that I probably last tried the spartan recipe.

Maybe I've eaten too many sugar cookies and am hallucinating. But I now envision that after church I will spend the afternoon relaxing with my family, especially my mother, listening to Christmas music, or reading the book I set aside before Thanksgiving, then assembling the rarebit at the last minute (I may throw in some crab meat), serving it with some good bread, lightly toasted, and a salad of bitter greens.

And maybe this rarebit recipe is not for you. But maybe you would like to think about your own simple plan this Christmas.

**Welsh Rabbit**

Adapted from a recipe in *The Fannie Farmer Cookbook* (11th Edition), revised by Wilma Lord Perkins (Little, Brown, 1965)

*Makes 1 cup sauce, enough for 4 servings*

Though I grew up with a rabbit (we called it "rarebit") made with beer or ale, this smoother version seems more appropriate for Christmas Day. If it looks too plain for you, think about some of the variations below or come up with your own simple plan that allows you to spend the day with those you love.

8 ounces cheddar cheese, as mild or sharp as you prefer, coarsely grated
1 tablespoon unsalted butter
Salt to taste
1 teaspoon Dijon-style mustard
Small pinch cayenne pepper
½ cup milk
1 egg, slightly beaten

In the top of a double boiler or in a heatproof dish fitted over a pot of simmering water, heat the cheese, butter, salt, mustard and cayenne, stirring occasionally, until the cheese melts.

Add the milk and egg and stir constantly until the mixture thickens. Taste and add more salt if desired. Pour over toast.

Per serving: 294 calories, 17 gm protein, 2 gm carbohydrates, 24 gm fat, 125 mg cholesterol, 15 gm saturated fat, 460 mg sodium, trace dietary fiber

**Variations**
Ale or beer: Instead of milk, use ale or beer.

Tomato: Spoon the rabbit over broiled tomatoes.

Chicken or Turkey: Spoon the rabbit over sliced cooked chicken or turkey breast on buttered toast. Top with a slice of partially cooked bacon and set under the broiler until the bacon crisps.

Seafood: Spoon the rabbit over bits of cooked lobster, crab meat or shrimp on rice or toast.

# Acknowledgments

We gratefully acknowledge all those who gave permission for written material to appear in this book. We have made every effort to trace and contact copyright holders. If an error or omission is brought to our notice we will be pleased to remedy the situation in future editions of this book. For further information, please contact the publisher.

"Kit" from *Appetite: So what do you want to eat today?* by Nigel Slater. Copyright © 2002 by Nigel Slater. Used by permission of Fourth Estate, a division of HarperCollins Publishers UK. ✤ "Cutting School" by Joyce Chang. Copyright © 2002 by Joyce Chang. Reprinted by permission. Originally appeared in the *New York Times Magazine*, October 9, 2002. ✤ "The Torch Is Passed, Handle First" by Amanda Hesser. Copyright © 2003 by the New York Times Co. Reprinted with permission. Originally appeared in the *New York Times*, March 5, 2003. ✤ "A Man and His Stove" by David Leite. Copyright © 2003 by David Leite and Leite's Culinaria. Used by permission. Originally appeared in *Bon Appétit*, February 2003. ✤ "Desperate Measures" by Matthew Amster-Burton. Copyright © 2003 by Matthew Amster-Burton. Used by permission of the author. Originally appeared on eGullet.com, April 7, 2003. ✤ "Makin' Groceries" excerpt from *Beyond Gumbo: Creole Fusion Food from the Atlantic Rim* by Jessica B. Harris. Copyright © 2003 by Jessica B. Harris. Reprinted with permission of Simon & Schuster Adult Publishing Group. ✤ "Slow Sausage" from *The Pleasures of Slow Food* by Corby Kummer. Copyright © 2002 by Corby Kummer. Used with permission of Chronicle Books LLC, San Francisco. Visit ChronicleBooks.com. ✤ "Travels with Captain Bacon" by Pete Wells. Copyright © 2003 by Pete Wells. Reprinted by permission of the author. First published in *Food & Wine*, May 2003. ✤ "Sustaining Vision" by Michael Pollan. Copyright © 2002 by Michael Pollan. Used by permission. Originally appeared in *Gourmet*, September 2002. ✤ "Earthy" by Margo True. Copyright

Onion" by Dave Gardetta. Copyright © 2002 by Los Angeles Magazine. Used by permission. Originally appeared in *Los Angeles Magazine*, August 2002. ❖ "Guess Who's Coming to Dinner" by Gabrielle Hamilton. Copyright © 2002 by Gabrielle Hamilton. Used by permission. Originally appeared in *Food & Wine*, July 2002. ❖ "Say Cheez" by Robb Walsh. Copyright © 2003 by Houston Press. Used by permission. Originally appeared in the *Houston Press*, February 20, 2003. ❖ "An Ode to Sloppy Joe, a Delicious Mess" by Andrea Strong. Copyright © 2002 by the New York Times Co. Reprinted with permission. Originally appeared in the *New York Times*, October 9, 2002. ❖ "Bread Winner" by Susan Choi. Copyright © 2002 by Susan Choi. Reprinted by permission of the author. First published in *Food & Wine*, July 2002. ❖ "Salumi" by Min Liao. Copyright © 2002 by Min Liao. Used by permission of the author. Originally appeared in *The Stranger,* September 5, 2002. ❖ "I See London, I See France" by Jonathan Gold. Copyright © 2002 by Jonathan Gold. Used by permission of the author. Originally appeared in *Gourmet*, November 2002. ❖ Excerpt from *Caviar: The Strange History and Uncertain Future of the World's Most Coveted Delicacy* by Inga Saffron. Copyright © 2002 by Inga Saffron. Used by permission of Broadway Books, a division of Random House, Inc. ❖ Excerpt from *Untangling My Chopsticks* by Victoria Abbott Riccardi. Copyright © 2002 by Victoria Abbott Riccardi. Used by permission of Broadway Books, a division of Random House, Inc. ❖ "Local Bounty" by Calvin Trillin. Copyright © 2003 by Calvin Trillin. Reprinted by permission of the author and by Lescher & Lescher. Originally appeared in the *New Yorker,* January 3, 2003. ❖ "The Cooking Game" by Adam Gopnik. Copyright © 2002 by Adam Gopnik. Reprinted by permission of the author. Originally appeared in the *New Yorker*, August 19-26, 2002. ❖ "Where Recipes Come From" by Benjamin Wallace. Copyright © 2003 by Benjamin Wallace. Used by permission. Originally appeared in *Philadelphia Magazine*, April 2003. ❖ "The Culinary Underground" by John T. Edge. Copyright © 2003 by John T. Edge. Reprinted by permission. Originally appeared in *Oxford American Magazine*, March/April 2003. ❖ "Life on the Line" by Jason Sheehan. Copyright © 2003 by Jason Sheehan. Reprinted with permission. Originally appeared in *Westword,*

# About the Editor

**Holly Hughes** is a writer, the former executive editor of Fodor's Travel Publications and author of *Frommer's New York City with Kids*.

# Submissions for Best Food Writing 2004

Submissions and nominations for *Best Food Writing 2004* should be forwarded no later than June 1, 2004, to Matthew Lore at *Best Food Writing 2004*, c/o Avalon Publishing Group, 245 W. 17th St., 11th floor, New York, NY 10011, or e-mailed to Matthew.Lore@avalonpub.com. We regret that, due to volume, we cannot acknowledge receipt of all submissions.

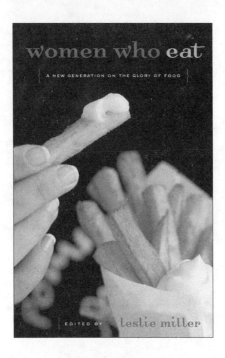

*Women Who Eat: A New Generation on the Glory of Food*
Edited by Leslie Miller

This long-overdue rebuttal to the notion that all women are on a diet puts a fresh spin on the joy of cooking—and eating and entertaining. Amanda Hesser praises the joys of simple food, and *Food & Wine* editor Kate Sekules discusses the importance of having a restaurant that feels like home. Theresa Lust describes her fondness for humble sauerkraut, and Elizabeth Nunez links her passion for Carvel ice cream to her childhood in Trinidad. Brimming over with generous helpings of great prose, this rich array of essays and recipes will whet your appetite and inspire you to pull out your pots and pans.
Bon appétit!

Published by Seal Press
www.sealpress.com
$15.95
ISBN 1-58005-092-1

Available at your local bookstore.